C00 956 682X

CONTENTS

Printed by Bell &
Maps produced by Alan Palfreyman
Contains OS data © Crown cop
Cover image Portmore, Peeblesshire copyright And

CHAIRMAN'S MESSAGE

It was, I suppose, predictable that after two consecutive warm and sunny summers, we would revert to a more normal Scottish summer in 2015. The spring was slow and cold which prolonged the snowdrop season here at home and our crocuses were quite glorious. Unfortunately despite a few warm days in June, the summer was not ideal either for gardeners or visitors, so could I start this introduction to our Guidebook for 2016 by thanking all those who opened their gardens last year for us and all those loyal visitors for their support. I sincerely hope that 2016 will be kind to us and we will once more enjoy some good growing conditions and many glorious gardens to visit. Our programme for this year is as enticing as ever with some beautiful new gardens to visit as well the return of some old favourites.

The last year has seen a major reorganisation of our head office. We have not been alone in seeing our costs, over which we have control, rising more quickly than our income streams over which we have almost no control. In the longer term a cost base rising faster than income is not sustainable so we took the decision to grasp the nettle and reduce our operating cost base.

In place of a full time Chief Executive we have appointed a part time National Organiser and I am delighted to welcome Terrill Dobson to head office. Terrill started her new role in October and she is working closely with our management team. Terrill has been the District Organiser for Angus for six years and two years ago became a Trustee, a role she has now relinquished, so she starts her new role with a very solid understanding of our purpose and culture.

More widely Terrill is known as the owner of the Herbalist's Garden at Logie in Kirriemuir which she has opened for Scotland's Gardens on various summer dates over many years. She has an extensive and varied background working in business and the third sector.

I should also like to congratulate David Mitchell on his appointment as Deputy Chairman. David will be well known to many of you and his background is in horticulture. Until last year he was a senior executive at the Royal Botanic Garden in Edinburgh.

The Guidebook has a slightly different feel to it this year and we have plans to gently change its format over the next few years but not to change its content. It remains a popular source of information amongst our garden visitors as well as being an interesting reference book to browse through. I am very grateful to our sponsors and all those who advertise in the guidebook for their continued support of Scotland's Gardens.

Whatever weather 2016 may bring, could I wish you an enjoyable and contented season of visiting gardens open for charity.

Mark Hedderwick
Chairman

Chris Jackson/Getty Images ©

Last summer was a testing time for gardeners with a cold May, an indifferent June and a miserably cold and wet July so it is a great tribute to all those who opened their gardens that this year's displays were so colourful and attractive. I know just how much garden visitors appreciate the hard work that goes into preparing and producing a garden so I would like to thank all those who opened their gardens in 2015, as well as all those District and Area organisers and volunteers, for everything they do to ensure the continuing success of Scotland's Gardens.

My congratulations go to all those people who invigorate the gardening calendar with new ideas such as the East Lothian Circle and the Fife and Angus Trail, and to everyone involved in the continuing success of the Snowdrop Festival and the Trails in Orkney. Of course, the traditional Sunday afternoon opening remains the visitors' favourite: they all enjoy seeing the gardens on display, the plants stalls and the wonderful teas that are so much part of Scotland's Gardens heritage.

As the President of Scotland's Gardens, I am so pleased that our appeal remains undiminished at a time of considerable change and uncertainty. This is due, in no small part, to our loyal garden owners, our local organisers and volunteers and that vital ingredient, our visitors, and my thanks go to them all.

I hope that 2016 will bring good weather, good gardening, and good visiting to you all!

Camilla

WHO'S WHO IN SCOTLAND'S GARDENS

MANAGEMENT TEAM

Mark Hedderwick
Chairman

Sarah Landale
Trustee

Sarah Barron
Trustee

Trish Kennedy
Trustee

David Mitchell
Deputy Chairman

Minette Struthers
Trustee

Richard Burns
Trustee

Max Ward
Trustee

Peter Yellowlees
Treasurer

Terrill Dobson
National Organiser

Lady Erskine
Trustee

James Wardrop
Trustee

Sally Lorimore
Trustee

Charlotte Hunt
Trustee

WHO'S WHO IN SCOTLAND'S GARDENS

PRESIDENT
HRH The Duchess of Rothesay

HEAD OFFICE
23 Castle Street,
Edinburgh EH2 3DN
T: 0131 226 3714
E: info@scotlandsgardens.org
W: www.scotlandsgardens.org

BANKERS
Adam & Company plc,
25 St Andrew Square, Edinburgh EH2 1AF

SOLICITORS
Turcan Connell, Princes Exchange,
Earl Grey Street, Edinburgh EH3 9EE

AUDITORS
Douglas Home & Co,
47-49 The Square, Kelso TD5 7HW

SCOTTISH CHARITY NO SC011337

ISSN   2054-3301
ISBN   978-0-901549-30-3

Elspeth Lindsay
Communications

Hazel Reid
Office Manager

Fiona Sloane
IT & Design

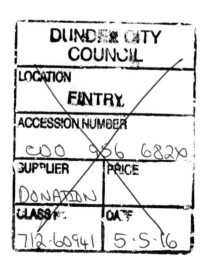

DUNDEE CITY COUNCIL
LOCATION   FINTRY
ACCESSION NUMBER
COO   986 682D
SUPPLIER   PRICE
DONATION
CLASS.   DATE
712·60941   5·5·16

Offices at: Bath Belfast Birmingham Bournemouth Cheltenham Edinburgh Exeter Glasgow Guildford Leeds Liverpool London Manchester Reigate Sheffield

Out of the Ordinary®

Investec
Wealth & Investment

Cultivating relationships, growing investments

We are proud to sponsor Scotland's Gardens. With 15 offices across the UK, we are a national network with a local feel, and our offices in Glasgow and Edinburgh are well placed to tend to your investments, pensions or other financial matters.

Our specialist teams manage £27 billion* on behalf of our clients, seeking the best and most tax-efficient returns on their capital. To see how we could best be of service to you please visit our website.

Please bear in mind that the value of investments and the income derived from them can go down as well as up and that you may not get back the amount that you have put in.

For more information on how we have supported Scotland's Gardens please visit **investecwin.co.uk/sponsorships**

Edinburgh – please contact Murray Mackay on **0131 226 5000**
Glasgow – please contact Stuart Light on **0141 333 9323**

*As at 31 March 2015. Member firm of the London Stock Exchange. Authorised and regulated by the Financial Conduct Authority. Investec Wealth & Investment Limited is registered in England. Registered No. 2122340. Registered Office: 2 Gresham Street, London EC2V 7QP.

WHAT HAPPENS TO THE MONEY RAISED?

Monies raised from our openings are split between the owner's choice of charity and our beneficiary charities which in 2016 will include the Queen's Nursing Institute Scotland, Maggie's Cancer Caring Centres, The Gardens Fund of the National Trust for Scotland and Perennial. Some of the other charities which will be supported in 2016 include:

ABF Soldiers' Charity ● Acting for Others ● Advocacy Service Aberdeen ● Alford Car Transport Service ● All Saints' Scottish Episcopal Church St Andrews ● Allergy UK ● Alzheimer Scotland ● Amnesty International ● Angus Toy Appeal ● Anthony Nolan ● Appin Village Hall ● Asbestos Action Tayside ● Association of Local Voluntary Organisations ● Auld Kirk, St Monans ● Barnardos ● Befriend A Child ● Ben Walton Trust ● Bennachie Guides ● Black Isle MacMillan Cancer Care ● Blairgowrie Black Watch Army Cadet Force ● Blebo Craigs Village Hall ● Bloodwise ● Borders Forest Trust ● Break the Silence ● British Heart Foundation ● British Horse Society Scotland ● British Limbless Ex-Servicemen's Association ● Brooke Hospital for Animals ● Bumblebee Conservation Trust ● Caddonfoot Parish Church Appeal ● Caerlaverock - Wildfowl and Wetlands Trust ● Caithness Samaritans ● Cambo Stables Project ● Camphill Blair Drummond ● Cancer Research ● Canine Partners ● Chest Heart & Stroke Scotland ● Children 1st ● Children's Hospice Association Scotland (CHAS) ● Children's Society ● Christ Church, Duns ● Clan Macpherson Museum ● CLASP ● CLIC Sargent ● Cloverglen Support Services Ltd ● Colinsburgh Town Hall Restoration Projects ● Compassion in World Farming ● Conservation Foundation ● Coronation Hall, Muckhart ● Corsock and Kirkpatrick Durham Church ● Cosgrove Care ● Coulter Library Trust ● Cowal Hospice ● Craigentinny Telferton Allotments ● Crail Cubs ● Crail Preservation Society ● Crichton Trust ● Crisis ● Croick Church ● Crossroads Caring Scotland ● Cruickshank Botanic Gardens Trust ● Daisy Chain Trust ● Dalhousie Day Care ● Dark Sky Observatory ● Diabetes UK ● Divine Innocence Trust ● Dogs for the Disabled ● Dogs Trust ● Dr Neil's Garden Trust ● Dundee and Glencarse Church ● Dunscore Church ● Elvanfoot Trust ● Environmental Justice Foundation ● Erskine Hospital ● Euan Macdonald Centre ● Fauna and Flora International ● Feedback Madagascar ● Fettercairn Community Allotments ● Firrholm Day Unit (Dementia) ● Forfar Open Garden Scheme ● Forgan Arts Centre ●Forget Me Not ● Forth Driving Group RDA ● Fortingall Church ● Freedom From Fistula Foundation ●Friends of Anchor ● Friends of Glasgow Botanic Gardens ● Friends of Hermitage Park ● Friends of Hillcrest ●Friends of Kirkcudbright Swimming Pool ● Friends of Loch Arthur Community ● Friends of St Modan's ● Friends of The Royal Botanic Garden Edinburgh ● Friends of Thor House ● Friendship Club ● Froglife ● Gairloch Museum ● Gardening Leave ● Gargunnock Community Trust ● Girl Guiding North Ayrshire ● Glasserton Parish Church ● Glencorse Church, Penicuik ● Green Routes ● Greenock Medical Aid Society ● Gunsgreen House Trust ● Gurkha Welfare Trust ● Help for Heroes ● Hessilhead Wildlife Rescue Trust ● Black Isle Bee Gardens ● Highland Hospice ● Hillfoot Harmony Barbershop Singers ● Hobkirk Church ● Home Start Stonehaven ● Hope Kitchen ● Horatio's Garden ● Humane Research Trust ● Jewish Care Scotland ● Jo Walters Trust ● John Buchan Museum, Peebles ● Julia Thomson Memorial Trust ● Juvenile Diabetes Research Foundation ● Katie McKerracher Trust ● Kew on Great Western Road Fund ● Kilbarchan Old Library ● Kilbryde Hospice ● Kincardine O'Neil Village Hall ● Kirkandrews Church ● Kirkcudbright Hospital League of Friends ● Kirkmahoe Parish Church ● Kirkpatrick Durham Church ● Laggan Church ● Lamancha & District Community Association ● Lanark Community Development Trust ● Lavender Touch ● Leighton Library ● Leuchie House ● Little Haven ● Local Animal Rescue Charities ● Loch Arthur Community (Camphill Trust) ● Lochdon School ● Lothian Cat Rescue ● LUPUS UK ● Lynton Centre (East Linton) ● Macmillan Cancer Support ● Maggie's Cancer Caring Centres ● Marie Curie Cancer Care ● Mary's Meals ● Medicins sans Frontieres ● Mercy Ships ● Mission to Seafarers ● Momentum Pathways ● Montrose Guides ● Motor Neurone Disease Association ● Multiple Sclerosis UK ● Muckhart Parish Church ● Muckhart Primary School ● Muckhart Village Hall ● Multiple Sclerosis UK ● Music in Hospitals Scotland ● Music in Lanark ● Newburgh Scout Group ● Oakfield, Easton Maudit ● Order of St John ● Orkidstudio ● Pain Association Scotland ● Palliative Care Unit, Dumfries Hospital ● Pancreatic Cancer ● Parkinson's UK ● Parklea "Branching Out" ● Penicuik Development Trust ● Perth & Kinross District Nurses ● Perthshire Abandoned Dogs Society ● Peter Pan Moat Brae Trust ● Pirnmill Village Association ● Plant Heritage ● Plantlife Scotland ●Poppy Scotland ● Port Logan Hall ● Practical Action ● RAF Benevolent Fund ● Red Cross ● Redhall Walled Garden SAMH ● Riding for the Disabled Association ● RIO Community Centre ● RNLI ● Dog Rescue ● ROKPA Tibetan Charity ● Rotary Polio Plus Campaign ● RUDA ● Saline Environmental Group ● Sandpiper Trust ● SANDS ● Save the Children ● Save the Elephant ● Scleroderma Society ● Scots Mining Company Trust ● Scottish Civic Trust ● Scottish Love in Action (SLA) ● Scottish Waterways Trust ● Silverburn Community ● Smile Train ● Sophie North Charitable Trust ● South of Scotland Wild Life Hospital ● Southton Smallholding ● SSAFA, the Armed Forces Charity ● SSPCA ● St Athernase Church, Leuchars ● St Columba's Hospice ● St Margaret's Parish Church ● St Mary's Episcopal Church ● St Peter's Episcopal Church ● St Vincents Hospice ● Stable Life ● Stobo & Drumelzier Kirk ● Stracathro Cancer Care Fund UK ● Strathcarron Hospice ● Student Foodbank, Dundee & Angus College ● Survival International ● Sustrans ● Tarland Community Garden ● Tayside Children's Hospital Appeal ● Tillicoultry Allotments Association ● Trees for Life and Community Café ● Trellis Scotland ● Type 1 Juvenile Diabetes Research Fund ● Unicorn Preservation Society ● Wellbeing of Women ● Whiting Bay Improvements and the Village Hall ● Willow Foundation ● Woodland Trust ● Worldwide Cancer Research ● WRVS ● Yorkhill Childrens Charity

Details of the charities chosen by each garden owner are provided within their garden listing.

Money is also donated via the Cattanach bequest to the National Trust for Scotland to train an apprentice gardener.

BENEFICIARY MESSAGES

maggie's

2016 is another year of growth for Maggie's, as we prepare to open our eighth Maggie's Centre in Scotland. This marks a major milestone in our history as a charity, giving Maggie's a presence at every major cancer treatment hospital in Scotland.

When it opens in summer 2016, Maggie's Forth Valley will be the first Maggie's Centre to be located beside water, sitting on the bank of an ornamental lochan and surrounded by green spaces, woodlands and a network of paths and walkways, in the grounds of Forth Valley Royal Hospital in Larbert. The Centre will offer a retreat from the outside world, whilst also celebrating the beauty of the landscape and the hope that nature offers.

2016 will also see the creation of a large, standalone garden adjacent to the Maggie's Centre in Edinburgh. This beautiful, winding outdoor space will be a visual and sensory experience to be enjoyed by the general public, whilst also allowing visitors to the centre to draw on the flora and fauna present through our courses in meditation, creative drawing, Tai Chi and relaxation.

Our co-founder Maggie Keswick Jencks was herself passionate about gardens and wrote one of the most important books published on Chinese gardens, and her original blueprint for Maggie's placed great emphasis on the role of the landscape and outdoor spaces in creating a relaxing environment, with the emphasis on healing. Holding true to this day, gardens remain an integral part of any Maggie's Centre. Our lushly planted gardens offer a sense of calm, designed to start the process of stress reduction and mindfulness the Centre aims to encourage.

I would like to take this opportunity to thank you all for your most welcome support of Maggie's in Scotland again this year. All of our Centres benefit from Scotland's Gardens donations.

With warmest wishes,

Laura Lee
Chief Executive
Please call 0300 123 1801 or visit
www.maggiescentres.org for more information.

Part of the garden at the Maggie's Centre in Edinburgh

BENEFICIARY MESSAGES

THE QUEEN'S NURSING INSTITUTE SCOTLAND

The history between Scotland's Gardens and the Queen's Nursing Institute of Scotland is well documented. Scotland's Gardens was initially set up in 1931 with the sole purpose of raising money for Queen's Nurses: nurses working in the community to provide healthcare across Scotland. The money raised supported the nurses from their training, through their working life and into retirement. With healthcare provision now provided centrally through the NHS, why do we still need support from Scotland's Gardens?

Currently, over 90% of health care is provided outside of hospital, a figure set to increase with the shift to health and social care integration. Community nursing includes a range of specialist roles, for example Health Visitors, District Nurses, School Nurses, Community Psychiatric Nurses, Criminal Justice Nurses and General Practice Nurses.

The role of the Institute has changed significantly over the years, but our central purpose today remains the same – to enable nurses working in the community to be the very best they can be to help improve the health and wellbeing of the people of Scotland.

While we no longer provide nurse training directly, we provide funding to allow nurses to take on opportunities for professional development – last year helping over 23 individuals and teams. In 2015 we also funded six projects under a programme of 'Catalysts for Change' seeking to address health inequalities for some overlooked communities, whilst developing nurse-led integration across agencies.

We still aim to provide recognition for the hard work and dedication of the community nursing workforce. In 2015, we awarded over 100 Long Service Awards to individuals who have devoted over 21 years of service to nursing in the community. Pictured here are some of the Greater Glasgow and Clyde nurses who received awards.

We continue to provide support for over 400 retired Queen's Nurses across Scotland, providing them with hardship grants, fellowship and companionship.

2016 will see the launch of our new strategy. It includes the reintroduction of the Queen's Nurse title, which has been enabled by funding from Scotland's Gardens. This important move will build on the rich tradition of Queen's Nursing in Scotland and develop the skills of contemporary nursing leaders in the community.

All that we have achieved over the past year, and indeed since 1931, has been supported with money raised by Scotland's Gardens, and we are proud to be a Beneficiary Charity. We would like to take this opportunity to pass on our thanks and appreciation to all the garden visitors, and particularly everyone who opens their gardens for their generous support of our work.

Clare Cable
Chief Executive and Nurse Director
Queen's Nursing Institute Scotland

BENEFICIARY MESSAGES

the National Trust
for Scotland
a place for everyone

On behalf of the National Trust for Scotland's Gardens Community I would like to thank all of Scotland's Gardens owners for their ongoing support to the National Trust for Scotland in general and its gardens portfolio in particular. We really appreciate the financial (and other) support you provide that enables so much of the work that goes on in our gardens. Our gardens and designed landscapes continue to flourish and grow, prove popular with our visitors, providing perfect places for sanctuary and reflection away from the pressures of modern daily life. We are grateful to everyone who supports our work and the future of Scottish gardens by continuing to visit and enjoy the places in our care.

In 2015 twenty-nine of our gardens supported Scotland's Gardens, with 47 successful events and activities held. For 2016 we plan to build on this by hosting 51 special events and including a special vegetable day at Threave Garden in association with the National Vegetable Society. For the first time, and new to Scotland's Gardens in 2016, we shall be welcoming visitors to see the early stages of the restoration of the Victorian Flower Garden at Newhailes in Musselburgh where recent archaeology has uncovered the elaborate former garden.

Through the School of Heritage Gardening, in part supported by Scotland's Gardens, the Trust continues to play an important part in growing future gardeners. There is a high quality framework to support gardener training in our gardens across the country with student placements at Threave Garden.

Thanks to your generous financial donation, visitors can continue to enjoy our gardens across the seasons and appreciate the expertise and labours of our dedicated gardens staff, who help to create, develop and conserve these beautiful places.

Simon Skinner
Chief Executive

Threave Garden, Kirkcudbrightshire

BENEFICIARY MESSAGES

PERENNIAL
GARDENERS' ROYAL BENEVOLENT SOCIETY
Helping Horticulturists In Need Since 1839

How Perennial helps

Kate Powell was employed for many years in nursery stock production until ill health forced her to stop working.

Kate and her partner were both horticulturists, independent and healthy, but when illness struck, as it can strike anyone, their circumstances changed rapidly. Kate's horticultural career was cut short when she became seriously ill with kidney failure and she relied on dialysis while she waited for a viable kidney transplant. They were struggling to make ends meet and it took her a huge amount of courage and swallowing of pride to contact Perennial to ask for help. But she did and recalls those first conversations with a lasting sense of relief:

Kate Powell

"We were visited by a Caseworker within days. She was, and still is, brilliant, a lifebelt in the flood. She seemed to know exactly what we needed and her advice and help was perfectly pitched. The Caseworkers are professional, discreet and they will go out of their way to do everything they can to help. Looking back we simply couldn't have coped without Perennial, and we still have their help and support."

Perennial helps hundreds of families like Kate's each year, providing bespoke solutions to clients until they are back on their feet. Highly confidential help is provided completely free by professional Caseworkers and Debt Advisers.

We regularly see families with young children worried about school costs. Here is how one client described the help they received during the year, "Perennial lifted the burden of going into debt while benefits were sorted out, and we were also given a voucher to receive emergency food supplies. Our children have been able to take part in their school activities and having enough food has lifted our morale."

Read about other people who have been helped by Perennial at www.perennial.org.uk/success-stories

We need your help!

We can only continue to provide services like these for the vulnerable horticulturists and their families who may need help and advice with the support from the garden loving public. Your visits to open gardens through the Scotlands Gardens scheme helps our charity throughout the year. If you would like to help more, why not make a personal donation to Perennial?

Go to www.perennial.org.uk/donate. If you know anyone who may need help please pass on our details.

Advice Line:	0800 093 8543
Debt Advice:	0800 093 8546
Donation Line:	0800 093 8792

Perennial, 115-117 Kingston Road,
Leatherhead, Surrey, KT22 7SU

Registered Charity Nos 1155156 | Scotland SC040180
Perennial's Debt Advice Service is regulated by the FCA.

GALLERY, MONTROSE

Occupying just over one acre the mid-18th century walled garden of Gallery lies immediately north of the house. Square piers supporting white painted iron railings allow a view from the outside. Historic features are the paths intersecting at the centre where the listed sundial erected by David Lyall in 1786 stands. The fine stone carving of a recumbent retriever lies over the antique wooden door at the north end. Beyond the north wall is a planting of varied heather interspersed with betula. The space beyond is home to a family group of Castlemilk Moorit sheep. The furthest fringe of trees tops a high bank overlooking the North Esk river with views over the Howe toward Cairn O' Mounth.

On entering the garden the customary route for visitors intending to see all parts will be to take the left exit from the circular entrance area adorned with mop head Quercus ilex.

This path laid with granite blaze and edged with trimmed box leads to a trellis carrying honeysuckle and hops. The apparent irregular planting of three Robinia reflects the ravages of winter. The borders, mainly of Campanula lactiflora, Achilea 'Moonshine' and Aconitum, provide an agreeable blue, yellow and cream colour combination.

Leaving this border on the path, round the edge of the large beech clipped in the shape of an egg, leads into the gold garden. The row of Mallus transitoria on the edge presents a cloud of white blossom contrasting with the laburnum on the adjoining edge. Zelkova 'Kiwi Sunset' occupies the centre space and Catalpa and Chamaecyparis surround the bench. The traditional prostrate conifer provides ground cover in the centre spaces.

Returning towards the entrance gate and turning left, this route takes us alongside the sunken garden ornamented with berberis, eleagnus and agapanthus accompanying an historic golden yew.

To the right of the path is a recently (2015) replanted hot bed including Papaver oriental alongside Phormium, poppies and dahlias.

Box-edged beds in full bloom © Ray Cox Photography

Beyond this is Anne's Garden at the foot of Cedrus atlantica and bordered by magnolia and hosta.

Round the corner is the arched entrance to the rose garden under a mass of 'Cerise Bouquet'. An ancient cherry occupies a central bed and others surrounding hold 'Buff Beauty', 'Fontin-Latour', 'Tuscany Superb', 'Mme Alice Garnier', 'De Rescht', Rosa fimbriata and many others. There is a supporting cast of Crambe, Philadelphus, geranium (including magnificus), Deutzia, with a variety of clematis clinging to the entrance arches. These include 'Veronica's Choice' and 'Beauty of Worcester'.

Leaving the rose garden through the hosta walk brings you to the summer lawn garden bordered with a generous hedge of 'Sally Holmes' roses. The southern shady end is planted to correspond in separate beds featuring rhododendron, box, and mahonia, supported by geum, heuchera and peonies. The south facing border at the foot of the wall was the first to be dug, manured and planted in 1999. It is characterised by the magnificent Crown Jewels, Fennels and 'Faust' delphiniums. These are supported by the collection of peonies, stanard rosa Ballerine, geranium, iris, hosta and others.

From the summer lawn the exit path leads to the

The white garden with fountain

entrance of the white garden, the central feature of which is a layered fountain and pool surrounded by raised beds. Separate stands of Delphinium 'Silver Jubilee', 'Moonbeam' and others are a principal feature whilst large spreads of Hydrangea 'Annabelle' face each other across the central pool. Weeping pears at the corners are a feature as is the collection of white roses. Anthemis cupaniana occupies centre stage around the pool.

Together, the clipped hedges and closely-mown lawns make a significant contribution to the atmosphere of order and calm which pervades the entire garden.

Delphiniums 'Faust' in the stunning south-facing border © Ray Cox Photography

Since 1999 there has, as described above, been a considerable embellishment of the Gallery garden. It followed the change of ownership in 1997 and is the achievement of a talented gardening team.

Head Gardener Ron Stephens is the full time working member of this team. The present excellent condition of the garden reflects his exceptional skill, hard work and commitment. These qualities were recognised by the award in 2015 for his contribution to gardening in Scotland from the Royal Caledonian Horticultural Society.

Veronica Adams' outstanding designs, on which the plant selection and planting plans are based, have been the other dominant factor in the restoration of the garden.

My late wife, Anne, a fellow student of Veronica's at the Ruskin School of Art, had the leading part in the early stages of the garden revival. Since her death in 2007 I like to think that the surviving members of this working group have successfully extended and carried forward the project she had so enthusiastically embarked upon.

Pink Rosa 'De Rescht'

Rosa 'Mme Alice Garnier'

Rosa 'Buff Beauty'

Mixed border thriving in the sunshine

DISCOVER SCOTTISH GARDENS

Discover Scottish Gardens was launched at Gardening Scotland in May 2015, at Ingliston. We are a new national tourism organisation aimed at inspiring more people from both home and abroad to explore Scottish gardens and to enjoy their beauty, heritage and variety.

The castles, whisky, golf and landscapes of Scotland are already well-known worldwide - but it is only now that our unique garden and plant history, diverse climatic conditions and impressive botanical offering is gaining the recognition it deserves.

Our unique plant hunter history is another special aspect of Scottish history, which remains under appreciated; some visitors already know about it but more will no doubt follow as we gain more profile.

Discover Scottish Gardens is encouraging more visitors to Scottish gardens and raising the profile of garden-related destinations. We are doing this by creating new, national seasonal festivals, a website which enables visitors to search for gardens and engagement through social media.

VisitScotland has shown tremendous support with £30,000 funding to launch Discover Scottish Gardens, ensuring the development of our website as well as a profile-raising campaign to spread the word and raise awareness, encouraging individual garden lovers to register their interest and hoping to inspire newcomers to investigate Scotland's unique garden offering.

Local groups such as Glorious Gardens of Argyll & Bute already exist while the famous Snowdrop Festival has gone from strength to strength. They benefit not only the gardens taking part but also local hotels and retailers who enjoy increased visitors for their activities.

Owners and managers of gardens throughout Scotland, and related businesses such as garden nurseries, horticultural organisations, specialist garden travel tour companies and accommodation providers are all welcome to join Discover Scottish Gardens.

Sunken garden at Attadale in September

We are keen to welcome more members so that through critical mass, garden owners and others involved in the sector can reach more potential visitors in an effective manner. Founding members include Scotland's Gardens themselves, the Royal Botanic Garden Edinburgh as well as the National Trust for Scotland.

Why not support us by liking us on Facebook (*facebook.com/discoverscottishgardens*) and following us on Twitter (*twitter.com/scottishgdns*)?

Plus www.discoverscottishgardens.org is full of information - have a look and do get in touch, whether as a prospective garden visitor or a possible member of the organisation, all are welcome.

Joanna Macpherson
Membership Director
Discover Scottish Gardens

DISC❀VER
SCOTTISH GARDENS

Branklyn Garden, Perth © NTS

© RBGE

OPEN BY ARRANGEMENT

Some hundred gardens will open 'by arrangement' for Scotland's Gardens in 2016 providing a convenient and leisurely way to visit gardens throughout the length and breadth of Scotland. All are different, many have rarely admitted visitors before and all have one thing in common- their owners would love to share their passion for gardening and garden design with you and raise money for charity in the process.

Representing nearly a fifth of our openings they are a very flexible way for visitors to see gardens: many open over a long period of the horticultural season and garden owners are often happy to fit opening times around visitor requirements. If you prefer a morning or afternoon visit or perhaps wish to take advantage of the long summer evenings and enjoy the peace and tranquillity of a garden at the end of a busy working day when the light is soft and wind has dropped, our garden owners would be pleased to discuss options.

"Whether you prefer a guided tour or to explore and investigate unaccompanied..."

Whether you prefer the majesty of a woodland garden with dramatic spring displays of rhododendron, azalea, magnolia, meconopsis and candelabra primula or admire gardens created out of rock base on a steep slope with alpines and other plants loving well drained soil, or enjoy the sight of wonderful mixed borders in full summer bloom gardens that open by arrangement reflect the vast range of possible garden styles. From recently created to renowned historic gardens all are unique and reflect the great talents of both professional and amateur gardeners alike.

Barham, Fife - a garden open by arrangement

One of the great advantages of visiting gardens by arrangement is that the owners will often provide guided tours. Others will also give presentations on the development of the garden followed by a guided tour. Be inspired by their garden and infected by their enthusiasm and passion for gardening and the garden design while accompanying them around their patch of paradise! Visitors who prefer to explore and investigate unaccompanied and enjoy the garden on their own are just as welcome!

"...what rare treasures can be discovered"

Some openings offer plants for sale. These plant stalls often offer locally sourced and grown plants and can be like no other: many of the gardens that open for Scotland's Gardens are privately owned and have been gardened for many years by keen gardener-owner plants women and men. The borders can be filled with rare and unusual plants collected over the years and with some plants unique to that garden where novel chance seedlings have been encouraged and nurtured. What rare treasures can be discovered at these plant stalls!

Many gardens are sited in spectacular locations with breath taking views and scenery others situated within a busy conurbation offering a tranquil retreat in the midst of the city. Wherever you live, planning to see an area for the first time or visit one of your favourite haunts, there is likely to be a garden open by arrangement nearby. Please do contact the garden owner and arrange a visit, you will get a very warm welcome. Some owners will provide teas and/or other refreshments on request.

"the owners really are keen to be contacted"

Blackmill Garden, Kilsyth - a garden open by arrangement

Parkhead House, Perth - a garden open by arrangement

Whether you are a group of keen gardeners, or friends looking for somewhere different to meet and socialise a beautiful scented garden is a wonderful place to gather, catch up and share the pleasure and exchange of ideas visiting a garden can provide.

Feedback from by arrangement openings of previous years has revealed that many potential garden visitors would love to visit but are wary of disturbing garden owners. We can assure you that the owners really are keen to be contacted to arrange a visit but, if you would prefer, a local volunteer organiser would be happy to be contacted in the first instance. We are trialling this approach in Stirlingshire, Perth and Kinross, Angus and Fife. These local organisers can answer any of your concerns or perhaps even suggest a group of gardens to visit over a day - your very own bespoke garden Trail!

Glenkyllachy Lodge, Inverness- a garden open by arrangement

The following district organisers are happy to give you advice on 'by arrangement' gardens or to help you organise your visits. A full list of these gardens can be found on pages 65-68.

STIRLINGSHIRE

Mandy Readman
T: 01786 821102
E: mandy@tebhan.com

PERTH & KINROSS

Margaret Gimblett
T: 01887 840288
E: gimblettsmill@aol.com

ANGUS

Terrill Dobson
T: 01575 570119
E: terrill@scotlandsgardens.org

FIFE

Sally Lorimore
T: 01382 542890
E: e.g.wright@dundee.ac.uk

NEW GARDENS FOR 2016

Aberdeenshire

Airdlin Croft
An Teallach

Angus & Dundee

Dundee & Angus College Gardens
Forfar Open Garden

Argyll

Braevallich Farm
Little Kilmory Cottage

Ayrshire

Craigengillan Estate and Dark Sky Observatory
Golf Course Road Gardens
South Logan Farm

Berwickshire

Kames

Dumfriesshire

Amisfield Tower
Barjarg Tower
The Crichton Rock Garden and Arboretum

Golf Course Road Gardens, Ayrshire

An-Grianan, Morayshire

Strathbungo Gardens, Glasgow & North Lanarkshire

Newhailes, East Lothian

Dunbartonshire

Stuckenduff

East Lothian

Newhailes

Edinburgh & West Lothian

Balerno Lodge
Brighton Gardens
Craigentinny and Telferton Allotments
Rivaldsgreen House

Fife

Boarhills Village Gardens
The Old Farmhouse

Glasgow & North Lanarkshire

Auchinstarry Sensory Garden
Glasgow Botanic Gardens
Strathbungo Gardens

Midlothian

Eskbank Gardens
Huntly Cot

Moray & Nairn

An-Grianan

Perth & Kinross

Kirkton Craig
Muckhart Village
The Garden at Craigowan

The Old Farmhouse, Fife

Craigengillan Estate & Dark Sky Observatory, Ayrshire
© Dr James Silvester

Glasgow Botanic Gardens

Kirkton Craig, Perth & Kinross

Renfrewshire

Highwood
Kilbarchan Village Gardens

Ross, Cromarty, Skye & Inverness

Craig Dhu House
Malin

Roxburghshire

Easter Weens

South Lanarkshire

Old Farm Cottage
The Castlebank Gardens
The Walled Garden, Shieldhill

Stirlingshire

Bridgend of Teith
Gardener's Cottage Walled Garden
Harvest Lunch at Easter Culmore
Kippenrait with St Blanes House
Manorcroft
Tillicoultry Allotments

Wigtownshire

Hill Cottage

The Garden at Craigowan, Perth & Kinross

Highwood, Renfrewshire

Easter Weens, Roxburghshire

Manorcroft, Stirlingshire

SNOWDROP OPENINGS

Celebrate the first signs of spring by exploring our beautiful Snowdrop Gardens.

New this year is a combined Snowdrops and Stars event at Craigengillan Estate and the Dark Sky Observatory.

VisitScotland support our openings under the popular Snowdrop Festival and are again promoting this very special time of year for visiting gardens.

The following properties will be opening and most will be participating in the Snowdrop Festival:

Aberdeenshire

Bruckhills Croft

Angus & Dundee

Lawton House

Pitmuies Gardens

Ayrshire

Blair House, Blair Estate

Craigengillan Estate & Dark Sky Observatory

Grougarbank House

Dumfriesshire

Barjarg Tower

Craig

East Lothian

Shepherd House

Fife

Lindores House

Kincardine & Deeside

Ecclesgreig Castle

Kirkcudbrightshire

Brooklands

Danevale Park

Lanarkshire

Cleghorn

SCOTTISH SNOWDROP FESTIVAL
SATURDAY 30 JAN - SUNDAY 13 MARCH

Moray & Nairn

10 Pilmuir Road West

Peeblesshire

Dawyck Botanic Garden
Kailzie Gardens

Perth & Kinross

Braco Castle
Cluny House
Kilgraston School

Renfrewshire

Ardgowan

Ross, Cromarty, Skye & Inverness

Abriachan Garden Nursery

Stirlingshire

Duntreath Castle
Gargunnock House Garden
Tamano
The Linns
West Plean House

Wigtownshire

Dunskey Garden and Maze
Logan Botanic Garden

If you have some lovely snowdrops please get in touch. Perhaps we can feature your garden in 2017!

PEEBLESSHIRE GARDEN TRIO MAY - AUGUST 2016

This superb trio of gardens will give you a taste of the wide variety of garden styles in the Peeblesshire area. See them develop from May to August with a season ticket, or spend a fabulous afternoon at your favourite.

Opening times

Saturday 28 May
1:30pm - 5:00pm   Haystoun

Sunday 29 May
1:30pm - 5:00pm   Haystoun and Glen House

Wednesday 22 June
1:30pm - 5:00pm   The Cottage, West Linton

Thursday 23 June
1:30pm - 5:00pm   Glen House

Wednesday 29 June
1:30pm - 5:00pm   Haystoun

Thursday 21 July
1:30pm - 5:00pm   The Cottage, West Linton

Thursday 25 August
1:30pm - 5:00pm   The Cottage, West Linton
                                  and Glen House

See page 286 for further details.

Charities

60% net of the proceeds from the Peeblesshire Garden Trio is shared between Scotland's Gardens' beneficiary charities:

* Maggie's Cancer Caring Centres
* Queen's Nursing Institute Scotland
* Gardens Fund of the National Trust for Scotland
* Perennial

The remaining 40% will go to the Conservation Foundation, the Ben Walton Trust and St Columba's Hospice.

Admission

£13.00 covering all three gardens and all seven dates. Single entry to either Glen House or Haystoun £5.00 and to The Cottage £3.00.

For further information or to book your ticket email Rose Parrott at **parrott@btinternet.com**.

Teas will be available at local tea rooms, details of these will be given with your ticket.

Haystoun

Glen House

The Cottage

TRAPRAIN GARDEN CIRCLE
MAY - JUNE 2016

Three distinctly different gardens, two of which have never previously opened, in rural East Lothian:

1 a bijou walled garden set in substantial policies

2 an exposed densely-planted garden

3 a traditional walled garden

Follow the unfolding of late spring and early summer in each garden on three afternoons over a month.

Opening times

Wednesday 25 May
Wednesday 15 June
Wednesday 29 June
11:00am - 6:00pm

See p262 for further details.

Admission

Season ticket £15.00, all gardens, all days
Single visit ticket £5.00 per garden
Tickets will be available on the day at all of the gardens.

Beneficiary Charities

60% net of the proceeds from the Traprain Garden Circle is shared between Scotland's Gardens' beneficiary charities:

- Maggie's Cancer Caring Centres
- Queen's Nursing Institute Scotland
- Gardens Fund of the National Trust for Scotland
- Perennial

The remaining 40% will go to Trellis Scotland which supports 300 gardening projects to improve physical, emotional and social wellbeing.

1 Garvald Grange

2 Granary House

3 Stevenson Steading Walled Garden

Granary House

Stevenson Steading Walled Garden

Garvald Grange

INDEX OF ADVERTISERS

Visit four Botanic Gardens to see one of the richest plant collections on Earth.

Royal Botanic Garden Edinburgh

Arboretum Place and Inverleith Row, Edinburgh EH3 5LR

Tel 0131 248 2909 | www.rbge.org.uk

Open every day from 10 am
(except 1 January and 25 December)
Garden is free
Entry charges apply to Glasshouses

Royal Botanic Garden Edinburgh at

Benmore

Dunoon,
Argyll PA23 8QU

Tel 01369 706261
www.rbge.org.uk/benmore

Open daily 1 March to 31 October
Admission charge applies

Royal Botanic Garden Edinburgh at

Logan

Port Logan, Stranraer,
Dumfries and Galloway DG9 9ND
Tel 01776 860231
www.rbge.org.uk/logan
Open daily 15 March to 31 October
and Sundays in February
Admission charge applies

Royal Botanic Garden Edinburgh at

Dawyck

Stobo, Scottish Borders
EH45 9JU

Tel 01721 760254
www.rbge.org.uk/dawyck

Open daily 1 February – 30 November
Admission charge applies

The Royal Botanic Garden Edinburgh is a Non Departmental Public Body (NDPB) sponsored and supported through Grant-in-Aid by the Scottish Government's Environment and Forestry Directorate (ENFOR).

Escape to Auchlochan Village to see our beautifully landscaped grounds, mature woodlands, spectacular gardens and expansive lochs.

Auchlochan Gardens

Escape to Auchlochan Garden Village to see our beautifully landscaped grounds, mature woodlands, spectacular gardens and lochs.

The gardens at Auchlochan are its undoubted glory, offering a wide range of attractions to visitors, walkers and residents alike.

Laid out over a 50 acre estate, the gardens feature not only the lochs that gave the village its name, but stunning herbaceous borders, terrace gardens, rhododendron beds and heather gardens. Along the River Nethan valley, the gardens merge with mature woodland which feature our prominent Sequoiadendron giganteum - giant Redwoods - which are native to California.

At Auchlochan's heart is the delightful 1.5 acre walled garden. Built around 1900, the garden was originally designed as a source of fruit and vegetables for the estate. Under the care of the current gardening team it has been transformed into a show garden.

The Auchlochan grounds attract many visitors - there is a 4 Star B&B and self catering accommodation available all year round - and enjoy a relaxing cup of tea or coffee or even lunch in our bistro, at the same time.

nd Grounds

Auchlochan
Garden Village

01555 893592
www.auchlochan.com

Auchlochan Garden Village, New Trows Road,
Lesmahagow, South Lanarkshire ML11 0GS

MHA Auchlochan, registered as a Charity - No.SC040155 • Company Limited by Guarantee - No. SC352117

SINCE 1931
SCOTLAND'S
GARDENS
GROWING AND GIVING

Two wonderful Private Garden Tours for 2016

Quoy of Houton, Orkney

Photo: Ray Cox

The Gardens and Castles of Mar

The county of Aberdeenshire has more castles per acre than anywhere else in the UK, certain of which are known collectively as the 'Castles of Mar'. It just so happens that the majority of these castles are surrounded by fine gardens, making this the ideal destination for a garden tour that has the added bonus of being set against a backdrop of romantic castles and houses which are bound up with the rich history of this handsome corner of Scotland.

We will be based at the comfortable Ardoe House Hotel and Spa just outside Aberdeen, itself a 19th century Scots Baronial-style mansion house set in tranquil grounds.

Departs July 24, 2016
Three nights' half board from **£515pp**
Single room supplement **£90**

What's included
Visits to the gardens of Brechin Castle, Leith Hall, Kildrummy Castle, Tillypronie, Hatton Castle, Fyvie Castle, Haddo House, Greenridge and Crathes Castle

Orkney's Garden Trail

Such was the success of our garden tour to Orkney last year, we have decided to repeat the chance to see the wonderful efforts of 'gardening on the edge'.

The high standard of gardens on 'Orkney's Garden Trail' along with the wonderful scenic beauty of the islands themselves makes it a pleasure to run this tour one more time along with visiting other fine private gardens not easily accessible in the far north of Scotland.

Departs July 8, 2016
Five nights' half board from **£825pp**
Single room supplement **£125**

What's included
Visits to the gardens of Old Allangrange, Langwell and the Castle of Mey; two private gardens in Thurso and some of the gardens of 'Orkney's Garden Trail'; guided tours of Orkney including the Ring of Brodgar, Standing Stones of Stenness, the Italian Chapel and archaeological sites at Skara Brae and Maeshowe.

For full details on both tours contact:
01334 657155

brightwater
holidays

Brightwater Holidays Ltd
Eden Park House,
Cupar, Fife KY15 4HS
info@brightwaterholidays.com
www.brightwaterholidays.com

Crathes Castle

BENNYBEG
PLANT
CENTRE

Plant Paradise

One of the widest selections of
garden plants in Scotland

Muthill Road, Crieff, Perthshire,
PH7 4HN T: 01764 656345 info@bennybeg.co.uk

JAMESFIELD
GARDEN CENTRE

For all your Garden needs

Next to
Jamesfield Farm Food
Shop & Restaurant

Abernethy, Perthshire, KY14 6EW
T: 01738 851176
www.jamesfieldgardencentre.co.uk

We are grateful for the support
of Scotland's Gardens and garden lovers everywhere.

Dougal Philip, Chair of Perennial's Board of Trustees and
owner of New Hopetoun Gardens, West Lothian, said:
*"Perennial has been around for over 175 years, supporting
all of us working in or retired from working in horticulture,
and our families. The bespoke service provided by
Perennial's highly trained Caseworkers and Debt Advisers
is often cited as a lifeline by our clients. With your support
we can help many more horticulturists get back on their
feet and achieve their potential."*

Perennial provides free, confidential advice, support and
financial assistance to gardeners of all ages working in or
retired from horticulture and their spouses, partners and
children for as long as it takes.

*Dougal Philip (left) and and RHS judge Jim Buttress (right) celebrating
with garden designers Amber Goudy and Martin Crowley, after their
garden for Perennial won Gold at Gardening Scotland in 2014.*

Supporting horticulturists since 1839

PERENNIAL
GARDENERS' ROYAL BENEVOLENT SOCIETY

To give us your support call us on 01372 373962
or visit our website www.perennial.org.uk/donate
A charity registered in Scotland no. SC040180 / YCOSGS

HAVE YOU DISCOVERED CARDWELL YET?

- Lots of quality trees, shrubs, bedding and houseplants
- Expert advice always available on all products
- Enormous selection of gifts, including a Scottish section
- 300 seat licensed restaurant serving food all day
- Indoor and outdoor furniture
- Arts, crafts and hobby centre
- Much, much more!

The Edinburgh Woollen Mill & PEACOCKS

ARE NOW OPEN AT CARDWELL

LOTS OF GREAT OFFERS IN STORE ALL YEAR ROUND

CARDWELL
GARDEN CENTRE

Scottish TOURIST BOARD ★★★★ TOURIST SHOP

Lunderston Bay, Gourock, Inverclyde, PA19 1BB
01475 521 536   www.cardwellgardencentre.co.uk

Munro
Greenhouses
& Garden Buildings

01786 357 400
info@munrogreenhouses.co.uk
www.munrogreenhouses.co.uk

Scotland's Independent Greenhouse Suppliers

Specialist Compost & Mulch Suppliers

We always advise our customers that you will only get back from the soil what you put in. Whether it is by digging in one of our soil improvers to improve the structure or protecting roots and soil by spreading our mulches over any bare ground, you are sure to see the benefits.

Find out more about our full range of Composts, Mulches and Soil Improvers online at www.gardensolutions.info or call 08000 430 450 to request a catalogue.

DISCOVER SCOTLAND

HOLIDAY COTTAGES

Quality self-catering holiday cottages for family holidays or short breaks.

www.discoverscotland.net
Tel 01556 504030

Quercus Garden Plants

A range of hardy and unusual plants for Scottish gardens

The nursery is one of an exciting group of businesses at Whitmuir Farm on the A701 just south of Leadburn. These include an award-winning organic farm shop, art gallery, crafts and cafe bistro.

We grow and sell a wide range of herbaceous plants, shrubs and trees, including old favourites and many unusual varieties. The majority of our plants are propagated and grown on site at 850 feet for at least a season, so are tough and acclimatised to Scottish growing conditions.

Whitmuir Farm, Lamancha, EH46 7BB   01968 660708   Open 10am - 5pm Wednesday - Sunday

www.quercusgardenplants.co.uk

DESIGNER, GOLDSMITH AND SILVERSMITH

91-95 High Street, Dunblane FK15 0ER
T: 01786 825244
www.grahamstewartsilversmith.co.uk

Casa Berti

Residential courses at
Casa Berti, Lucca, Tuscany
Spring and Autumn 2016
include...

- Tuscan villa gardens tours
- Wax modelling to
  Bronze sculpture with
  Dido Crosby
- Photography
- Watercolour and drawing
- Art History tour
- Yoga retreat
- Mindfulness

Casa Berti is a private family estate situated in the foothills of the Apuan Alps on a sunlit spur ten miles from the splendid walled city of Lucca, comprising extensive olive groves, gardens and woodland. At its heart, is a handsome and beautifully appointed 17th century manor house offering outstanding views on all sides. Our residential courses offer luxurious accommodation, catering and exceptional course leaders.

The property accommodates up to 16 guests and is available for private rental.

Contact: bengooder@casaberti.com   casaberti.com

Stephen Ogilvie
garden design, build & horticulture

Creative designs from our professional studio; from the traditional to the contemporary, Stephen Ogilvie delivers outstanding gardens and landscapes.

Design is the heart of our company. Our Head Designer Nick Starnes would be delighted to discuss your ideas for an inspirational garden. Professional 3D modelling, Virtual garden tours and beautifully detailed hand drawn designs create a stunning client package.

A combination of our Design studio and own highly skilled Construction team allows close communication on your project and results in exceptional finishes.

Creative planting schemes bring designs to life. We source plants locally as well as through Europe's best nursery growers to deliver stunning borders. We are specialists in the implementation of 'instant' planting schemes and the installation of large specimen trees and shrubs.

Stephen Ogilvie Garden Design Build and Horticulture has gained recognition over the past 20 years for its innovative design team and its exceptional garden construction skills across Scotland. We would welcome the opportunity to be involved in your project.

106 Biggar Road, Edinburgh, Office: 0131 4470145 Stephen: 07776 295541 Nick: 07872 818113
Email: stephen@stephenogilvie.co.uk nick@stephenogilvie.co.uk
www.stephenogilvie.co.uk

BY APPOINTMENT TO
HER MAJESTY THE QUEEN
WINE MERCHANTS
CORNEY & BARROW LIMITED
LONDON

BY APPOINTMENT TO
HRH THE PRINCE OF WALES
WINE MERCHANTS
CORNEY & BARROW LIMITED
LONDON

For tastings, personal cellar and gift suggestions, please visit our Edinburgh office.

Call **01875 321921** or
email **edinburgh@corneyandbarrow.com**

www.corneyandbarrow.com

**Corney & Barrow Ltd
Oxenfoord Castle
Pathhead
Midlothian
EH37 5UB**

Guiding our clients every step of the way

The Turcan Connell Group is the country's leading firm of legal, wealth management and tax advisers with an interdisciplinary team of lawyers, tax planners, investment managers and financial planners working together out of offices in Edinburgh, Glasgow, London and Guernsey. We provide our clients with all the services and expertise they need under one roof:

- Wealth Management*
- Charity Law and Philanthropy
- Charity Office
- Divorce and Family Law
- Employment Law
- Family Businesses
- Financial Planning*
- Pensions*

- Land and Property
- Litigation and Dispute Resolution
- Tax Compliance
- Wills, Estate Planning and Succession
- Turcan Connell Family Office*
- Investment Management*
- Renewables

TURCAN CONNELL
LEGAL • WEALTH MANAGEMENT • TAX

Edinburgh   Glasgow   London

Princes Exchange, 1 Earl Grey Street, Edinburgh EH3 9EE Tel: 0131 228 8111
Sutherland House, 149 St Vincent Street, Glasgow G2 5NW Tel: 0141 441 2111

Follow us on Twitter 🐦 @TurcanConnell
enquiries@turcanconnell.com   www.turcanconnell.com

Turcan Connell is a Partnership of Scottish Solicitors regulated by The Law Society of Scotland
Turcan Connell Asset Management Limited is authorised and regulated by the Financial Conduct Authority
*Indicates services supplied by Turcan Connell Asset Management Limited

NEW HOPETOUN GARDENS

...so much more than just a garden centre

The perfect place for a relaxed visit at any time of year. Set in six acres of woodland with 20 small themed gardens to explore and probably the biggest range of garden plants for sale in Scotland.

The Orangery tearoom will revive you and the gift shop will tempt you with the most exciting range of presents for everyone.

art in the garden runs during July and August and features original works of art by artists working in Scotland installed in the gardens.

(Entry is always free to our gardens.)

OPEN EVERY DAY 10.00AM – 5.30PM
New Hopetoun Gardens, by Winchburgh
West Lothian EH52 6QZ   01506 834433
www.newhopetoungardens.co.uk

FREE TEA or COFFEE
for Two Garden Lovers
in July or August 2016
Present this voucher in the
Orangery tearoom in
exchange for tea/coffee
for 2 people

35 inspirational gardens to visit. Right on your doorstep.

Discover one of the National Trust for Scotland's 35 magnificent gardens. Located throughout Scotland, each one is a feast for the senses and the imagination. A magical world awaits.

Step into a world of wonder.
Visit *www.nts.org.uk/visitgardens*

the National Trust for Scotland

a place for everyone

The National Trust for Scotland for Places of Historic Interest or Natural Beauty is a charity registered in Scotland, Charity Number SC 007410

Become a Friend
and help the Garden grow

Join the Royal Botanic Garden Edinburgh as a Friend and help us to explore, conserve and explain the world of plants for a better future.

Call the Membership Office on **0131 552 5339** or join online **www.rbge.org.uk/membership**

The Royal Botanic Garden Edinburgh is a charity registered in Scotland (number SC007983)

Plant Sales

Your opportunity to purchase from an enviable collection of plants at truly wonderful prices

All proceeds help support the work of the Royal Botanic Garden Edinburgh

Edinburgh – Sunday 8th May from 2pm-4pm
Dawyck – Sunday 15th May from 10am-3pm
Benmore – Sunday 29th May from 12noon
Logan – Sunday 28th August from 10.30am-3pm
Dawyck – Sunday 9th October from 10am-12.30pm

www.rbge.org.uk

The Royal Botanic Garden Edinburgh is a charity registered in Scotland (number SC007983)

Meet Connor.

At the age of 10

he became the

man of the house.

Connor's dad died of a stroke at age 42.

He was the picture of health.

It was the last thing anyone expected.

Make the end a new beginning.

A gift in your Will can mean life to those suffering from chest, heart and stroke illness in Scotland.

The funding that gifts in Wills provide is crucial to our work.

Chest Heart & Stroke Scotland

We are Scotland's Health Charity

Research • Advice • Support • Action

FundRaising
Standards Board

0300 1212 555 | gifts@chss.org.uk | www.chss.org.uk

Registered with and regulated by the Office of the Scottish Charity Regulator (no SC018761),
Chest Heart & Stroke Scotland is a wholly Scottish charity.
It also operates as CHSS and is registered in Scotland as a company limited by guarantee, no SC129114.

Supporting gardening in the heart of communities

Supporting Members

- Great days out to over 150 UK gardens, including 26 Partner Gardens in Scotland.
- Priority booking for the world-renowned RHS Flower Shows.
- Personalised gardening advice and The Garden Magazine.

Supporting Communities

- Supporting over 1350 schools in Scotland to learn and grow.
- Helping communities to transform their open spaces.
- Promoting horticultural education, training & volunteering.

Royal Horticultural Society

Sharing the best in Gardening

RHS in Scotland
Community Outreach Team

scotland@rhs.org.uk

rhs.org.uk/communities

RHS Registered Charity No: 222879/SC038262 Image: Shona Cooley Photography

PLANT HERITAGE
National Council for the Conservation of Plants & Gardens

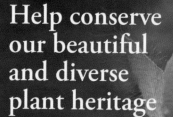

NCCPG

Help conserve our beautiful and diverse plant heritage

Join one of our five Scottish Groups for only £28 and meet fellow enthusiasts, hear experts speak and acquire rare and unusual plants.

Your support will help secure the future of our garden plants.

Meconopsis grandis © Stan Farrow

www.plantheritage.com
01483 447540 for further details
Reg Charity: 1004009/SC041785

There are over 60 National Plant Collections in Scotland - 'living libraries' of garden plants – all worth a visit!

ngs gardens open for charity

OVER 3,800 GARDENS OPEN FOR CHARITY IN ENGLAND AND WALES

Berriedale, Cumbria. Image: Val Corbett.

For more information visit our website
www.ngs.org.uk or telephone 01483 211535
The National Gardens Scheme registered charity number 1112664

Growing the
future...
of Horticulture in Scotland

The Caley has been supporting Horticulture and Gardening in Scotland since 1809. Scotland's Gardens showcases many different gardens in Scotland, some of which have received **RCHS awards** in recognition of their work.

This year The Caley is as **busy as a bee** supporting gardeners, professional and amateur, across Scotland.

Awards, Lectures, Demonstration Allotment, Gardening for Children, Educational Initiatives, National Horticultural Conference, Garden Tours, Spring Bulb Show AND SO MUCH MORE!

Join us today

£26 for individuals
£32 family membership

The Caley
Royal Caledonian Horticultural Society
Supporting Horticulture & Gardening in Scotland since 1809

For more information visit our website www.rchs.co.uk | Scottish Charity Number SC 006522

Every one of our retirement homes comes with a 40 acre garden.

And a gardening team.

Remember Flower Power? It's alive and well in the gardens at Inchmarlo.

You can enjoy the handiwork of our green-fingered workers everywhere (they do the spadework so you don't have to).

Then, slightly off the well-manicured path, our woods are home for red squirrels, deer and all kinds of birds.

And while woodland and gardens surround the village, the whole estate is surrounded by the regal grandeur of Royal Deeside.

Homes at Inchmarlo range from one-bedroom apartments to four bedroom houses, all well proportioned and all carefully designed for retirement living.

An added comfort is Inchmarlo House. This magnificent Georgian mansion is now a care home, so as your needs change, help and support is right on your doorstep.

Here too is a private lounge for Home Owners' events and a bar/restaurant serving dishes inspired by Michelin starred chefs.

To find out more call +44 (1330) 824981 or email info@inchmarlo-retirement.co.uk

Then come and see why Inchmarlo is the ideal spot to put down some roots.

INCHMARLO
RETIREMENT VILLAGE

Where Gracious Living Comes Naturally

GARDEN LISTINGS

GENERAL INFORMATION

MAPS
A map of each region and district is provided. These
show the general areas and location of gardens.
Directions can be found in the garden descriptions.

HOUSES
Houses are not open unless specifically stated; where
the house or part of the house is open, an additional
charge is usually made.

TOILETS
Private gardens do not normally have outside toilets.
For security reasons owners have been advised not
to admit visitors into their houses.

PHOTOGRAPHY
No photographs taken in a garden may be used for sale
or reproduction without the prior permission of the
garden owner.

CHILDREN
Children are generally welcome but must be
accompanied by an adult. Some of our gardens have
children's activities; details in the garden descriptions.

CANCELLATIONS
All cancellations will be posted on our website
www.scotlandsgardens.org

KEY TO SYMBOLS

 New in 2016

 Teas

 Cream teas

 Homemade teas

 Dogs on a lead allowed

 Wheelchair access

 Accommodation

 Plant stall

 Scottish Snowdrop Festival

REGIONAL MAP OF SCOTLAND

Scotland's Gardens 2016 Guidebook is sponsored by **INVESTEC WEALTH & INVESTMENT**

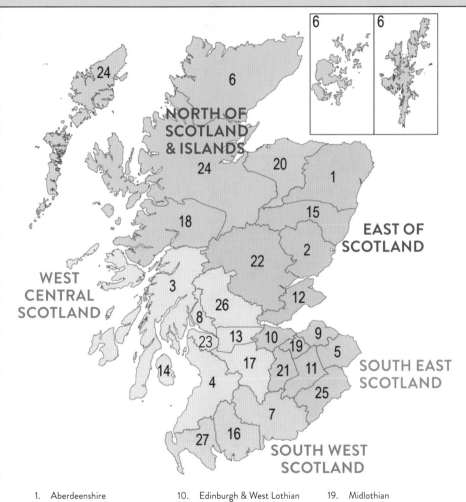

1. Aberdeenshire
2. Angus & Dundee
3. Argyll
4. Ayrshire
5. Berwickshire
6. Caithness, Sutherland, Orkney & Shetland
7. Dumfriesshire
8. Dunbartonshire
9. East Lothian
10. Edinburgh & West Lothian
11. Ettrick & Lauderdale
12. Fife
13. Glasgow & North Lanarkshire
14. Isle of Arran
15. Kincardine & Deeside
16. Kirkcudbrightshire
17. South Lanarkshire
18. Lochaber
19. Midlothian
20. Moray & Nairn
21. Peeblesshire
22. Perth & Kinross
23. Renfrewshire
24. Ross, Cromarty, Skye & Inverness
25. Roxburghshire
26. Stirlingshire
27. Wigtownshire

GARDENS OPEN ON A SPECIFIC DATE

Dates to be advised

Argyll	Maolachy's Garden, Lochavich, by Taynuilt
Kirkcudbrightshire	Danevale Park, Crossmichael

February

Sunday 7 February

Peeblesshire	Kailzie Gardens, Peebles
Wigtownshire	Logan Botanic Garden, Port Logan, by Stranraer

Saturday 13 February

Wigtownshire	Dunskey Gardens and Maze, Portpatrick, Stranraer

Sunday 14 February

Ayrshire	Blair House, Blair Estate, Dalry, Ayrshire
Wigtownshire	Dunskey Gardens and Maze, Portpatrick, Stranraer
Wigtownshire	Logan Botanic Garden, Port Logan, by Stranraer

Saturday 20 February

East Lothian	Shepherd House, Inveresk, Musselburgh
Kincardine & Deeside	Crathes Castle Garden, Banchory
Wigtownshire	Dunskey Gardens and Maze, Portpatrick, Stranraer

Sunday 21 February

Ayrshire	Craigengillan Estate and Dark Sky Observatory
Dumfriesshire	Craig, Langholm
East Lothian	Shepherd House, Inveresk, Musselburgh
South Lanarkshire	Cleghorn, Stable House, Cleghorn Farm, Lanark
Perth & Kinross	Kilgraston School, Bridge of Earn
Renfrewshire	Ardgowan, Inverkip
Wigtownshire	Dunskey Gardens and Maze, Portpatrick, Stranraer
Wigtownshire	Logan Botanic Garden, Port Logan, by Stranraer

Wednesday 24 February

Dumfriesshire	Barjarg Tower, Auldgirth

Thursday 25 February

Dumfriesshire	Barjarg Tower, Auldgirth

Saturday 27 February

Dumfriesshire	Barjarg Tower, Auldgirth

Sunday 24 April

Argyll	Benmore Botanic Garden, Benmore, Dunoon
Fife	46 South Street, St Andrews
Moray & Nairn	Brodie Castle, Brodie, Forres
Stirlingshire	The Pass House, Kilmahog, Callander
Wigtownshire	Claymoddie Garden, Whithorn, Newton Stewart

May

Sunday 1 May

Angus & Dundee	Brechin Castle, Brechin
Dumfriesshire	Portrack House, Holywood
Edinburgh & West Lothian	101 Greenbank Crescent, Edinburgh
Edinburgh & West Lothian	Moray Place and Bank Gardens, Edinburgh
Perth & Kinross	Branklyn Garden, 116 Dundee Road, Perth

Saturday 7 May

Aberdeenshire	Castle Fraser Garden, Sauchen, Inverurie
Angus & Dundee	3 Balfour Cottages, Menmuir
East Lothian	Shepherd House, Inveresk, Musselburgh
Fife	The Tower, 1 Northview Terrace, Wormit
Lochaber	Canna House Walled Garden, Isle of Canna
Midlothian	Huntly Cot, Moorfoot, by Temple, Midlothian
Stirlingshire	Gartmore Village Plant Sale, Gartmore

Sunday 8 May

Aberdeenshire	Castle Fraser Garden, Sauchen, Inverurie
Argyll	Arduaine Garden, Oban
East Lothian	Shepherd House, Inveresk, Musselburgh
Edinburgh & West Lothian	Roscullen, 1 Bonaly Road, Edinburgh
Fife	Kellie Castle Spring Plant Sale, Pittenweem
Kirkcudbrightshire	Threave Garden, Castle Douglas
Lochaber	Arisaig House, Beasdale, Arisaig

Thursday 12 May

East Lothian	Humbie Dean, Humbie

Saturday 14 May

Angus & Dundee	Dundee & Angus College Gardens, Dundee
Argyll	Braevallich Farm, by Dalmally
Dumfriesshire	Drumpark, Irongray
Edinburgh & West Lothian	Redcroft, 23 Murrayfield Road, Edinburgh

Sunday 15 May

Angus & Dundee	Dalfruin, Kirktonhill Road, Kirriemuir
Argyll	Braevallich Farm, by Dalmally
Argyll	Crarae Garden, Inveraray
Dumfriesshire	Capenoch, Penpont, Thornhill

Saturday 28 May

Angus & Dundee	Gallery, Montrose
Argyll	Knock Cottage, Lochgair
Kincardine & Deeside	Drum Castle Garden, Drumoak, by Banchory
Peeblesshire	The Peeblesshire Garden Trio
Ross, Cromarty, Skye & Inverness	Malin, Glenaldie, Tain
Ross, Cromarty, Skye & Inverness	Oldtown of Leys Garden, Inverness

Sunday 29 May

Argyll	Knock Cottage, Lochgair
Ayrshire	1 Burnside Cottages, Sundrum, Coylton
Dumfriesshire	Dalswinton House, Dalswinton
Dunbartonshire	High Glenan and Westburn, Helensburgh
Fife	Earlshall Castle, Leuchars
Kincardine & Deeside	Drum Castle Garden, Drumoak, by Banchory
Kirkcudbrightshire	Corsock House, Corsock, Castle Douglas
Lochaber	Aberarder with Ardverikie, Kinlochlaggan
Peeblesshire	8 Halmyre Mains, West Linton
Peeblesshire	The Peeblesshire Garden Trio
Perth & Kinross	Rossie House, Forgandenny
Ross, Cromarty, Skye & Inverness	Malin, Glenaldie, Tain
Stirlingshire	Kippenrait with St Blanes House, Sheriffmuir, Dunblane

June

Wednesday 1 June

Ross, Cromarty, Skye & Inverness	Inverewe Garden and Estate, Poolewe, Achnasheen

Thursday 2 June

Perth & Kinross	Bradystone House, Murthly
Ross, Cromarty, Skye & Inverness	Dundonnell House, Little Loch Broom, Wester Ross

Saturday 4 June

Argyll	Braevallich Farm, by Dalmally
Ayrshire	Holmes Farm, Drybridge, by Irvine
Fife	Newton Mains and Newton Barns, Auchtermuchty
Ross, Cromarty, Skye & Inverness	Old Allangrange, Munlochy

Sunday 5 June

Aberdeenshire	Kildrummy Castle Gardens, Alford
Aberdeenshire	Tillypronie, Tarland
Argyll	Braevallich Farm, by Dalmally
Argyll	Torosay Castle Gardens, Craignure, Isle of Mull
Ayrshire	Holmes Farm, Drybridge, by Irvine
Dumfriesshire	Amisfield Tower, Amisfield
Dunbartonshire	Geilston Garden, Main Road, Cardross
East Lothian	Stenton Village, East Lothian
Edinburgh & West Lothian	Dean Gardens, Edinburgh
Ettrick & Lauderdale	The Yair, Galashiels

Sunday 26 June (contd.)

Berwickshire	East Gordon Smiddy, Gordon
Caithness & Sutherland	Duncan Street Gardens, Thurso
Dumfriesshire	Newtonairds Lodge, Newtonairds
Dumfriesshire	The Gardens of Middleshaw, Kettleholm, Lockerbie
Fife	Rofsie Arts Garden, by Collessie
Glasgow & North Lanarkshire	123 Waterfoot Road, Newton Mearns, Glasgow
Kincardine & Deeside	Finzean House, Finzean, Banchory
Kirkcudbrightshire	Glenlivet with The Limes, Tongland Road, Kirkcudbright
Kirkcudbrightshire	The Limes with Glenlivet, Kirkcudbright
Moray & Nairn	An-Grianan, Rafford, Forres
Renfrewshire	Gardening Leave, Erskine Hospital, Bishopton
Ross, Cromarty, Skye & Inverness	House of Aigas and Field Centre, by Beauly
Stirlingshire	Thorntree, Arnprior

Tuesday 28 June

Edinburgh & West Lothian	Malleny Garden, Balerno

Wednesday 29 June

East Lothian	Traprain Garden Circle
Midlothian	Newhall, Carlops
Peeblesshire	The Peeblesshire Garden Trio
Peeblesshire	The Potting Shed, Broughton Place, Broughton, Biggar

Thursday 30 June

Isle of Arran	Brodick Castle & Country Park, Brodick, Isle of Arran
Perth & Kinross	Bradystone House, Murthly

July

Saturday 2 July

Angus & Dundee	Forfar Open Garden, 36 Lochside Road, Forfar
Fife	The Old Farmhouse, Straiton Farm, Balmullo
Ross, Cromarty, Skye & Inverness	The New House, Wester Alness Ferry, by Balblair

Sunday 3 July

Aberdeenshire	Bruckhills Croft, Rothienorman, Inverurie
Ayrshire	Gardening Leave, c/o Gardens Unit, SAC Auchincruive
Berwickshire	Lennel Bank, Coldstream
Berwickshire	Netherbyres, Eyemouth
Caithness & Sutherland	Bighouse Lodge, by Melvich
Dumfriesshire	Dalgonar, Dunscore, Dumfries
East Lothian	Tyninghame House and The Walled Garden, Dunbar
Fife	Boarhills Village Gardens, St Andrews
Glasgow & North Lanarkshire	Strathbungo Gardens
Kirkcudbrightshire	Southwick House, Southwick
Perth & Kinross	Wester Cloquhat , Bridge of Cally
Roxburghshire	Easter Weens, Bonchester Bridge, Hawick
Wigtownshire	Ardoch with Damnaglaur House , Drummore, Stranraer

Sunday 17 July

Berwickshire	Kames, Greenlaw
Dunbartonshire	7 The Birches with West Garemount, Shandon
Fife	Crail: Small Gardens in the Burgh
Fife	Falkland Palace and Garden, Falkland, Cupar
Glasgow & North Lanarkshire	Auchinstarry Sensory Garden, Kilsyth Marina
Midlothian	Eskbank Gardens, 23 Lasswade Road, Eskbank
Peeblesshire	8 Halmyre Mains, West Linton
Peeblesshire	Drumelzier Old Manse, Drumelzier, nr Broughton
South Lanarkshire	Dippoolbank Cottage, Carnwath

Wednesday 20 July

Kincardine & Deeside	Drum Castle Garden, Drumoak, by Banchory
Midlothian	Newhall, Carlops
Peeblesshire	Portmore, Eddleston
Peeblesshire	The Potting Shed, Broughton Place, Broughton, Biggar

Thursday 21 July

Aberdeenshire	Leith Hall Garden, Huntly
East Lothian	Humbie Dean, Humbie
Peeblesshire	The Peeblesshire Garden Trio
Perth & Kinross	Bradystone House, Murthly

Saturday 23 July

Argyll	Caol Ruadh, Colintraive
Edinburgh & West Lothian	Rivaldsgreen House, 48 Friars Brae, Linlithgow
Moray & Nairn	Haugh Garden, College of Roseisle

Sunday 24 July

Argyll	Caol Ruadh, Colintraive
Ayrshire	Cairnhall House, Mauchline Road, Ochiltree
Fife	Balcaskie with Kellie Castle, Pittenweem
Glasgow & North Lanarkshire	Kamares, 18 Broom Road, Newton Mearns, Glasgow
Kirkcudbrightshire	Crofts, Kirkpatrick Durham, Castle Douglas
Ross, Cromarty, Skye & Inverness	House of Aigas and Field Centre, by Beauly
South Lanarkshire	Wellbutts, Elsrickle, by Biggar
Stirlingshire	Bridgend of Teith, Doune
Wigtownshire	Hill Cottage, Portlogan, Stranraer

Tuesday 26 July

Aberdeenshire	Haddo House, Methlick, Ellon

Wednesday 27 July

Kincardine & Deeside	Drum Castle Garden, Drumoak, by Banchory
Midlothian	Newhall, Carlops
Peeblesshire	Portmore, Eddleston

Thursday 28 July

Isle of Arran	Brodick Castle & Country Park, Brodick, Isle of Arran
Perth & Kinross	Bradystone House, Murthly

Saturday 30 July

Argyll	Little Kilmory Cottage, Rothesay, Isle of Bute
Caithness & Sutherland	House of Tongue, Tongue, Lairg
Ettrick & Lauderdale	Harmony Garden with Priorwood Garden, St Mary's Road, Melrose
Fife	The Tower, 1 Northview Terrace, Wormit
Ross, Cromarty, Skye & Inverness	Malin, Glenaldie, Tain

Sunday 31 July

Angus & Dundee	The Herbalist's Garden at Logie, Logie House, Kirriemuir
Argyll	Ardchattan Priory, North Connel
Argyll	Little Kilmory Cottage, Rothesay, Isle of Bute
Ayrshire	Golf Course Road Gardens, Girvan
Caithness & Sutherland	Langwell, Berriedale
Ross, Cromarty, Skye & Inverness	Malin, Glenaldie, Tain
Roxburghshire	West Leas, Bonchester Bridge
South Lanarkshire	Beeches Cottage Nursery and Smallholding, High Boreland, nr Hawksland, Lesmahagow
Stirlingshire	The Tors, 2 Slamannan Road, Falkirk

August

Wednesday 3 August

Peeblesshire	Portmore, Eddleston

Saturday 6 August

Ross, Cromarty, Skye & Inverness	Hugh Miller's Birthplace Cottage & Museum, Cromarty

Sunday 7 August

Aberdeenshire	Pitmedden Garden, Ellon
Argyll	Torosay Castle Gardens, Craignure, Isle of Mull
Edinburgh & West Lothian	Craigentinny and Telferton Allotments, Edinburgh
Kincardine & Deeside	Glenbervie House, Drumlithie, Stonehaven
Kirkcudbrightshire	Cally Gardens, Gatehouse of Fleet
Kirkcudbrightshire	Threave Garden, Castle Douglas
Midlothian	Silverburn Village, nr Penicuik
Perth & Kinross	Drummond Castle Gardens, Crieff
Perth & Kinross	Mount Tabor House, Mount Tabor Road, Perth
South Lanarkshire	The Walled Garden, Shieldhill, Quothquan, Biggar

Wednesday 10 August

Peeblesshire	Portmore, Eddleston

GARDENS OPEN BY ARRANGEMENT

NORTH OF SCOTLAND & ISLANDS

Lochaber

Ard-Daraich, Ardgour, by Fort William	On request

Moray & Nairn

10 Pilmuir Road West , Forres	30 January - 13 March and 1 July - 1 September
Castleview, Auchindoun, Dufftown	1 June - 31 August
Haugh Garden, College of Roseisle	1 June - 31 August

Ross, Cromarty, Skye & Inverness

Brackla Wood, Culbokie, Dingwall	1 May - 31 May and 1 July - 31 July
Cardon, Balnafoich, Farr	1 March - 30 September
Dundonnell House, Little Loch Broom	1 April - 31 October
Glenkyllachy Lodge, Tomatin	1 May - 31 July and 1 September - 31 October
House of Aigas and Field Centre, by Beauly	1 April - 28 October
Leathad Ard, Upper Carloway, Isle of Lewis	1 April - 30 September
The Lookout, Kilmuir, North Kessock	On request

Shetland

Cruisdale, Sandness	On request
Keldaberg, Cunningsburgh	1 June - 31 October
Lindaal, Tingwall	1 June - 30 September
Nonavaar, Levenwick	10 April - 25 September

EAST OF SCOTLAND

Aberdeenshire

Airdlin Croft, Ythanbank, Ellon	21 May - 31 July
An Teallach, Largue, Huntly	1 May - 30 September
Birken Cottage, Burnhervie, Inverurie	1 May - 31 August
Blairwood House, Blairs	13 June - 28 August
Bruckhills Croft, Inverurie	6 February - 13 March and 1 July - 31 July
Grandhome, Danestone, Aberdeen	1 April - 31 October

EAST OF SCOTLAND (CONTD.)

Aberdeenshire (contd.)

Greenridge, Craigton Road, Cults	1 July - 31 August
Hatton Castle, Turriff	On request
Laundry Cottage, Huntly	On request
Middle Cairncake, Cuminestown, Turriff	1 May - 18 September

Angus & Dundee

Dunninald Castle, Montrose	On request for groups
Gallery	1 May - 30 September
Kirkton House, Kirkton of Craig, Montrose	1 May - 30 September
The Herbalist's Garden at Logie, Kirriemuir	1 June - 31 August

Fife

Barham, Bow of Fife	1 April - 31 July
Helensbank, Kincardine	1 June - 31 July
Logie House, Crossford, Dunfermline	1 April - 31 October
South Flisk, Blebo Craigs, Cupar	15 April - 19 June
The Old Farmhouse, Straiton Farm, Balmullo	On request
The Tower, 1 Northview Terrace, Wormit	1 April - 30 September
Willowhill, Forgan, Newport-on-Tay	1 May - 31 August
Wormistoune House, Crail	1 April - 30 September

Perth & Kinross

Briglands House, Rumbling Bridge	1 April - 15 June and 1 October - 31 October
Carig Dhubh, Bonskeid	1 May - 30 October
Croftcat Lodge, Grandtully	14 May - 16 October
Delvine, Murthly	15 April - 15 October
Dowhill, Cleish	On request
Glenlyon House, Fortingall	On request
Hollytree Lodge, Dollar	25 March - 10 April 1 May - 30 June and 1 September - 31 October
Kirkton Craig, Abernyte	3 May - 26 July
Latch House, Abernyte	1 May - 31 August
Little Tombuie, Aberfeldy	1 May - 31 July
Mill of Forneth, Blairgowrie	1 May - 30 September
Parkhead House, Perth	1 May - 30 September
Pitcurran House, Abernethy	1 April - 30 September
Pitnacree House , Pitnacree, Pitlochry	1 May - 31 July
The Garden at Craigowan, Ballinluig	15 April - 30 June
The Steading at Clunie, Blairgowrie	8 May - 25 June 11 June - 19 June

WEST CENTRAL SCOTLAND

Argyll

Braevallich Farm, by Dalmally	16 April - 30 June
Eas Mhor, Oban	1 May - 31 August
Kinlochlaich Gardens, Appin	15 October - 13 March
Knock Cottage, Lochgair	15 April - 15 June

Ayrshire

Burnside, Littlemill Road, Drongan	1 April - 14 September
Grougarbank House, Kilmarnock	1 February - 29 February 16 April - 11 September
High Fulwood, Stewarton	1 May - 31 August

Glasgow & North Lanarkshire

Kilsyth Gardens, Allanfauld Road, Kilsyth	1 April - 30 September

South Lanarkshire

Carmichael Mill, Hyndford Bridge, Lanark	On request
The Scots Mining Company House, Biggar	1 April - 30 September

Stirlingshire

Arndean, by Dollar	16 May - 17 June
Duntreath Castle, Blanefield	1 February - 30 November
Gardener's Cottage Walled Garden, Killearn	1 May - 31 October
Kilbryde Castle, Dunblane	1 April - 30 September
Manorcroft, Blairlogie	1 May - 15 July
Milseybank, Bridge of Allan	1 April - 31 May
Plaka, Bridge of Allan	1 June - 30 September
Rowberrow, 18 Castle Road, Dollar	1 February - 31 December
The Linns, Sheriffmuir, Dunblane	15 February - 30 September
The Steading at Dollar, Yetts O'Muckhart	1 April - 15 October
The Tors, 2 Slamannan Road, Falkirk	1 May - 30 September
Thorntree, Arnprior	1 April - 15 October

SOUTH WEST SCOTLAND

Kirkcudbrightshire

Anwoth Old Schoolhouse, Anwoth	15 February - 15 November
Brooklands, Crocketford	1 February - 1 October
Corsock House, Corsock, Castle Douglas	1 April - 30 June
Stockarton, Kirkcudbright	1 April - 31 July
The Mill House at Gelston, Gelston	12 July - 13 September

SOUTH WEST SCOTLAND (CONTD.)

Wigtownshire

Dunskey Gardens and Maze, Stranraer	22 February - 24 March
Woodfall Gardens, Glasserton	On request

SOUTH EAST SCOTLAND

Berwickshire

Anton's Hill, Leitholm, Coldstream	On request
Lennel Bank, Coldstream	On request
Netherbyres, Eyemouth	1 May - 31 August

Edinburgh & West Lothian

61 Fountainhall Road, Edinburgh	1 April - 30 October
Hunter's Tryst, Edinburgh	On request
Laverockdale House, Edinburgh	1 August - 31 August
Redcroft, Edinburgh	23 September - 14 October

Peeblesshire

Portmore, Eddleston	1 June - 7 September

Roxburghshire

West Leas, Bonchester Bridge	On request

GARDENS OPEN ON A REGULAR BASIS

NORTH OF SCOTLAND & ISLANDS

Caithness & Sutherland

The Castle & Gardens of Mey	18 May - 24 July and 9 August - 30 September

Lochaber

Ardtornish, by Lochaline, Morvern	Daily

Ross, Cromarty, Skye & Inverness

Abriachan Garden Nursery, Loch Ness Side	1 February - 30 November
Applecross Walled Garden, Strathcarron	1 March - 31 October
Attadale, Strathcarron	1 April - 29 October closed on Sundays
Balmeanach House, Isle of Skye	7 May - 30 October Mondays and Thursdays only
Dunvegan Castle and Gardens, Isle of Skye	1 April - 15 October
Highland Liliums, 10 Loaneckheim, Kiltarlity	Daily
Leathad Ard, Upper Carloway, Isle of Lewis	16 May - 31 August not open Sundays or 3 August
Oldtown of Leys Garden, Inverness	Daily
The Lookout, Kilmuir, North Kessock	1 May - 31 August open Sundays only

Shetland

Highlands, East Voe, Scalloway	1 May - 30 September
Lea Gardens, Tresta	1 April - 31 October closed Thursdays
Nonavaar, Levenwick	10 April - 25 September Friday and Sunday only
Norby, Burnside, Sandness	Daily

EAST OF SCOTLAND

Aberdeenshire

Fyvie Castle, Turriff	4 January - 23 December

Angus & Dundee

Dunninald Castle, Montrose	2 July - 31 July excluding Mondays
Gallery, Montrose	1 June - 31 August Tuesdays only
Hospitalfield Gardens, Arbroath	14 May - 24 September Saturdays only
Pitmuies Gardens, by Forfar	30 January - 13 March and 1 April - 31 October
The Herbalist's Garden at Logie, Kirriemuir	1 August - 31 August Sundays only

EAST OF SCOTLAND (CONTD.)

Fife

Willowhill, Forgan, Newport-on-Tay	4 June - 27 August Saturdays only

Perth & Kinross

Ardvorlich, Lochearnhead	1 May - 1 June
Blair Castle Gardens, Blair Atholl	25 March - 31 October
Bolfracks, Aberfeldy	Daily
Braco Castle, Braco	1 February - 31 October
Cluny House, Aberfeldy	Daily
Drummond Castle Gardens, Crieff	1 May - 31 October
Glendoick, by Perth	1 April - 31 May
Glenericht House, Blairgowrie	Daily

WEST CENTRAL SCOTLAND

Argyll

Achnacloich, Connel, Oban	25 March - 31 October Saturdays only
Ardchattan Priory, North Connel	25 March - 31 October
Ardkinglas Woodland Garden, Cairndow	Daily
Ardmaddy Castle, by Oban	Daily
Ascog Hall, Ascog, Isle of Bute	1 April - 31 October
Barguillean's "Angus Garden", Taynuilt	Daily
Benmore Botanic Garden, Benmore, Dunoon	1 March - 31 October
Crinan Hotel Garden, Crinan	1 May - 31 August
Druimneil House, Port Appin	25 March - 31 October
Fairwinds, 14 George Street, Hunter's Quay, Dunoon	1 April - 31 October
Inveraray Castle Gardens, Inveraray	1 April - 31 October
Kinlochlaich Gardens, Appin	14 March - 14 October
Oakbank, Ardrishaig	1 May - 31 August

Dunbartonshire

Glenarn, Glenarn Road, Rhu, Helensburgh	21 March - 21 September

Stirlingshire

Gargunnock House Garden, Gargunnock	1 February - 13 March and 16 April - 30 September Mondays - Fridays

SOUTH WEST SCOTLAND

Wigtownshire

Claymoddie Garden, Whithorn, Newton Stewart	1 April - 30 September
Dunskey Gardens and Maze, Portpatrick, Stranraer	25 March - 30 September
Glenwhan Gardens, Dunragit, by Stranraer	1 April - 31 October
Logan Botanic Garden, Port Logan, by Stranraer	15 March - 31 October
Logan House Gardens, Port Logan, by Stranraer	1 March - 30 September

SOUTH EAST SCOTLAND

Berwickshire

Bughtrig, nr Leitholm, Coldstream	1 June - 1 September

East Lothian

Shepherd House, Inveresk, Musselburgh	9 February - 3 March and 12 April - 14 July Tuesdays and Thursdays

Edinburgh & West Lothian

Newliston, Kirkliston	1 May - 4 June except Mondays and Tuesdays
Redhall Walled Garden, Edinburgh	1 January - 31 December Monday to Friday
The Glasshouses at the Royal Botanic Garden Edinburgh	2 January - 31 December, closed 25 December

Peeblesshire

Dawyck Botanic Garden, Stobo	Daily
Kailzie Gardens, Peebles	Daily

Roxburghshire

Floors Castle, Kelso	25 March - 30 April 1 May - 30 September 1 October - 30 October
Monteviot, Jedburgh	1 April - 31 October, closed 27 and 28 May

PLANT SALES

Fife

Cambo House Spring Plant and Craft Fair, Kingsbarns	Sunday 17 April	11:00am - 4:00pm

Renfrewshire

Kilmacolm Plant Sale, Kilmacolm	Saturday 23 April	10:00am - 12:00pm

Stirlingshire

Gartmore Village Plant Sale, Gartmore	Saturday 7 May	10:00am - 12:30pm

Fife

Kellie Castle Spring Plant Sale, Pittenweem	Sunday 8 May	10:30am - 4:00pm

Peeblesshire

8 Halmyre Mains, West Linton	Sunday 29 May	10:00am - 12:00pm

Perth & Kinross

Rossie House, Forgandenny	Sunday 29 May	2:00pm - 5:00pm

Dunbartonshire

Hill House Plant Sale, Helensburgh	Sunday 28 August	11:00am - 4:00pm

Renfrewshire

Kilmacolm Plant Sale, Kilmacolm	Saturday 10 September	10:00am - 12:00pm

Dunbartonshire

Glenarn, Helensburgh	Sunday 11 September	2:00pm - 5:00pm

Fife

Hill of Tarvit Plant Sale and Autumn Fair, Cupar	Sunday 2 October	10:30am - 4:00pm

Kincardine & Deeside

Drum Castle Garden, by Banchory	Saturday 8 October	11:00am - 4:00pm
Drum Castle Garden, by Banchory	Sunday 9 October	11:00am - 4:00pm

NORTH OF SCOTLAND & ISLANDS

Scotland's Gardens 2016 Guidebook is sponsored by **INVESTEC WEALTH & INVESTMENT**

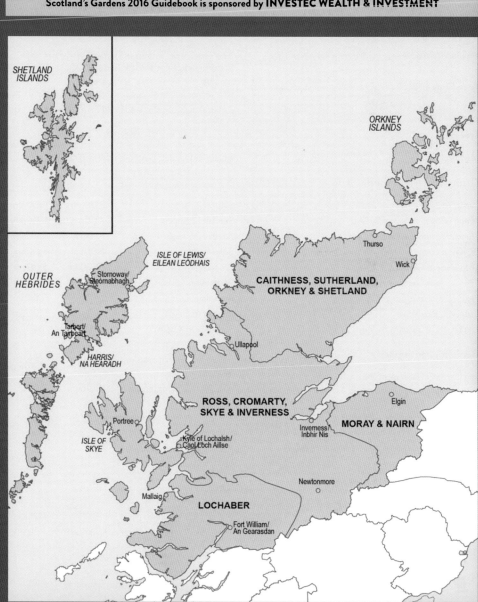

SHETLAND ISLANDS

ORKNEY ISLANDS

ISLE OF LEWIS/ EILEAN LEÒDHAIS

OUTER HEBRIDES

Stornoway/ Steòrnabhagh

Thurso

Wick

CAITHNESS, SUTHERLAND, ORKNEY & SHETLAND

Tarbert/ An Tairbeart

HARRIS/ NA HEARADH

Ullapool

Portree

ROSS, CROMARTY, SKYE & INVERNESS

Elgin

MORAY & NAIRN

ISLE OF SKYE

Kyle of Lochalsh/ Caol Loch Aillse

Inverness/ Inbhir Nis

Newtonmore

Mallaig

LOCHABER

Fort William/ An Gearasdan

CAITHNESS & SUTHERLAND

Scotland's Gardens 2016 Guidebook is sponsored by INVESTEC WEALTH & INVESTMENT

District Organiser

Mrs Judith Middlemas	22 Miller Place, Scrabster, Thurso KW14 7UH E: caithness@scotlandsgardens.org

Area Organisers

Mrs Jonny Shaw	Amat, Ardgay, Sutherland IV24 3BS

Treasurer

Mr Chris Hobson	Braeside, Dunnet, Caithness KW14 8YD

Gardens open on a specific date

Amat, Ardgay	Saturday 11 June	2:00pm	- 5:00pm
Amat, Ardgay	Sunday 12 June	2:00pm	- 5:00pm
Duncan Street Gardens, Thurso	Sunday 26 June	1:00pm	- 5:00pm
Bighouse Lodge, by Melvich	Sunday 3 July	2:00pm	- 5:00pm
The Castle & Gardens of Mey	Wednesday 6 July	10:00am	- 5:00pm
The Castle & Gardens of Mey	Wednesday 13 July	10:00am	- 5:00pm
House of Tongue, Tongue, Lairg	Saturday 30 July	2:00pm	- 6:00pm
Langwell, Berriedale	Sunday 31 July	1:00pm	- 5:00pm
The Castle & Gardens of Mey	Saturday 13 August	10:00am	- 5:00pm

Gardens open regularly

The Castle & Gardens of Mey	18 May - 24 July 9 August - 30 September	10:00am	- 5:00pm

Key to symbols

New in 2016	Homemade teas	Accommodation
Teas	Dogs on a lead allowed	Plant stall
Cream teas	Wheelchair access	Scottish Snowdrop Festival

GARDEN LOCATIONS IN CAITHNESS & SUTHERLAND

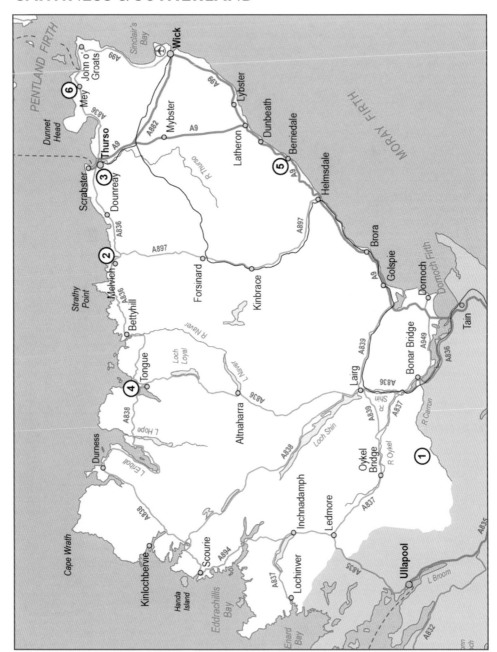

CAITHNESS & SUTHERLAND

AMAT
Ardgay IV24 3BS
Jonny and Sara Shaw
E: sara.amat@aol.co.uk

Riverside garden surrounded by the old Caledonian Amat Forest. Herbaceous borders and rockery set in a large lawn looking onto a salmon pool. Old and new rhododendrons with woodland and river walk plus large specimen trees in policies.

Directions: Take the road from Ardgay to Croick nine miles. Turn left at the red phone box and the garden is 500 yards on the left.

Disabled Access:
Partial

Opening Times:
Saturday 11 June
2:00pm - 5:00pm
Sunday 12 June
2:00pm - 5:00pm

Admission:
£4.50, teas £3.50

Charities:
Gardening Leave receives 20%, Croick Church receives 20%, the net remaining to SG Beneficiaries

BIGHOUSE LODGE
by Melvich KW14 7YJ
Bighouse Estate
E: info@bighouseestate.com   www.bighouseestate.com

Bighouse Lodge is situated on the north coast of Sutherland at the mouth of the River Halladale. The two acre walled garden, originally laid out in 1715, consists of a central axis leading to a charming bothy with lawn, herbaceous borders, a sunken garden and four separate conceptual gardens behind the hedgerows. Each garden contains a sculpture to reflect the aspects of the Bighouse Estate namely the River, the Forest, the Strath and the Hill. The garden has recently been restored and is now a most interesting place to visit.

Other Details: There are gravelled paths. Homemade teas are available priced £3.50

Directions: Off A836 ½ mile East of Melvich.

Disabled Access:
Partial

Opening Times:
Sunday 3 July
2:00pm - 5:00pm

Admission:
£4.00, children under 12
£1.00

Charities:
RNLI receives 40%, the net remaining to SG Beneficiaries

DUNCAN STREET GARDENS
Thurso KW14 7HU
The Gardeners of Duncan Street

Four town gardens with their own micro climate, offering a good selection of interesting shrubs and trees, roses and herbaceous plants with landscaping on different levels. Each garden has its specialties including bonsai, alpines, cactus and succulents and water features.

Other Details: Wheelchair access is limited due to narrow paths and steps.

Directions: Visitors to the gardens should start at 7 Duncan Street, Thurso.

Disabled Access:
Partial

Opening Times:
Sunday 26 June
1:00pm - 5:00pm

Admission:
£4.50

Charities:
Caithness Samaritans receives 10%, Friends of Thor House receives 10%, Anthony Nolan receives 10%, Chest, Heart and Stroke receives 10%, the net remaining to SG Beneficiaries

HOUSE OF TONGUE
Tongue, Lairg IV27 4XH
The Countess of Sutherland
E: richardrowe37@gmail.com

Seventeenth century house on Kyle of Tongue. Walled garden with herbaceous borders, lawns, old fashioned roses, vegetables, soft fruit and small orchard.

Other Details: Teas available at the Hostel at beginning of the causeway.

Directions: Half a mile from Tongue village. House just off the main road approaching causeway. The garden is well signposted.

Disabled Access:
Partial

Opening Times:
Saturday 30 July
2:00pm - 6:00pm

Admission:
£4.00, children £1.00

Charities:
Children 1st receives 40%, the net remaining to SG Beneficiaries

---

LANGWELL
Berriedale KW7 6HD
Welbeck Estates T: 01593 751278/751237
E: macanson@hotmail.com

A beautiful and spectacular old walled garden with outstanding borders situated in the secluded Langwell Strath. Charming wooded access drive with a chance to see deer.

Other Details: Teas and homebaking will be served in the Berriedale Portland Hall which is just off the A9 on the north side of Berriedale Braes 100 metres downhill from and opposite the Berriedale Church.

LANGWELL ARE CELEBRATING THEIR 75TH GARDEN OPEN DAY FOR SCOTLAND'S GARDENS IN 2016

Directions: Turn off the A9 at Berriedale Braes, up the private (tarred) drive signposted Private - Langwell House. It is around 1¼ miles from the A9.

Disabled Access:
Partial

Opening Times:
Sunday 31 July
1:00pm - 5:00pm

Admission:
£4.00, children under 12 free

Charities:
RNLI receives 40%, the net remaining to SG Beneficiaries

THE CASTLE & GARDENS OF MEY
Mey KW14 8XH
The Queen Elizabeth Castle of Mey Trust T: 01847 851473
E: enquiries@castleofmey.org.uk www.castleofmey.org.uk

Originally a Z plan castle bought by the Queen Mother in 1952 and then restored and improved. The walled garden and the East Garden were also created by the Queen Mother. An animal centre has been established over the last three years and is proving very popular with all ages. New herbaceous border, east facing, nestled under the West Wall contains Agapanthus, Phlox, Pink Aconitum, Sidalcea, Verbascum and Knautia among others.

Other Details: Tearoom, shop and animal centre. Visitor Centre, Animal Centre and Gardens open 10:00am - 5:00pm. Castle opens 10:20am and last entries are at 4:00pm.

Directions: On A836 between Thurso and John O'Groats.

Disabled Access:
Partial

Opening Times:
Weds 6 & 13 July & Sat 13 Aug.
18 May - 24 Jul & 9 Aug - 30
Sept. 10:00am - 5:00pm

Admission:
Gardens only £6.50, children £3.00, family £19.00
Castle & Gardens £11.00, concessions £9.75, children £6.50, family £29.00

Charities:
Donation to SG Beneficiaries

LOCHABER

Scotland's Gardens 2016 Guidebook is sponsored by **INVESTEC WEALTH & INVESTMENT**

District Organiser

Norrie and Anna Maclaren	Ard-Daraich, Ardgour, nr Fort William PH33 7AB E: lochaber@scotlandsgardens.org

Area Organiser

Angela Simpson	The Larch House, Camusdarach, Arisaig PH39 4NT

Treasurer

Norrie Maclaren	Ard-Daraich, Ardgour, nr Fort William PH33 7AB

Gardens open on a specific date

Canna House Walled Garden, Isle of Canna	Saturday 7 May	10:00am - 4:30pm
Arisaig House, Beasdale, Arisaig	Sunday 8 May	11:00am - 4:00pm
Aberarder with Ardverikie, Kinlochlaggan	Sunday 29 May	2:00pm - 5:30pm
Canna House Walled Garden, Isle of Canna	Saturday 13 August	10:00am - 4:30pm

Gardens open regularly

Ardtornish, by Lochaline, Morvern	Daily	10:00am - 6:00pm

Gardens open by arrangement

Ard-Daraich, Ardgour, by Fort William	Daily	01855 841384

Key to symbols

	New in 2016		Homemade teas		Accommodation
	Teas		Dogs on a lead allowed		Plant stall
	Cream teas		Wheelchair access		Scottish Snowdrop Festival

GARDEN LOCATIONS
IN LOCHABER

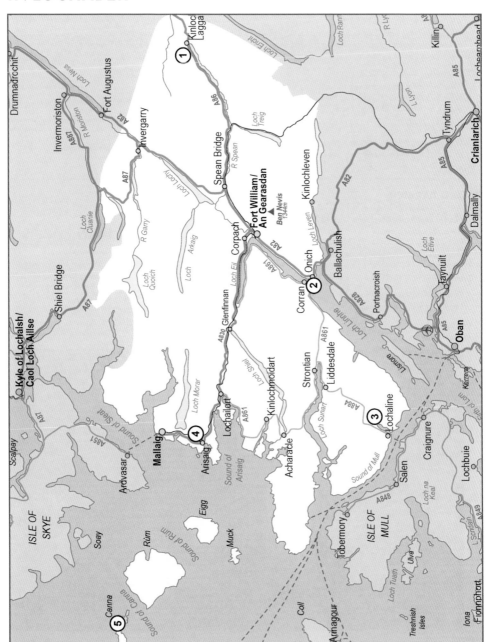

LOCHABER

ABERARDER WITH ARDVERIKIE
Kinlochlaggan   PH20 1BX
The Feilden Family and Mrs P Laing & Mrs E T Smyth-Osbourne

Aberarder T: 01528 544300
The garden has been laid out over the last 20 years to create a mixture of spring and autumn plants and trees, including rhododendrons, azaleas and acers. The elevated view down Loch Laggan from the garden is exceptional.

Ardverikie T: 01528 544300
Lovely setting on Loch Laggan with magnificent trees. Walled garden with large collection of acers, shrubs and herbaceous. Architecturally interesting house (not open). Site of the filming of the TV series *Monarch of the Glen*.

Other Details: Teas at Aberarder for an additional charge.

Directions: On A86 between Newtonmore and Spean Bridge. Entrance at east end of Loch Laggan by gate lodge over bridge.

Disabled Access:
Partial

Opening Times:
Sunday 29 May
2:00pm - 5:30pm

Admission:
£5.00 includes entrance to both gardens.

Charities:
Highland Hospice receives 20%, Laggan Church receives 20%, the net remaining to SG Beneficiaries

ARD-DARAICH
Ardgour, by Fort William   PH33 7AB
Norrie and Anna Maclaren   T: 01855 841384
www.arddaraich.co.uk

Glorious seven acre hill garden, in a spectacular setting, with many fine and uncommon rhododendrons, an interesting selection of trees and shrubs and a large collection of camellias, acers and sorbus.

Directions: West from Fort William, across the Corran Ferry, turn left and a mile on the right further west.

Disabled Access:
None

Opening Times:
By arrangement on request

Admission:
£4.00

Charities:
Donation to SG Beneficiaries

ARDTORNISH
By Lochaline, Morvern PA80 5UZ
Mrs John Raven

Wonderful gardens of interesting mature conifers, rhododendrons, deciduous trees, shrubs and herbaceous, set amid magnificent scenery.

Directions: A884 Lochaline three miles.

Disabled Access:
None

Opening Times:
Daily 10:00am - 6:00pm

Admission:
£4.00

Charities:
Donation to SG Beneficiaries

ARISAIG HOUSE
Beasdale, Arisaig PH39 4NR
Ms. Emma Weir T: 01687 450730
E: sarahwi@arisaighouse.co.uk www.arisaighouse.co.uk

Arisaig House, designed in 1864 by Philip Webb, is a luxurious family run Country House Hotel, offering dinner, bed and breakfast. Wander through twenty acres of well-established and cared for woodlands and gardens. Extensive collection of specimen trees, rhododendrons and shrubs. Exquisite terrace with formal rose and herb beds. Visit the kitchen garden with its orchard, soft fruit cages, productive polytunnel, and vegetable beds. Whatever can be found in the garden that day is on the menu that night! Birds and wildlife abound.

Other Details: Live music on the terrace. Delicious homemade teas in the dining room. Works by local artists on sale in the house.

Directions: Arisaig House is 32 miles from Fort William on the A830 road to Mallaig. Approximately 1.2 miles from Beasdale train station turn left into junction signposted Arisaig House and Cottages.

Disabled Access:
None

Opening Times:
Sunday 8 May
11:00am - 4:00pm

Admission:
£4.00

Charities:
Local Feis receives 40%, the net remaining to SG Beneficiaries

CANNA HOUSE WALLED GARDEN
Isle of Canna PH44 4RS
National Trust for Scotland T: 01687 462998
E: llogan@nts.org.uk www.nts.org.uk

Formerly derelict two acre walled garden brought back to life following a five year restoration project. There are soft fruits, top fruits, vegetables, ornamental lawns and flower beds. There is also a stunning 80 foot Escallonia arch. The garden has been replanted to attract bees, butterflies and moths. The woodland walks outside walls are not to be missed along with the spectacular views of neighbouring islands. Don't miss your chance to see this gem.

Directions: Access Isle of Canna via Calmac ferry from Mallaig pier.

Disabled Access:
Partial

Opening Times:
Saturday 7 May
10:00am - 4:30pm
Saturday 13 August
10:00am - 4:30pm

Admission:
£3.00 (including NTS members). N.B. Prices correct at the time of going to print

Charities:
Donation to SG Beneficiaries

MORAY & NAIRN

Scotland's Gardens 2016 Guidebook is sponsored by **INVESTEC WEALTH & INVESTMENT**

District Organiser

Mr James Byatt	Lochview Cottage, Scarffbanks, Pitgaveny IV30 5PQ E: moraynairn@scotlandsgardens.org

Area Organisers

Mrs Lorraine Dingwall	10 Pilmuir Road West, Forres IV36 2HL
Mrs Rebecca Russell	12 Duff Avenue, Elgin, Moray IV30 1QS
Mrs Annie Stewart	33 Albert Street, Nairn IV12 4HF

Treasurer

Mr Michael Barnett	Drumdelnies, Nairn IV12 5NT

Gardens open on a specific date

Brodie Castle, Brodie, Forres	Saturday 23 April	10:30am	- 4:00pm
Brodie Castle, Brodie, Forres	Sunday 24 April	10:30am	- 4:00pm
Haugh Garden, College of Roseisle	Saturday 25 June	2:00pm	- 5:00pm
An-Grianan, Rafford, Forres	Sunday 26 June	11:00am	- 4:00pm
Haugh Garden, College of Roseisle	Saturday 23 July	2:00pm	- 5:00pm
Haugh Garden, College of Roseisle	Saturday 20 August	2:00pm	- 5:00pm
Gordonstoun, Duffus, near Elgin	Sunday 11 September	2:00pm	- 4:30pm

Gardens open by arrangement

10 Pilmuir Road West , Forres	30 January - 13 March and 1 July - 1 September	01309 674634
Castleview, Auchindoun, Dufftown	1 June - 31 August	01340 820941
Haugh Garden, College of Roseisle	1 June - 31 August	01343 835790

Key to symbols

	New in 2016		Homemade teas		Accommodation
	Teas		Dogs on a lead allowed		Plant stall
	Cream teas		Wheelchair access		Scottish Snowdrop Festival

GARDEN LOCATIONS IN MORAY & NAIRN

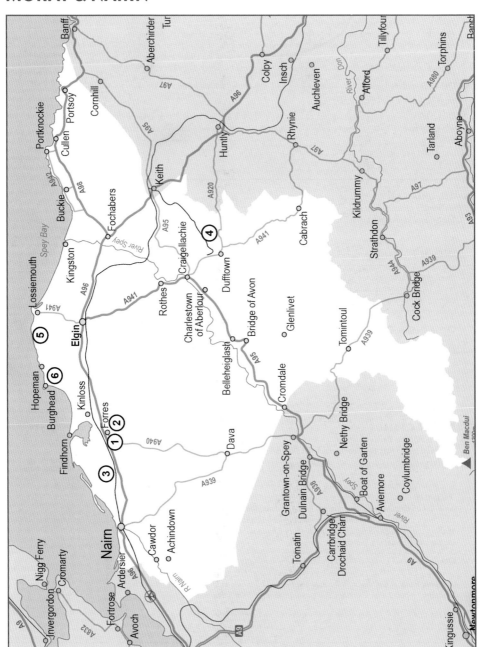

10 PILMUIR ROAD WEST
Forres IV36 2HL
Mrs Lorraine Dingwall T: 01309 674634
E: fixandig@aol.com www.simplesite.com/hosta

Plantsman's small town garden with over 300 cultivars of hostas, an extensive collection of hardy geraniums together with many other unusual plants. Managed entirely without the use of artificial fertilizers or chemicals, the owner encourages hedgehogs, toads and wild birds to control slugs. In early spring there are approximately 150 named snowdrops to be seen, some of which are very rare.

Other Details: Please phone to arrange a visit as parking is limited and weather variable during snowdrop season.

Directions: From Tesco roundabout at Forres continue along Nairn Road. Take first left onto Ramflat Road, then go right at the bottom and first left onto Pilmuir Road West.

Disabled Access:
None

Opening Times:
By arrangement
30 January - 13 March
for the Snowdrop Festival
and 1 July - 1 September
Groups welcome

Admission:
£3.00

Charities:
Macmillan Cancer Support receives 40%, the net remaining to SG Beneficiaries

---

AN-GRIANAN
Rafford, Forres IV36 2RT
Susan and Howard Stollar T: 07843 795053

Delightful four acre garden. There are beautiful herbaceous borders which will appeal to the beginner and conoisseur alike; a herb area and rockery; as well as a mature orchard, vegetable garden and polytunnel which supply the owners with fresh food all year round. Enjoy a tranquil walk through semi-mature woodland, and enjoy the abundant birdsong and the sight of the wild flowers growing freely in the meadow and wooded areas.

Other Details: Parking available.

Directions: Head out of Forres on St Leonards Road towards Rafford. In Rafford take the sharp right for Dallas Dhu Distillery. An-Grianan is approximately ¾ mile along this road on the right.

Disabled Access:
None

Opening Times:
Sunday 26 June
11:00am - 4:00pm

Admission:
£4.00

Charities:
Trees for Life and Community Café, Forres receives 40%, the net remaining to SG Beneficiaries

---

BRODIE CASTLE
Brodie, Forres IV36 2TE
The National Trust for Scotland T: 01309 641371
E: sferguson@nts.org.uk www.nts.org.uk

The grounds of Brodie Castle are carpeted with daffodils in the spring and include a National Collection of over 110 different cultivars bred at the property by a former laird. Good displays of other spring bulbs and shrubs including dog's tooth violet and rhododendrons. On these special days Garden staff will be leading guided tours of the garden and talking about the history of the daffodil collection at Brodie in support of Scotland's Gardens.

Other Details: National Plant Collection®: Narcissus (Brodie cvs.). Tea, coffee and cakes will be available to purchase in the Tea Room. The servery in the castle will be open. Pots of daffodils, including a very limited stock of Brodie cultivars will be available to purchase. Contact the property for further information.

Directions: Off A96 4½ miles west of Forres and 24 miles east of Inverness.

Disabled Access:
Full

Opening Times:
Saturday 23 April
10:30am - 4:00pm
Sunday 24 April
10:30am - 4:00pm

Admission:
Usual NTS admission charges apply. Garden tour £3.00 (including NTS members).

Charities:
Donation to SG Beneficiaries

CASTLEVIEW
Auchindoun, Dufftown AB55 4DY
Mr and Mrs Ian Sharp T: 01340 820941
E: castleview10@hotmail.com

A small secluded riverside garden, created on three levels from scrub land by two enthusiastic beginners in 2005. The garden consists of two interconnected ponds, one formal, one natural and an abundance of herbaceous plants and shrubs. There are several sitting areas where you can admire the garden from many viewpoints.

Directions: From Dufftown on the A920, travel approximately three miles towards Huntly. Drive until a small cluster of houses is reached; garden on the left is approximately twenty yards off the main road.

Disabled Access:
None

Opening Times:
By arrangement
1 June - 31 August

Admission:
£3.00 (honesty box)

Charities:
All proceeds to
SG Beneficiaries

GORDONSTOUN
Duffus, near Elgin IV30 5RF
Gordonstoun School T: 01343 837837
E: richardss@gordonstoun.org.uk www.gordonstoun.org.uk

The gardens consist of good formal herbaceous borders around lawns, a terrace and an orchard. The school grounds include Gordonstoun House, a Georgian House of 1775/6 incorporating an earlier 17th century house built for the 1st Marquis of Huntly, and the school chapel, both of which will be open to visitors. There is also a unique circle of former farm buildings known as the Round Square and a scenic lake.

Directions: Entrance off B9012, four miles from Elgin at Duffus Village.

Disabled Access:
Full

Opening Times:
Sunday 11 September
2:00pm - 4:30pm

Admission:
£4.00, children £2.00

Charities:
All proceeds to
SG Beneficiaries

HAUGH GARDEN
College of Roseisle IV30 5YE
Gwynne and David Hetherington T: 01343 835790

We are now in the fourth year of developing our two acre garden with walks through mature woodland extensively planted with shade loving plants and young woodland. Large lawns bordered by extensive herbaceous borders. Ongoing work to develop the garden around the ruins of an 18th century farmhouse continues.There is a wildlife pond with adjacent bog garden, fruit trees and a soft fruit and vegetable garden. The garden also has a greenhouse and large polytunnel.

Other Details: Car parking at Roseisle Village Hall but drop-off available at the house. There will be a well-stocked plant stall.

Directions: From Elgin take the A96 west, then the B9013 Burghead Road to the crossroads at the centre of College of Roseisle. The garden is on the right, enter from the Duffus Road. Village Hall car parking is to the left off Kinloss Road.

Disabled Access:
Partial

Opening Times:
Saturdays
25 June, 23 July and 20 Aug
2:00pm - 5:00pm
By arrangement
1 June - 31 August

Admission:
£4.00

Charities:
CHAS receives 20%,
Alzheimer's Scotland receives
20%, the net remaining to
SG Beneficiaries

ROSS, CROMARTY, SKYE & INVERNESS

Scotland's Gardens 2016 Guidebook is sponsored by **INVESTEC WEALTH & INVESTMENT**

District Organiser

Lady Lister-Kaye	House of Aigas, Beauly IV4 7AD E: rosscromarty@scotlandsgardens.org

Area Organiser

Emma MacKenzie	Glenkyllachy, Tomatin IV13 7YA

Treasurer

Mrs Sheila Kerr	Lilac Cottage, Struy, by Beauly IV4 7JU

Gardens open on a specific date

Dundonnell House, Little Loch Broom, Wester Ross	Thursday 21 April	2:00pm	- 5:00pm
Inverewe Garden and Estate, Poolewe, Achnasheen	Wednesday 18 May	10:00am	- 5:30pm
Malin, Glenaldie, Tain	Saturday 28 May	11:00am	- 5:00pm
Oldtown of Leys Garden, Inverness	Saturday 28 May	2:00pm	- 5:00pm
Malin, Glenaldie, Tain	Sunday 29 May	11:00am	- 5:00pm
Inverewe Garden and Estate, Poolewe, Achnasheen	Wednesday 1 June	9:30am	- 6:00pm
Dundonnell House, Little Loch Broom, Wester Ross	Thursday 2 June	2:00pm	- 5:00pm
Old Allangrange, Munlochy	Saturday 4 June	11:00am	- 5:30pm
The New House, Wester Alness Ferry, by Balblair	Saturday 11 June	12:00pm	- 4:00pm
Field House, Belladrum, Beauly	Sunday 12 June	2:00pm	- 4:30pm
Gorthleck, Stratherrick	Friday 17 June	10:00am	- 9:00pm
House of Gruinard, Laide, by Achnasheen	Wednesday 22 June	2:00pm	- 5:00pm
House of Aigas and Field Centre, by Beauly	Sunday 26 June	2:00pm	- 5:00pm
The New House, Wester Alness Ferry, by Balblair	Saturday 2 July	12:00pm	- 4:00pm
House of Aigas and Field Centre, by Beauly	Sunday 24 July	2:00pm	- 5:00pm
Malin, Glenaldie, Tain	Saturday 30 July	11:00am	- 5:00pm
Malin, Glenaldie, Tain	Sunday 31 July	11:00am	- 5:00pm
Hugh Miller's Birthplace Cottage & Museum, Cromarty	Saturday 6 August	12:00pm	- 5:00pm
Craig Dhu House, Laggan	Sunday 14 August	1:00pm	- 5:00pm
Dundonnell House, Little Loch Broom, Wester Ross	Thursday 18 August	2:00pm	- 5:00pm
2 Durnamuck, Little Loch Broom, Wester Ross	Sat/Sun 20 & 21 August	12:00pm	- 5:00pm
Skye Forest Gardens, Sleat, Isle of Skye	Sunday 21 August	10:30am	- 5:00pm
Highland Liliums, 10 Loaneckheim, Kiltarlity	Sunday 28 August	12:00pm	- 4:00pm
Old Allangrange, Munlochy	Saturday 3 September	11:00am	- 5:30pm
2 Durnamuck, Little Loch Broom, Wester Ross	Saturday 10 September	12:00pm	- 5:00pm

ROSS, CROMARTY, SKYE & INVERNESS

Dundonnell House, Little Loch Broom, Wester Ross	Thursday 15 September	2:00pm	- 5:00pm

Gardens open regularly

Abriachan Garden Nursery, Loch Ness Side	1 February - 30 November	9:00am	- Dusk
Applecross Walled Garden, Strathcarron	1 March - 31 October	Dawn	- Dusk
Attadale, Strathcarron	1 April - 29 October	10:00am	- 5:30pm
Balmeanach House, Isle of Skye	7 May - 30 October	10:30am	- 3:30pm
Dunvegan Castle and Gardens, Isle of Skye	1 April - 15 October	10:00am	- 5:30pm
Highland Liliums, 10 Loaneckheim, Kiltarlity	Daily	9:00am	- 5:00pm
Leathad Ard, Upper Carloway, Isle of Lewis	16 May - 31 August	10:00am	- 6:00pm
Oldtown of Leys Garden, Inverness	Daily	8:00am	- 8:00pm
The Lookout, Kilmuir, North Kessock	1 May - 31 August	12:00pm	- 4:00pm

Gardens open by arrangement

Brackla Wood, Culbokie, Dingwall	1 May - 31 May &	
	1 July - 31 July	01349 877765
Cardon, Balnafoich, Farr	1 March - 30 September	01808 521389
Dundonnell House, Little Loch Broom, Wester Ross	1 April - 31 October	07789 390028
Glenkyllachy Lodge, Tomatin	1 May - 31 July &	
	1 Sep - 31 October	emmaglenkyllachy@gmail.com
House of Aigas and Field Centre, by Beauly	1 April - 28 October	01463 782443
Leathad Ard, Upper Carloway, Isle of Lewis	1 April - 30 September	01851 643204
The Lookout, Kilmuir, North Kessock	1 January - 31 December	01463 731489

Key to symbols

	New in 2016		Homemade teas		Accommodation
	Teas		Dogs on a lead allowed		Plant stall
	Cream teas		Wheelchair access		Scottish Snowdrop Festival

GARDEN LOCATIONS IN
ROSS, CROMARTY, SKYE & INVERNESS

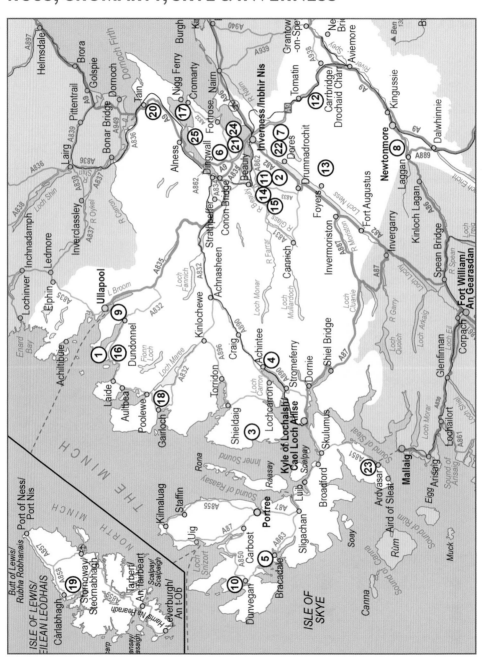

2 DURNAMUCK
Little Loch Broom, Wester Ross IV23 2QZ
Will Soos and Susan Pomeroy T: 01854 633761
E: sueandwill@icloud.com

Our garden is situated on the edge of Little Loch Broom and is south east facing. It is a coastal plantsman's garden with a rich mix of herbaceous borders, trees and shrubs, vegetables, drystone wall planting, South African plants, Mediterranean plants, wild meadow and stunning views. Many of the plants have been collected from all over the world and growing them in Durnamuck has provided the obvious challenges but with an overall pleasing outcome. The ground in places is a bit stony, including the drive.

Other Details: Teas available Sunday 21 August and Saturday 10 September.

Directions: On the west coast take the A832, then take the turning along the single track road signed Badcaul, continue to yellow salt bin, turn right, go to bottom of the hill and it is the house with the red roof. There is parking down by the house if needed.

Disabled Access:
None

Opening Times:
Saturday 20 August
12:00pm - 5:00pm
Sunday 21 August
12:00pm - 5:00pm
Saturday 10 September
12:00pm - 5:00pm

Admission:
£3.00

Charities:
Save the Elephant receives 40%, the net remaining to SG Beneficiaries

ABRIACHAN GARDEN NURSERY
Loch Ness Side IV3 8LA
Mr and Mrs Davidson T: 01463 861232
E: info@lochnessgarden.com   www.lochnessgarden.com

This is an outstanding garden. Over four acres of exciting plantings with winding paths through native woodlands. Seasonal highlights - snowdrops, hellebores, primulas, meconopsis, hardy geraniums and colour-themed summer beds. Views over Loch Ness.

Other Details: Working retail nursery.

Directions: On A82 Inverness/Drumnadrochit road, approximately eight miles south of Inverness.

Disabled Access:
Partial

Opening Times:
1 February - 30 November
9:00am - 7:00pm or Dusk
During summer the garden will close at 7:00pm

Admission:
£3.00

Charities:
Highland Hospice receives 40%, the net remaining to SG Beneficiaries

APPLECROSS WALLED GARDEN
Strathcarron IV54 8ND
Applecross Organics T: 01520 744440

Immaculate garden with neat and tidy borders and not a weed in sight - well, that's definitely not us! We have a one and a quarter acre walled garden planted with emphasis on design, plant combinations and not least, on wildlife as nature intended. The Garden is also home to our award winning café/restaurant, which is open every day from March to October. Peek into Mr MacCowan's 1920s garden bothy. Peace and tranquility await you in Applecross Walled Garden.

Other Details: Restaurant open from 8:30am till late, last orders 8:30pm.

Directions: Take the spectacular Bealach na Ba hill road after Kishorn. At the T-junction in Applecross, turn right for half a mile. Entrance to Applecross House is immediately in front of you.

Disabled Access:
Full

Opening Times:
1 March - 31 October
8:30am or Dawn
- 8:30pm or Dusk

Admission:
By donation

Charities:
Smile Train receives 40%, the net remaining to SG Beneficiaries

ATTADALE
Strathcarron IV54 8YX
Mr and Mrs Ewen Macpherson T: 01520 722603
E: info@attadalegardens.com www.attadalegardens.com

The Gulf Stream, surrounding hills and rocky cliffs, create a microclimate for 20 acres of outstanding water gardens, old rhododendrons, unusual trees and a fern collection in a geodesic dome. There is also a sunken fern garden developed on the site of an early 19th century drain, a waterfall into a pool with dwarf rhododendrons, a sunken garden and kitchen garden. Other features include a conservatory, Japanese garden, sculpture collection and giant sundial.

Other Details: Disabled car parking by the house.

Directions: On A890 between Strathcarron and South Strome.

Disabled Access:
Partial

Opening Times:
1 April - 29 October
10:00am - 5:30pm
closed on Sundays

Admission:
£6.00, OAPs £4.00,
children £1.00, free entry for wheelchair users

Charities:
Highland Hospice receives 40%, the net remaining to SG Beneficiaries

BALMEANACH HOUSE
Balmeanach House, Balmeanach, near Struan, Isle of Skye IV56 8FH
Mrs Arlene Macphie T: 01470 572320
E: info@skye-holiday.com   www.skye-holiday.com

During the late 1980s, a ⅓ acre of croft land was fenced in to create a garden.
Now there is a glorious herbaceous border, bedding plants area and a small azalea/
rhododendron walk. In addition, there is a woodland dell with fairies, three ponds
and a small shrubbery.

Other Details: Plant stall at Plants 'n Stuff, Atholl Service Station.
Teas at Waterside Cafe, Atholl Service Station.

Directions: A87 to Sligachan, turn left, Balmeanach is five miles north of Struan
and five miles south of Dunvegan.

Disabled Access:
None

Opening Times:
7 May - 30 October
10:30am - 3:30pm
Mondays and Thursdays only

Admission:
£3.00

Charities:
SSPCA receives 40%,
the net remaining to
SG Beneficiaries

BRACKLA WOOD
Culbokie, Dingwall IV7 8GY
Susan and Ian Dudgeon T: 01349 877765
E: smdbrackla@aol.com

Mature one acre plot consisting of woodland, wildlife features, ponds, mixed
borders, a kitchen garden, rockery and mini-orchard. Spring bulbs and hellebores,
rhododendrons, wisteria and roses followed by crocosmia, clematis and deciduous
trees provide continuous colour and interest throughout the seasons. There is always
the chance to see red squirrels.

Other Details: Strictly no dogs except guide dogs.

Directions: From north - Take the A9 and turn off to Culbokie. At the far end of
village, turn right after playing fields signposted Munlochy. A mile up the road, turn
right into No Through Road signposted Upper Braefindon.
From south - Take A9 and turn off to Munlochy. At far end of village, turn right and
then sharp left up road signposted Culbokie and Killen. After about 4½ miles turn left
onto road signposted Upper Braefindon. Brackla Wood is the first house on the left.

Disabled Access:
Partial

Opening Times:
By arrangement
1 May - 31 May
By arrangement
1 July - 31 July

Admission:
£3.00, children free

Charities:
Black Isle MacMillan Cancer
Care receives 40%, the net
remaining to SG Beneficiaries

CARDON
Balnafoich, Farr IV2 6XG
Caroline Smith T: 01808 521389
E: csmith@kitchens01.fsnet.co.uk   www.holidaylettings.co.uk

The garden is set in approximately five acres of woodlands with a feature pond and
lawn area. There are also rockeries, wild woodland areas and cottage style plantings.

Other Details: Self-catering accommodation available at Cardon House. See
website for details.

Directions: From Inverness - head south, turn right to Daviot (seven miles) and
head to Balnafoich. Cardon is 3½ miles.
From Inverness Academy - take B861. After 4½ miles take the left to Daviot and
the garden is 400 yards on the left.

Disabled Access:
Full

Opening Times:
By arrangement
1 March - 30 September

Admission:
£3.00, children free

Charities:
Local charities will receive
40%, the net remaining to
SG Beneficiaries

8 CRAIG DHU HOUSE
Laggan PH20 1BS
Mrs Valerie Macpherson T: 01528 544200

Craig Dhu sits above the River Spey with a dramatic rockface background and surrounded by magnificent trees including Silver and Douglas fir, Western Hemlock, Wellingtonia, aspen and birch. There are stunning views. Flower and shrub border, rhododendron path, woodland walks, vegetable patch and an orchard - all at nearly 1000 feet.

Directions: Three miles west of Newtonmore on the A86. Turn in by the red sentry box.

Disabled Access:
None

Opening Times:
Sunday 14 August
1:00pm - 5:00pm

Admission:
£4.00, children free

Charities:
Clan Macpherson Museum receives 20%, Laggan Church receives 20%, the net remaining to SG Beneficiaries

9 DUNDONNELL HOUSE
Little Loch Broom, Wester Ross IV23 2QW
Dundonnell Estates T: 07789 390028

Camellias, magnolias and bulbs in spring, rhododendrons and laburnum walk in this ancient walled garden. Exciting planting in new borders gives all year colour centred around one of the oldest yew trees in Scotland.

A new water sculpture, midsummer roses, restored Edwardian glasshouse, riverside walk, arboretum - all in the valley below the peaks of An Teallach.

Other Details: Champion Trees: Yew and Holly. On 2 June homemade teas are available in the house. On other dates teas are available at Maggie's Tearoom three miles towards Little Loch Broom.

Directions: Off A835 at Braemore on to A832. After 11 miles take Badralloch turn for half a mile.

Disabled Access:
Partial

Opening Times:
Thurs 21 April, 2 Jun, 18 Aug, 15 Sep 2:00pm - 5:00pm
By appointment 1 April - 31 October weekdays only

Admission:
£3.50, children free

Charities:
Environmental Justice Foundation & Gairloch Museum each receive 20% the net remaining to SG Beneficiaries

10 DUNVEGAN CASTLE AND GARDENS
Isle of Skye IV55 8WF
Hugh Macleod of Macleod T: 01470 521206
E: info@dunvegancastle.com www.dunvegancastle.com

The five acres of formal gardens began life in the 18th century. In stark contrast to the barren moorland that dominates Skye's landscape, the gardens are a hidden oasis featuring an eclectic mix of plants, woodland glades, shimmering pools fed by waterfalls and streams flowing down to the sea. After experiencing the Water Garden with its ornate bridges and islands replete with a rich and colourful plant variety, wander through the elegant surroundings of the formal Round Garden. Visit The Walled Garden to see its colourful herbaceous borders and recently added Victorian style glasshouse. In what was formerly the castle's vegetable garden, there is a Garden Museum and a range of plants & flowers which complement the attractive features including a waterlily pond, a neoclassical urn and a Larch pergola. A considerable amount of replanting and landscaping has taken place over the last 30 years to restore and develop these gardens.

Directions: One mile from Dunvegan Village, 23 miles west of Portree. Follow the signs for Dunvegan Castle.

Disabled Access:
Partial

Opening Times:
1 April - 15 October
10:00am - 5:30pm

Admission:
Gardens only £10.00, children £7.00, concs £8.00. Castle & Gardens: £12.00, children 5-15 £9.00, family ticket £31.00, concs £10.00

Charities:
Donation to SG Beneficiaries

FIELD HOUSE
Belladrum, Beauly IV4 7BA
Mr and Mrs D Paterson
www.dougthegarden.co.uk

An informal country garden in a one acre site with mixed borders and some unusual plants - a plantsman's garden. Featured in *The Beechgrove Garden*.

Directions: Four miles from Beauly on A833 Beauly to Drumnadrochit road, then follow signs to Belladrum.

Disabled Access:
None

Opening Times:
Sunday 12 June
2:00pm - 4:30pm

Admission:
£4.00

Charities:
Highland Hospice receives 40%, the net remaining to SG Beneficiaries

GLENKYLLACHY LODGE
Tomatin IV13 7YA
Mr and Mrs Philip Mackenzie
E: emmaglenkyllachy@gmail.com

In a remote highland glen and at an altitude of 1150 feet this is a glorious garden of shrubs, herbaceous, rhododendrons and trees planted round a pond with a backdrop of a juniper and birch covered hillside. There are many unusual trees (some grown from seed), and a new embryonic arboretum. Interesting rhododendrons up the drive flower in June, an annual wild flower meadow flowering in September, a poly tunnel and vegetable garden. Various original sculptures are situated round the garden and a wondrous wall/ folly with many fascinating features provides year round interest. There is a second pond with oriental bridges and ornamental ducks.

Other Details: Teas are available by prior arrangement.

Directions: Turn off the A9 at Tomatin and take the Coignafearn and Garbole single track road down the north side of the River Findhorn, there is a cattle grid and gate on the right 500 metres after the sign to Farr.

Disabled Access:
Partial

Opening Times:
By appointment
1 May - 31 July and
1 September - 31 October

Admission:
£5.00, children free

Charities:
Marie Curie Cancer Care receives 40%, the net remaining to SG Beneficiaries

GORTHLECK
Stratherrick IV2 6UJ
Steve & Katie Smith T: 07710 325903
E: visit@gorthleckgarden.co.uk

Gorthleck is an unusual 20 acre woodland garden built in an unlikely place, on and around an exposed rocky ridge. The layout of the garden works with the natural features of the landscape, with numerous paths, hedges and shelter belts creating clearly defined spaces that enable a large collection of plants and trees to thrive. It has extensive collections of both rhododendrons and bamboos. The challenges presented by the site become a bonus with the ridge offering long views of the surrounding countryside in the 'borrowed landscape' tradition of Japanese gardens. It didn't exist ten years ago and Gorthleck is very much a work-in-progress that is well-maintained by plantsman Graham Chattington and groundsman Lindsay MacDonald.

Directions: From A9, join the B862. Go through Errogie. Approx. 1 mile after sharp left hand bend there is a small church on left. Gorthleck drive is directly opposite church and house can be seen on hill to the left as you follow the drive (follow it to the left of the new house). Park outside house on the gravel.

Disabled Access:
None

Opening Times:
Friday 17 June
10:00am - 9:00pm

Admission:
£5.00

Charities:
All proceeds to
SG Beneficiaries

ROSS, CROMARTY, SKYE & INVERNESS

14 HIGHLAND LILIUMS
10 Loaneckheim, Kiltarlity IV4 7JQ
Neil and Frances Macritchie T: 01463 741365
E: neil.macritchie@btconnect.com www.highlandliliums.co.uk

A working retail nursery with spectacular views over the Beauly valley and Strathfarrar hills. A wide selection of home grown plants available including alpines, ferns, grasses, herbaceous, herbs, liliums, primulas and shrubs.

Other Details: Teas on 28 August only.

Directions: Signposted from Kiltarlity village, which is just off the Beauly to Drumnadrochit road (A833), approximately 12 miles from Inverness.

Disabled Access:
Full

Opening Times:
Sunday 28 August
12:00pm - 4:00pm
1 January - 31 December
9:00am - 5:00pm

Admission:
Free but donations welcome

Charities:
Highland Hospice receives 40%, the net remaining to SG Beneficiaries

---

15 HOUSE OF AIGAS AND FIELD CENTRE
By Beauly IV4 7AD
Sir John and Lady Lister-Kaye T: 01463 782443
E: sheila@aigas.co.uk www.aigas.co.uk

The House of Aigas has a small arboretum of named Victorian specimen trees and modern additions. The garden consists of extensive rockeries, herbaceous borders, ponds and shrubs. Aigas Field Centre rangers lead regular guided walks on nature trails through woodland, moorland and around a loch.

Other Details: Champion Trees: Douglas fir, Atlas Cedar and Sequoiadendron. Homemade teas in the house on both 26 June and 24 July. Lunches/teas are available on request on other dates. Check out Aigas website for details of other events.

Directions: Four and a half miles from Beauly on A831 Cannich/Glen Affric road.

Disabled Access:
Partial

Opening Times:
Sunday 26 June
2:00pm - 5:00pm
Sunday 24 July
2:00pm - 5:00pm
By arrangement
1 April - 28 October

Admission:
£4.00, children free

Charities:
Highland Hospice (Aird branch) receives 40%, the net remaining to SG Beneficiaries

---

16 HOUSE OF GRUINARD
Laide, by Achnasheen IV22 2NQ
The Hon Mrs A G Maclay T: 01445 731235
E: office@houseofgruinard.com

Superb hidden and unexpected garden developed in sympathy with stunning west coast estuary location. Wide variety of interesting herbaceous and shrub borders with water garden and extended wild planting.

Directions: On A832 twelve miles north of Inverewe and nine miles south of Dundonnell.

Disabled Access:
None

Opening Times:
Wednesday 22 June
2:00pm - 5:00pm

Admission:
£3.50, children under 16 free

Charities:
MacMillan Nurses receives 40%, the net remaining to SG Beneficiaries

HUGH MILLER'S BIRTHPLACE COTTAGE & MUSEUM
Church Street, Cromarty IV11 8XA
The National Trust for Scotland T: 01381 600245
E: millersmuseum@nts.org.uk www.nts.org.uk

Two gardens: the Garden of Wonders, created in 2008, with its theme of natural history, features fossils, exotic ferns, ornamental letter-cutting and a 'mystery' stone. The sculptural centrepiece of this award-winning small but beautiful area is a scrap metal ammonite created by Helen Denerley. Also walk around the garden named after Hugh's wife, Lydia. The crescent-shaped, sandstone path of fragrant climbing roses, herbs and wild plant areas which reflect Miller's own love of nature and curiosity in the natural landscape.

Directions: By road via Kessock Bridge and A832 to Cromarty. Twenty-two miles north east of Inverness.

Disabled Access:
None

Opening Times:
Saturday 6 August
12:00pm - 5:00pm
(Last entry 4:30pm)

Admission:
Free - normal Trust admission applies to museum buildings.

Charities:
Donation to SG Beneficiaries

INVEREWE GARDEN AND ESTATE
Poolewe, Achnasheen IV22 2LG
The National Trust for Scotland T: 01445 781200
E: inverewe@nts.org.uk www.nts.org.uk

Magnificent 54 acre Highland garden, surrounded by mountains, moorland and sea loch. Created by Osgood Mackenzie in the late 19th century, it now includes a wealth of exotic plants from Australian tree ferns to Chinese rhododendrons to South African bulbs. Recent plantings include a grove of Wollemi pines and other 'fossil' trees. We have an electric buggy and two wheelchairs that are available to use free of charge. Please book in advance to avoid disappointment.

Other Details: National Plant Collection®: Olearia, Rhododendron (subsect. Barbata, subsect. Glischra, subsect. Maculifera). Champion Trees: Over twenty.
18 May - The Head Gardener's walk will focus on Woodland Gardening.
1 June - The First Gardener's walk will look at the National Collection plantings. Meet at Visitor Centre at 2:00pm for all walks. Shop and self-service restaurant.

Directions: Signposted on A832 by Poolewe, six miles northeast of Gairloch.

Disabled Access:
Partial

Opening Times:
Wednesday 18 May
10:00am - 5:30pm
Wednesday 1 June
9:30am - 6:00pm

Admission:
Normal Trust admission applies.

Charities:
Donation to SG Beneficiaries

LEATHAD ARD
Upper Carloway, Isle of Lewis HS2 9AQ
Rowena and Stuart Oakley T: 01851 643204
E: stuart.oakley1a@gmail.com www.whereveriam.org/leathadard

A one acre sloping garden with stunning views over East Loch Roag. It has evolved along with the shelter hedges that divide the garden into a number of areas giving a new view at every corner. With shelter and raised beds, the different conditions created permit a wide variety of plants to be grown. Beds include herbaceous borders, cutting borders, bog gardens, grass garden, exposed beds, patio, a new pond and vegetable and fruit patches, some of which are grown to show.

Other Details: Rowena and Stuart are happy to show visitors around in the afternoons, although this could take a couple of hours.

Directions: A858 Shawbost - Carloway. First right after Carloway football pitch. First house on right. The Westside circular bus ex Stornoway to road end, ask for the Carloway football pitch.

Disabled Access:
None

Opening Times:
16 May - 31 August
10:00am - 6:00pm
Not open Suns or 3rd Aug.
By arrangement 1 Apr
- 30 Sep excluding Sundays.

Admission:
Recomm. min donation is
£4.00 per head, children free

Charities:
Red Cross receives 40%,
the net remaining to
SG Beneficiaries

20

MALIN
Glenaldie, Tain IV19 1ND
Ivan Brock
E: ikbrock@btinternet.com

The garden has a wide range of trees, shrubs and other plants including alpines, roses and perennials. In a damp area hostas and primulas grow with many ferns. A pergola has a vine and other climbers including wisteria and jasmine. Rhododendrons and azaleas have been planted in the woodland and main garden. There are two ponds, one with 60 ducks and geese, and a stream with rogersia, gunnera and meconopsis. The garden also has a polytunnel, greenhouses and an alpine house.

Other Details: The two acre garden has been lovingly developed by Mary and Ivan over the past 20 years mostly from a bare farm field. The garden is being opened in memory of Mary, who sadly died in April 2015.

Directions: From the south near Tain, on the A9, turn left signposted Glenaldie and Rosemount. Just over ½ mile along this road at the end of the woodland the garden entrance is on the left.

Disabled Access:
Partial

Opening Times:
Sat/Sun28 & 29 May
11:00am - 5:00pm
Sat/Sun 30 & 31 July
11:00am - 5:00pm

Admission:
£3.00, homemade teas £3.00

Charities:
Highland Hospice receives 20%, Macmillan Cancer Support receives 20%, the net remaining to SG Beneficiaries

 21

OLD ALLANGRANGE
Munlochy IV8 8NZ
J J Gladwin T: 01463 811304
E: jayjaygladwin@gmail.com

A 17th century lime washed house is the backdrop to a formal(ish) garden. There is an ice house, horse path, vegetable garden, a mound and an orchard. The garden uses sculpted hedges to play with perspective and to block or expose views. Because the garden is planted for wildlife, particularly bees, wildflowers and beneficial weeds are encouraged. There is a grove of ancient yew trees which are particularly fine, linking the formal garden with the rest of the garden.

Other Details: Champion Trees: Yew. We garden and farm organically, work with the BBCT to develop bee habitat and have our own charitable society which creates gardens to benefit people and bees; Balck Isle Bee Gardens. There will be a bee identification walk with Katy Malone of the Bumble Bee Conservation Trust.

Directions: From Inverness head four miles north on A9, and follow the directions for Black Isle Brewery. Park in brewery car park and get directions in the shop.

Disabled Access:
Partial

Opening Times:
Saturday 4 June
11:00am - 5:30pm
Saturday 3 September
11:00am - 5:30pm

Admission:
£6.00 including organic teas

Charities:
Black Isle Bee Gardens receives 40%, the net remaining to SG Beneficiaries

 22

OLDTOWN OF LEYS GARDEN
Inverness IV2 6AE
David and Anne Sutherland T: 01463 238238
E: ams@oldtownofleys.com

Large garden established ten years ago on the outskirts of Inverness and overlooking the town. Herbaceous beds with lovely rhododendron and azalea displays in spring. There are specimen trees, three ponds surrounded by waterside planting and a small woodland area. A new rockery area was created in 2015 and is still developing.

Directions: Turn off Southern distributor road (B8082) at Leys roundabout towards Inverarnie (B861). At T-junction turn right. After fifty metres turn right into Oldtown of Leys.

Disabled Access:
Partial

Opening Times:
Saturday 28 May
2:00pm - 5:00pm
1 January - 31 December
8:00am - 8:00pm

Admission:
28th May: £4.00, children £1.00, under 2s free
Other days: by donation

Charities:
Local Charities receive 40%, the net remaining to SG Beneficiaries

23

SKYE FOREST GARDENS
Skye Permaculture, Rhuba Phoil, Armadale Pier Road, Ardvasar, Sleat, Isle of
Skye IV45 8RS
Sandy Masson T: 01471 844700
E: rubhaphoil@yahoo.co.uk www.skyeforestgarden.com

A wild natural forest garden managed on permaculture principles with a woodland
walk to seal and bird islands. Look out for otters and other wildlife! There is an
interesting Alchemy Centre with a composting display.

Other Details: Accommodation is available in tent/bothy retreat.
Follow us on Facebook at *www.facebook.com/RubhaPhoil* and
www.facebook.com/skyepermaculture

Directions: Turn right at the car park on Armadale Pier.

Disabled Access:
Partial

Opening Times:
Sunday 21 August
10:30am - 5:00pm

Admission:
£4.00, children free

Charities:
Donation to SG Beneficiaries

 24

THE LOOKOUT
Kilmuir, North Kessock IV1 3ZG
David and Penny Veitch T: 01463 731489
E: david@veitch.biz

A ¾ acre elevated coastal garden with incredible views over the Moray Firth which
is only for the sure-footed. This award winning garden is created out of a rock base
with shallow pockets of ground, planted to its advantage to encourage all aspects
of wildlife. There is a small sheltered courtyard, raised bed vegetable area, pretty
cottage garden, scree and rock garden, rose arbour, rhododendrons, flowering
shrubs, bamboos, trees and lily pond with waterside plants.

Other Details: Coffee, tea and home baking outside if weather permits. Studio with
exhibition of landscape pictures for sale.

Directions: From Inverness, take North Kessock left turn from A9, and third left
at roundabout to underpass then sharp left onto Kilmuir road. From Tore, take slip
road for North Kessock and first right for Kilmuir. Follow signs for Kilmuir (3 miles)
until you reach shore. Garden is near far end of village with a large palm tree on grass.

Disabled Access:
None

Opening Times:
1 May - 31 August
12:00pm - 4:00pm
Open Sundays only.
By arrangement on request

Admission:
£3.00, children under 16 free

Charities:
Alzheimers Scotland receives
40%, the net remaining to
SG Beneficiaries

25

THE NEW HOUSE
Wester Alness Ferry, by Balblair, Dingwall IV7 8LJ
Mrs Adele Farrar T: 01381 610755
E: Adelefarrar@outlook.com

A woodland garden with lots of interesting plants. There are raised beds, herbaceous
borders and alpine plants. The garden overlooks the Cromarty Firth with lots of
birds enjoying the view there too.

Other Details: Small seating areas in the garden.

Directions: Turn off the A9, head through Culbokie on to Resolis. When you reach
the school, across the road is a war memorial - go down to the bottom of the lane.

Disabled Access:
Partial

Opening Times:
Saturday 11 June
12:00pm - 4:00pm
Saturday 2 July
12:00pm - 4:00pm

Admission:
£3.00, children free

Charities:
MS Centre (Therapy Centre)
receives 40%, the net
remaining to SG Beneficiaries

SHETLAND

Scotland's Gardens 2016 Guidebook is sponsored by **INVESTEC WEALTH & INVESTMENT**

Area Organisers

Mrs Mary Leask	VisitScotland, Market Cross, Lerwick ZE1 0LU
Mr Steve Mathieson	VisitScotland, Market Cross, Lerwick ZE1 0LU
	E: shetland@scotlandsgardens.org

Treasurer

Mr Chris Hobson	Braeside, Dunnet, Caithness KW14 8YD

Gardens open regularly

Highlands, East Voe, Scalloway	1 May - 30 September	9:00am	- 9:00pm
Lea Gardens, Tresta	1 April - 31 October Closed Thursdays	2:00pm	- 5:00pm
Nonavaar, Levenwick	10 April - 25 September Fridays and Sundays only	11:00am	- 6:00pm
Norby, Burnside, Sandness	Daily	Dawn	- Dusk

Gardens open by arrangement

Cruisdale, Sandness	On request	01595 870739
Keldaberg, Cunningsburgh	1 June - 31 October	01950 477331
Lindaal, Tingwall	1 June - 30 September	01595 840420
Nonavaar, Levenwick	10 April - 25 September	01950 422447

Key to symbols

	New in 2016		Homemade teas		Accommodation
	Teas		Dogs on a lead allowed		Plant stall
	Cream teas		Wheelchair access		Scottish Snowdrop Festival

GARDEN LOCATIONS IN SHETLAND

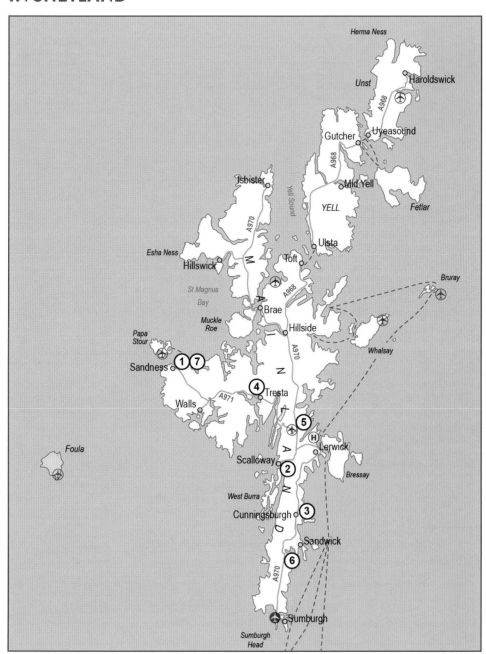

SHETLAND

1 CRUISDALE
Sandness ZE2 9PL
Alfred Kern T: 01595 870739

The garden is in a natural state with many willows, several ponds and a variety of colourful hardy plants that grow well in the Shetland climate. It is a work in progress, started about 13 years ago and growing bigger over the years with more work planned.

Directions: From Lerwick head north on the A970, then at Tingwall take the A971 to Sandness, on the west side of Shetland. Opposite the school, on the right hand side with a wind generator in the field.

Disabled Access:
None

Opening Times:
By arrangement on request

Admission:
£3.00

Charities:
WRVS receives 40%, the net remaining to SG Beneficiaries

2 HIGHLANDS
East Voe, Scalloway ZE1 0UR
Sarah Kay T: 01595 880526
E: info@easterhoull.co.uk www.easterhoull.co.uk

The garden is in two parts. The upper garden is mostly a rockery, with a large selection of plants, shallow pond, seating area and newly built 'polycrub' and green house. The lower garden is on a steep slope with a spectacular sea view over the village of Scalloway. There is a path to lead visitors around. The garden features a large collection of plants, vegetable patch, deep pond and pergola. It was awarded a Shetland Environmental Award in 2014 for its strong theme of recycling.

Other Details: There is self catering accommodation available next to the garden. See website for details.

Directions: Follow A970 main road towards village of Scalloway. Near the top of the hill heading towards Scalloway take a sharp turn to the left, signposted Easterhoull Chalets. Follow road to chalets (painted blue with red roofs) and you will see the yellow SG sign for the garden.

Disabled Access:
None

Opening Times:
1 May - 30 September
9:00am - 9:00pm

Admission:
£3.50

Charities:
Yorkhill Childrens Charity receives 40%, the net remaining to SG Beneficiaries

3 KELDABERG
Cunningsburgh ZE2 9HG
Mrs L Johnston T: 01950 477331
E: linda.keldaberg@btinternet.com

A 'secret garden' divided into four areas. A beach garden of grasses, flowers and driftwood. The main area is a sloping perennial border leading down to a greenhouse, vegetable plot, up to a decked area with containers and exotic plants including agaves, pineapple lilies, cannas and gunneras. The new part has trees, raised vegetable beds, a rockery, retaining walls and an arbour in which to rest. There is a pond complete with goldfish, golden orf and koi plus aquatic plants, and a water lily.

Directions: On the A970 south of Lerwick is Cunningsburgh, take the Gord junction on the left after passing the village hall. Continue along the road to the first house past the Kenwood sign.

Disabled Access:
Partial

Opening Times:
By arrangement
1 June - 31 October
Must phone first to avoid disappointment

Admission:
£3.00

Charities:
Chest Heart & Stroke Scotland receives 40%, the net remaining to SG Beneficiaries

Lea Gardens © Andrea Jones

 LEA GARDENS
Tresta ZE2 9LT
Rosa Steppanova T: 01595 810454

Lea Gardens, started in the early 1980s, now covers almost two acres. The plant collection, the largest north of Inverewe Gardens, consists of 1,500 different species and cultivars from all over the world, including phyto-geographic elements of collections of plants from New Zealand, South Africa and South America. Planted to provide all year round interest it has been divided into a variety of habitats: woodland and shade, borders, wetland, raised beds, and acid and lime lovers. A winner of the 2011 Shetland Environmental Award.

Directions: From Lerwick take A970 north, turn left at Tingwall onto A971 past Weisdale along Weisdale Voe and up Weisdale hill. Coming down, Lea Gardens is on your right surrounded by trees.

Disabled Access:
Partial

Opening Times:
1 April - 31 October
2:00pm - 5:00pm
Closed Thursdays

Admission:
£4.00

Charities:
Donation to SG Beneficiaries

 LINDAAL
Tingwall ZE2 9SG
Mr Adam Leslie T: 01595 840420
E: lindaal@btinternet.com

An established garden of almost one acre. Flat area around the house leading up a slope to a small woodland area with conifers and deciduous trees. In the garden there are four ponds and a well, tubs and hanging baskets with a mix of perennial plants and annuals. Good for wildlife with frogs and birds.

Directions: Go north from Lerwick to Tingwall taking the Laxfirth junction on your right past the local hall and school, round the end of the loch and straight up the hill to first wooden house on the right.

Disabled Access:
Partial

Opening Times:
By arrangement
1 June - 30 September
Please phone first

Admission:
£3.00

Charities:
MS Society Shetland Branch receives 40%, the net remaining to SG Beneficiaries

SHETLAND

 6

NONAVAAR
Levenwick ZE2 9HX
James B Thomason T: 01950 422447

This is a delightful country garden, sloping within drystone walls, overlooking magnificent coastal views. It contains ponds, terraces, trees, bushes, varied perennials, annuals, vegetable garden and greenhouse.

Other Details: There is an Arts & Crafts studio.

Directions: Head south from Lerwick. Turn left at Levenwick sign soon after Bigton turnoff. Follow road to third house on left after Midway stores. Park where there is a Garden Open sign.

Disabled Access:
None

Opening Times:
10 April - 25 September
11:00am - 6:00pm
Fridays and Sundays only.
Other days by arrangement during this period. Please phone first.

Admission:
£3.00

Charities:
Cancer Research receives 40%, the net remaining to SG Beneficiaries

© Andrea Jones

 7

NORBY
Burnside, Sandness ZE2 9PL
Mrs Gundel Grolimund T: 01595 870246
E: gislinde@tiscali.co.uk

A small but perfectly formed garden and a prime example of what can be achieved in a very exposed situation. Blue painted wooden pallets provide internal wind breaks and form a background for shrubs, climbers and herbaceous plants, while willows provide a perfect wildlife habitat. There are treasured plants such as chionocloa rubra, pieris, Chinese tree peonies, and a selection of old-fashioned shrub roses, lilies, hellebores, grasses from New Zealand etc.

Directions: Head north on the A970 from Lerwick then west on the A971 at Tingwall. At Sandness, follow the road to Norby, turn right at the Methodist Church, Burnside at end of road.

Disabled Access:
None

Opening Times:
Daily
Dawn - Dusk
If no one is in please feel free to wander around.

Admission:
£3.00

Charities:
Survival International receives 40%, the net remaining to SG Beneficiaries

Each visit you make to one of our gardens in 2016 will raise money for our beneficiary charities:

In addition, funds will be distributed to a charity of the owner's choice.
For South West Scotland, these include:

Alzheimer's Scotland

Anthony Nolan

Black Isle Bee Gardens

Black Isle MacMillan Cancer Care

Caithness Samaritans

Cancer Research

CHAS

Chest, Heart and Stroke

Community Café, Forres

Children 1st

Clan Macpherson Museum

Croick Church

Environmental Justice Foundation

Friends of Thor House

Gairloch Museum

Gardening Leave

Highland Hospice

Highland Hospice (Aird branch)

Laggan Church

Local Feis

Macmillan Cancer Support

MacMillan Nurses

Marie Curie Cancer Care

MS Centre (Therapy Centre)

MS Society Shetland Branch

Red Cross

RNLI

Save the Elephant

Smile Train

SSPCA

Survival International

Trees for Life

WRVS

Yorkhill Childrens Charity

Children's Hospice Association Scotland

Sharing the Caring

EAST OF SCOTLAND

Scotland's Gardens 2016 Guidebook is sponsored by **INVESTEC WEALTH & INVESTMENT**

ABERDEENSHIRE

Scotland's Gardens 2016 Guidebook is sponsored by **INVESTEC WEALTH & INVESTMENT**

District Organiser

Mrs V Walters	Tillychetly, Alford AB33 8HQ
	E: aberdeenshire@scotlandsgardens.org

Area Organisers

Mrs Gill Cook	Old Semeil, Strathdon AB36 8XJ
Mrs H Gibson	6 The Chanonry, Old Aberdeen AB24 1RP
Mrs F G Lawson	Asloun, Alford AB33 8NR
Mrs Penny Orpwood	Middle Cairncake, Cuminestown, Turriff AB53 5YS
Mrs A Robertson	Drumblade House, Huntly AB54 6ER
Mrs H Rushton	Bruckhills Croft, Rothienorman, Inverurie AB51 8YB

Treasurer

Mr A H J Coleman	Templeton House, Arbroath DD11 4QP

Gardens open on a specific date

Auchmacoy, Ellon	Sunday 17 April	1:00pm	- 4:00pm
Westhall Castle, Oyne, Inverurie	Sunday 17 April	1:00pm	- 4:00pm
Castle Fraser Garden, Sauchen, Inverurie	Saturday 7 May	11:00am	- 4:00pm
Castle Fraser Garden, Sauchen, Inverurie	Sunday 8 May	11:00am	- 4:00pm
Leith Hall Garden, Huntly	Thursday 26 May	7:00pm	
Kildrummy Castle Gardens, Alford	Sunday 5 June	10:00am	- 5:00pm
Tillypronie, Tarland	Sunday 5 June	2:00pm	- 5:00pm
Birken Cottage, Burnhervie, Inverurie	Sunday 12 June	2:00pm	- 5:00pm
Leith Hall Garden, Huntly	Thursday 23 June	7:00pm	
Mansefield, Alford	Sunday 26 June	2:00pm	- 5:00pm
Bruckhills Croft, Rothienorman, Inverurie	Sunday 3 July	12:00pm	- 5:00pm
Glenkindie House, Glenkindie, Alford	Wednesday 6 July	12:00pm	- 3:00pm
Leith Hall Garden, Huntly	Thursday 21 July	7:00pm	
Haddo House, Methlick, Ellon	Tuesday 26 July	11:00am	- 4:00pm
Pitmedden Garden, Ellon	Sunday 7 August	10:00am	
Haddo House, Methlick, Ellon	Sunday 14 August	11:00am	- 4:00pm
Leith Hall Garden, Huntly	Thursday 25 August	7:00pm	
Tillypronie, Tarland	Sunday 28 August	2:00pm	- 5:00pm
Cruickshank Botanic Gardens, Aberdeen	Wednesday 7 September	6:00pm	- 8:30pm
Kildrummy Castle Gardens, Alford	Sunday 2 October	10:00am	- 5:00pm

ABERDEENSHIRE

Garden open regularly

Fyvie Castle, Fyvie, Turriff	4 January - 23 December	9:00am - Dusk

Gardens open by arrangement

Airdlin Croft, Ythanbank, Ellon	21 May - 31 July	01358 761491
An Teallach, Largue, Huntly	1 May - 30 September	01464 871471
Birken Cottage, Burnhervie, Inverurie	1 May - 31 August	01467 623013
Blairwood House, South Deeside Road, Blairs	13 June - 28 August	01224 868301 M:07732 532276
Bruckhills Croft, Rothienorman, Inverurie	6 February - 13 March and 1 July - 31 July	01651 821596
Grandhome, Danestone, Aberdeen	1 April - 31 October	01224 722202
Greenridge, Craigton Road, Cults	1 July - 31 August	01224 860200 Fax: 01224 860210
Hatton Castle, Turriff	Daily	01888 562279
Laundry Cottage, Culdrain, Gartly, Huntly	Daily	01466 720768
Middle Cairncake, Cuminestown, Turriff	1 May - 18 September	01888 544432

Bruckhills Croft

Key to symbols

	New in 2016		Homemade teas		Accommodation
	Teas		Dogs on a lead allowed		Plant stall
	Cream teas		Wheelchair access		Scottish Snowdrop Festival

GARDEN LOCATIONS
IN ABERDEENSHIRE

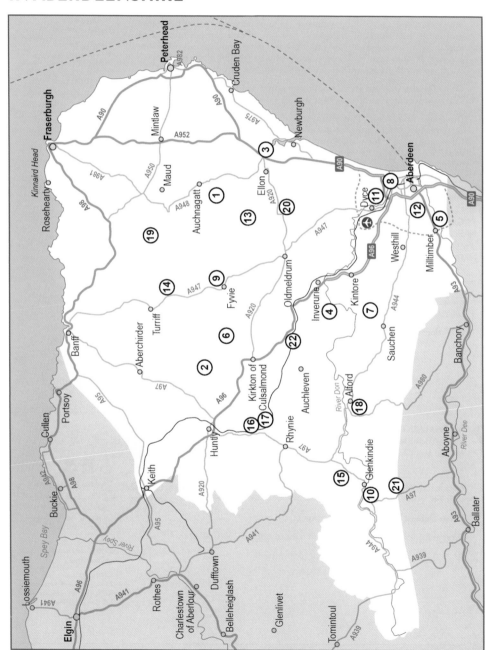

ABERDEENSHIRE

AIRDLIN CROFT
Ythanbank, Ellon AB41 7TS
Richard and Ellen Firmin T: 01358 761491
E: rsf@airdlin.com

A large woodland garden, eventually destined to fill our five-acre croft, features species Rhododendrons, Hydrangeas, Viburnums, Hostas, ferns and other shade-tolerant plants. A sheltered, sunny terrace hosts some tender exotics. One of two polytunnels houses the 'library collection' of more than 450 Hosta cultivars. We go out of our way to attract wildlife - 99 bird species recorded here since 1983.

Other Details: Disabled access to plant nursery only. Please, no dogs.
Teas available at Haddo House or Formartine's, about five miles away.

Directions: From A948, three miles north of Ellon, take the left turn towards Drumwhindle. After another couple of miles take the second left towards Cairnorrie. Proceed for nearly a mile, ignoring the first Airdlin Croft at Coalmoss, and turn left at the first bend down our 0.2 mile track, parking in the field at the bottom.

Disabled Access:
Partial

Opening Times:
By arrangement
21 May - 31 July

Admission:
£4.00

Charities:
Fauna and Flora International receives 40%, the net remaining to SG Beneficiaries

---

AN TEALLACH
Largue, Huntly AB54 6HS
Gary and Victoria Morrison T: 01464 871471
E: vstevens70@gmail.com

This young cottage garden, of approximately one acre (and growing), was created in 2013 and has become established in a remarkably short time. Surrounded by uninterrupted views of rolling hills and farmland, the garden includes a charming variety of colourful, herbaceous, mixed borders, a terraced woodland bank, rose garden, fruit and vegetable beds, and an (as-yet) untamed quarry area. The growing collection of plants and flowers provide interest from May to October.

Directions: Leaving Largue on the B9001, head towards Rothienorman.
An Teallach is the first track on the left, after the national speed limit sign.

Disabled Access:
None

Opening Times:
By arrangement
1 May - 30 September

Admission:
£3.00

Charities:
Dogs Trust receives 40%, the net remaining to SG Beneficiaries

---

AUCHMACOY
Ellon AB41 8RB
Mr and Mrs Charles Buchan

Auchmacoy House's attractive policies feature spectacular displays of thousands of daffodils.

Other Details: Homemade teas and soup.

Directions: A90 from Aberdeen. Turn right to Auchmacoy/Collieston.

Disabled Access:
Partial

Opening Times:
Sunday 17 April
1:00pm - 4:00pm

Admission:
£3.00, concessions £2.50, children free

Charities:
Mission to Seafarers receives 40%, the net remaining to SG Beneficiaries

---

BIRKEN COTTAGE
Burnhervie, Inverurie AB51 5JR
Clare and Ian Alexander T: 01467 623013
E: i.alexander@abdn.ac.uk

This steeply sloping garden of just under one acre is packed with plants. It rises from a wet streamside gully and woodland, past sunny terraces and a small parterre, to dry flowery banks.

Directions: Burnhervie is about three miles west of Inverurie. Leave Inverurie by the B9170 (Blackhall Road) or B993 (St James' Place).

Disabled Access:
None

Opening Times:
Sunday 12 June
2:00pm - 5:00pm
By arrangement
1 May - 31 August

Admission:
£4.00

Charities:
Friends of Anchor receives 40%, the net remaining to SG Beneficiaries

BLAIRWOOD HOUSE
South Deeside Road, Blairs AB12 5YQ
Ilse Elders T: 01224 868301 M:07732 532276
E: ilse.elders@yahoo.co.uk

Over the past three years we have changed our 17 year old, ½ acre garden in several ways. By re-routing part of the driveway we created space for a pond (using local stones) and a small stream. Many new flowering shrubs are used to extend seasonal interest and to provide a good backdrop for less substantial herbaceous perennials. We revamped the entire herb garden for ease of maintenance, and began a new kitchen garden. The garden sits well in the surrounding countryside and provides pleasure through its plant combinations. Short walk from garden to the river Dee is recommended.

Other Details: Refreshments available at two nearby hotels. Teas for parties of ten and over by request.

Directions: Blairs, on the B9077, five minutes by car from Bridge of Dee, Aberdeen. Very close to Blairs Museum.

Disabled Access:
Partial

Opening Times:
By arrangement
13 June - 28 August

Admission:
£4.00

Charities:
Elvanfoot Trust receives 40%, the net remaining to SG Beneficiaries

BRUCKHILLS CROFT
Rothienorman, Inverurie AB51 8YB
Paul and Helen Rushton T: 01651 821596
E: helenrushton1@aol.com

An informal country cottage garden extending to ¾ acre with a further acre as wildflower meadow and pond. Numerous borders are packed with a huge variety of plants, and include a white border and a blue and yellow border. Do some wildlife spotting down by the river, take a turn round the labyrinth, or relax in the pavilion with a cuppa and homebake.

Other Details: There are plenty of home raised plants in the plant sales area including some of the 320 plus named varieties of snowdrop we have. The Snowdrop Festival openings are by appointment only, due to unpredictability of spring weather and because of limited parking. Please advise if you would like teas provided.

Directions: At Rothienorman take the B9001 North, just after Badenscoth Nursing Home turn left, in one mile you will be directed where to park depending if it is the winter or summer opening.

Disabled Access:
None

Opening Times:
Sunday 3 July
12:00pm - 5:00pm
By arrangement 6 February - 13 March and 1 - 31 July

Admission:
£4.00, children free

Charities:
Advocacy Service Aberdeen receives 20%, Befriend A Child, Aberdeen receives 20%, the net remaining to SG Beneficiaries

ABERDEENSHIRE

 CASTLE FRASER GARDEN
Sauchen, Inverurie AB51 7LD
The National Trust for Scotland T: 01330 833463
E: castlefraser@nts.org.uk www.nts.org.uk

Castle Fraser's designed landscape and parkland are the work of Thomas White dating from 1794. Castle Fraser, one of the most spectacular of the Castles of Mar, has a traditional walled garden of trees, shrubs and herbaceous plantings, a medicinal and culinary border and organically grown fruit and vegetables. You can stroll through the woodland garden with its azaleas and rhododendrons or take the young at heart to the Woodland Secrets adventure playground and trails.

Other Details: A sale of herbaceous plants lifted straight from the castle garden. Pick up a colourful addition to enhance your own garden from the Castle Fraser collection; reliably hardy for Aberdeenshire.

Directions: Near Kemnay, off A944.

Disabled Access:
Partial

Opening Times:
Saturday 7 May
11:00am - 4:00pm
Sunday 8 May
11:00am - 4:00pm

Admission:
All donations welcome.

Charities:
Donation to SG Beneficiaries

CRUICKSHANK BOTANIC GARDENS
23 St Machar Drive, Aberdeen AB24 3UU
Cruickshank Botanic Garden Trust, Aberdeen University
www.abdn.ac.uk/botanic-garden/

An evening tour with the Curator, Mark Paterson and Head Gardener, Richard Walker. The garden comprises a sunken garden with alpine lawn, a rock garden built in the 1960s complete with waterfalls and pond system, a long unbroken herbaceous border, a formal rose garden with drystone walling, and an arboretum. It has a large collection of flowering bulbs and rhododendrons, and many unusual shrubs and trees including two mature Camperdown Elms. It is sometimes known as The Secret Garden of Old Aberdeen.

Directions: Come down St Machar Drive over the mini roundabout, just before the first set of traffic lights turn left into the Cruickshank Garden car park. The pedestrian garden entrance is off The Chanonry.

Disabled Access:
Partial

Opening Times:
Wednesday 7 September
6:00pm - 8:30pm

Admission:
£5.00 includes tea/coffee and biscuits.

Charities:
Cruickshank Botanic Gardens Trust receives 40%, the net remaining to SG Beneficiaries

Cruickshank Botanics Rose Garden © George McKay University of Aberdeen

9 FYVIE CASTLE
Fyvie, Turriff AB53 8JS
The National Trust for Scotland T: 01651 891363 / 891266
E: gthomson@nts.org.uk www.nts.org.uk

An 18th century walled garden developed as a garden of Scottish fruits and vegetables. There is also the American garden, Rhymer's Haugh woodland garden, a loch and parkland to visit. Expert staff are always on hand to answer any questions. Learn about the collection of Scottish fruits and their cultivation, and exciting projects for the future. Check the Fyvie Castle Facebook page for up-to-date information on fruit and vegetable availability.

Other Details: A wide selection of seasonal, fresh, organically grown produce for sale from our Fruit Store shop in the walled garden. Proceeds to be donated to Scotland's Gardens.

Directions: Off A947 eight miles south east of Turriff and twenty-five miles north west of Aberdeen.

Disabled Access:
Full

Opening Times:
4 January - 23 December
9:00am - Dusk
The walled garden is closed during the Christmas holidays.

Admission:
Usual NTS admission applies. Free entrance to the garden and grounds.

Charities:
Donation to SG Beneficiaries

10 GLENKINDIE HOUSE
Glenkindie, Alford AB33 8SU
Mr and Mrs J P White

Glenkindie House gardens are laid out around the house in an Arts and Crafts style. The lawns are resplendent with unusual topiary figures: look out for teddy bears, soldiers and Alice in Wonderland characters. There are ancient rubble walls, rose beds planted with R. 'Braveheart', herbaceous borders and a large pond.

Other Details: New for 2016! Soup lunch will be served in the house. There is limited disabled access in the house due to stairs. Bring-and-buy plant stall, to include a wonderful selection of plants for sale, all locally grown. We welcome donations of plants, labelled if possible.

Directions: On the A97 Alford/Strathdon road, 12 miles west of Alford.

Disabled Access:
Partial

Opening Times:
Wednesday 6 July
12:00pm - 3:00pm

Admission:
£8.00 to include soup lunch

Charities:
Willow Foundation receives 20%, Save the Children receives 20%, the net remaining to SG Beneficiaries

11 GRANDHOME
Danestone, Aberdeen AB22 8AR
Mr and Mrs D R Paton T: 01224 722202
E: davidpaton@btconnect.com

Eighteenth century walled garden, incorporating rose garden (replanted 2010); policies with daffodils, tulips, rhododendrons, azaleas, mature trees and shrubs.

Directions: From north end of North Anderson Drive, continue on the A90 over Persley Bridge, turning left at Tesco roundabout. 1¾ miles on the left, through the pillars on a left hand bend.

Disabled Access:
Partial

Opening Times:
By arrangement
1 April - 31 October

Admission:
£4.00

Charities:
Children 1st receives 40%, the net remaining to SG Beneficiaries

ABERDEENSHIRE

GREENRIDGE
Craigton Road, Cults AB15 9PS
BP Exploration T: 01224 860200 or Fax 01224 860210
E: greenrid@bp.com

Large secluded garden surrounding 1840 Archibald Simpson house. For many years winner of Britain in Bloom *Best Hidden Garden*. The garden has mature specimen trees and shrubs, a kitchen garden and sloping, walled rose garden and terraces.

Directions: Will be advised when booking.

Disabled Access:
Partial

Opening Times:
By arrangement
1 July - 31 August

Admission:
£3.50

Charities:
Cancer Research Scotland receives 40%, the net remaining to SG Beneficiaries

HADDO HOUSE
Methlick, Ellon AB41 7EQ
The National Trust for Scotland T: 01651 851 440
E: haddo@nts.org.uk www.nts.org.uk

The gardens at Haddo have recently been restored to their original Victorian glory and showcase geometric beds planted in a modern interpretation of Victorian formal bedding schemes. Meet the gardeners and learn about this project, the history of the gardens and our plans for the future. Visitors will also enjoy the secluded glades and knolls. A magnificent avenue of lime trees leads to adjacent Haddo country park with its lakes, monuments, walks and wildlife.

Other Details: Garden quiz and crafts for kids – get creative with our gardeners and bring home your own little piece of Haddo. Guided tours 12:30pm and 3:30pm.

Directions: Off B999 near Tarves, at Raxton crossroads, 19 miles north of Aberdeen, four miles north of Pitmedden and ten miles NW of Ellon. Cycle - one mile from NCN 1. Bus Stagecoach Bluebird from Aberdeen bus station 01224 212666, circa four mile walk.

Disabled Access:
Partial

Opening Times:
Tuesday 26 July
11:00am - 4:00pm
Sunday 14 August
11:00am - 4:00pm

Admission:
Usual NTS admission applies
Guided tours £4.00, Children under 12 £2.00
Kid's quiz £1.00 and Kid's crafts by donation

Charities:
Donation to SG Beneficiaries

HATTON CASTLE
Turriff AB53 8ED
Mr and Mrs D James Duff T: 01888 562279
E: jjdgardens@btinternet.com

Hatton Castle has a two acre walled garden featuring mixed borders and shrub roses with yew and box hedges and alleys of pleached hornbeam. Also, a kitchen garden, fan trained fruit trees, a lake and woodland walks.

Directions: On A947, two miles south of Turriff.

Disabled Access:
Full

Opening Times:
By arrangement on request

Admission:
£5.00, children free

Charities:
Juvenile Diabetes Research Foundation receives 40%, the net remaining to SG Beneficiaries

15 KILDRUMMY CASTLE GARDENS
Alford AB33 8RA
Kildrummy Garden Trust
www.kildrummy-castle-gardens.co.uk

These gardens were created in the ancient quarry below the Castle. The bridge spanning the garden is a copy of famous brig o' Balgownie and reflects beautifully on the largest of the four ponds which plays host to a wide range of water plants. Rhododendrons and azaleas feature from April (frost permitting). In June the lovely blue of the Meconopsis can be enjoyed and September/October brings colchicums and brilliant colour with acers, fothergillas and viburnums.

Directions: On A97, ten miles from Alford, seventeen miles from Huntly. Car park free inside hotel main entrance. Coaches park up at hotel delivery entrance.

Disabled Access:
Partial

Opening Times:
Sunday 5 June
10:00am - 5:00pm
Sunday 2 October
10:00am - 5:00pm

Admission:
£4.50, concessions £4.00,
children free

Charities:
Aberdeen Branch Multiple
Sclerosis Society receives
40%, the net remaining to
SG Beneficiaries

16 LAUNDRY COTTAGE
Culdrain, Gartly, Huntly AB54 4PY
Simon and Judith McPhun T: 01466 720768
E: simon.mcphun@btinternet.com

An informal, cottage-style garden of about 1½ acres. Upper garden around the house of mixed borders, vegetables and fruit. Steep grass banks to the south and east are planted with native and non-native flowers, specimen trees and shrubs. Narrow grass paths, not suitable for wheelchairs, lead down to the River Bogie.

Directions: Four miles south of Huntly on A97.

Disabled Access:
Partial

Opening Times:
By arrangement on request

Admission:
£4.00, children free

Charities:
Amnesty International
receives 40%, the net
remaining to SG Beneficiaries

17 LEITH HALL GARDEN
Huntly AB54 4NQ
The National Trust for Scotland T: 01464 831148
E: leithhall@nts.org.uk www.nts.org.uk

A series of evening guided tours with the Head Gardener. The west garden was made by Charles and Henrietta Leith-Hay around the beginning of the 20th century. In summer the magnificent zigzag herbaceous and serpentine catmint borders provide a dazzling display. A lot of project work has been ongoing in the garden, including a rose catenary along with large borders which have been redeveloped in a Gertrude Jekyll style and a Laburnum archway with spring interest borders. The carefully reconstructed rock garden is an ongoing work in progress with new planting being added throughout the season.

Other Details: The guided tours with the Head Gardener start at 7:00pm and include refreshments. Booking is essential.

Directions: On B9002 one mile west of Kennethmont.

Disabled Access:
Partial

Opening Times:
Thursday 26 May 7:00pm
Thursday 23 June 7:00pm
Thursday 21 July 7:00pm
Thursday 25 August 7:00pm

Admission:
£5.00 for the guided tour

Charities:
Donation to SG Beneficiaries

MANSEFIELD

Alford AB33 8NL
Diane and Derek Neilson T: 019755 63086
E: info@mansefieldgarden.co.uk www.mansefieldgarden.co.uk

A three acre country garden surrounding a Georgian manse, adjacent to the original Alford church. The garden is bounded by the Leochel Burn and features woodland areas and a burnside walk. There is an 18th century partly walled garden that is informally planted as well as a more formal Victorian walled garden with numerous herbaceous and mixed borders.

Directions: On A980 Alford/Lumphanan Road, adjacent to Alford West Church.

Disabled Access:
Partial

Opening Times:
Sunday 26 June
2:00pm - 5:00pm

Admission:
£4.00, children under 12 free

Charities:
Alford Car Transport Service receives 40%, the net remaining to SG Beneficiaries

MIDDLE CAIRNCAKE

Cuminestown, Turriff AB53 5YS
Mr and Mrs N Orpwood T: 01888 544432

Our garden has evolved from grass circling the house and steading to a series of small garden areas with places to sit and enjoy the surroundings. Our aim has been to create a pleasing environment to delight the senses through different garden themes and planting. It includes cottage gardens, a pond, formal rose garden, heathers and a productive kitchen garden for self-sufficiency. We have many trees and the lower woodland walk completes the garden.

Directions: Middle Cairncake is on the A9170 between New Deer and Cuminestown. It is clearly signposted.

Disabled Access:
Partial

Opening Times:
By arrangement
1 May - 18 September

Admission:
£3.50, children free

Charities:
Parkinson's UK receives 40%, the net remaining to SG Beneficiaries

PITMEDDEN GARDEN

Ellon AB41 7PD
The National Trust for Scotland T: 01651 842352
E: sburgess@nts.org.uk www.nts.org.uk

Join Property Manager/Head Gardener Susan Burgess on one of a series of mini guided walks conducted throughout the afternoon in the tranquil setting of Pitmedden's historic walled garden. Enjoy the sights and scents of the rose border and fine herbaceous borders, and marvel at the immaculate boxwood parterres brimming with summer annuals. Hear about the planning and preparation which goes into creating and presenting this highly acclaimed formal garden.

Other Details: Self-catering accommodation available. Tearoom and gift shop.

Directions: On A920, one mile west of Pitmedden village and fourteen miles north of Aberdeen.

Disabled Access:
Partial

Opening Times:
Sunday 7 August 10:00am onwards.
Guided tours at 1:00, 2:00 and 3:00pm

Admission:
Usual admission charges apply. Donations for guided walk.

Charities:
Donation to SG Beneficiaries

21 TILLYPRONIE
Tarland AB34 4XX
The Hon Philip Astor

Late Victorian house, for which Queen Victoria laid the foundation stone, with superb views over the Dee Valley. There are herbaceous borders, heather beds, a water garden and rockery with alpines. The Golden Jubilee garden contains trees, shrubs and plants of a golden hue. There is a fine collection of trees, including recently planted acers and a well-established pinetum with rare specimens. There is also a fruit garden and greenhouses. In June there is a wonderful show of azaleas, rhododendrons and spring heathers.

Other Details: Please note there is no disabled toilet. There is a plant stall at the June opening only.

Directions: Off A97 between Ballater and Strathdon.

Disabled Access:
Partial

Opening Times:
Sunday 5 June
2:00pm - 5:00pm
Sunday 28 August
2:00pm - 5:00pm

Admission:
£5.00, children £2.00

Charities:
All proceeds to
SG Beneficiaries

22 WESTHALL CASTLE
Oyne, Inverurie AB52 6RW
Mr Gavin Farquhar and Mrs Pam Burney T: 01224 214301
E: enquiries@ecclesgreig.com

Set in an ancient landscape in the foothills of the impressive foreboding hill of Bennachie. A circular walk through glorious daffodils with outstanding views. Interesting garden in early stages of restoration, with large groupings of rhododendrons and specimen trees. Westhall Castle is a 16th century tower house, incorporating a 13th century building of the Bishops of Aberdeen. There were additions in the 17th, 18th and 19th centuries. The castle is semi-derelict, but stabilised from total dereliction. A fascinating house encompassing 600 years of alteration and additions.

Directions: Marked from the A96 at Old Rayne and from Oyne Village.

Disabled Access:
Partial

Opening Times:
Sunday 17 April
1:00pm - 4:00pm

Admission:
£4.00, children free

Charities:
Bennachie Guides receives
40%, the net remaining to
SG Beneficiaries

ANGUS & DUNDEE

Scotland's Gardens 2016 Guidebook is sponsored by **INVESTEC WEALTH & INVESTMENT**

District Organiser

Mrs Terrill Dobson	Logie House, Kirriemuir DD8 5PN
	E: angus@scotlandsgardens.org

Area Organisers

Mrs Helen Brunton	Cuthlie Farm, Arbroath DD11 2NT
Mrs Moira Coleman	Templeton House, Arbroath DD11 4QP
Mrs Katie Dessain	Lawton House, Inverkeilor, by Arbroath DD11 4RU
Mrs Mary Gifford	Kinnordy House, Kinnordy, Kirriemuir DD8 5ER
Mrs Jeanette Ogilvie	House of Pitmuies, Guthrie DD8 2SN
Mrs Rosanne Porter	West Scryne Farm, Carnoustie DD7 6LL
Mrs Gladys Stewart	Ugie-Bank, Ramsay Street, Edzell DD9 7TT
Mrs Claire Tinsley	Ethie Mains, Ethie DD11 5SN

Treasurer

Mrs Mary Stansfeld	Dunninald Castle, by Montrose DD10 9TD

Gardens open on a specific date

Lawton House, Inverkeilor, by Arbroath	Sunday 13 March	2:00pm	-	5:00pm
Brechin Castle, Brechin	Sunday 1 May	2:00pm	-	5:00pm
3 Balfour Cottages, Menmuir	Saturday 7 May	1:00pm	-	5:00pm
Dundee & Angus College Gardens, Kingsway Campus	Saturday 14 May	11:00am	-	4:00pm
Dalfruin, Kirktonhill Road, Kirriemuir	Sunday 15 May	2:00pm	-	5:00pm
Dunninald Castle, Montrose	Sunday 22 May	2:00pm	-	5:00pm
Gallery, Montrose	Saturday 28 May	2:00pm	-	5:00pm
Edzell Village & Castle, Edzell	Sunday 19 June	1:00pm	-	5:00pm
Forfar Open Garden, 36 Lochside Road, Forfar	Saturday 2 July	2:00pm	-	5:00pm
Hospitalfield Gardens, Westway, Arbroath	Saturday 9 July	2:00pm	-	5:00pm
Gallery, Montrose	Saturday 16 July	2:00pm	-	5:00pm
The Herbalist's Garden at Logie, Kirriemuir	Sunday 31 July	2:00pm	-	5:00pm

Gardens open by arrangement

Dunninald Castle, Montrose	For groups	visitorinformation@dunninald.com
Gallery, Montrose	1 May - 30 Sept	galleryhf@googlemail.com
Kirkton House, Kirkton of Craig, Montrose	1 May - 30 Sept	01674 673604
The Herbalist's Garden at Logie, Kirriemuir	1 June - 31 August	terrill@angusherbalists.co uk

ANGUS & DUNDEE

Gardens open regularly

Dunninald Castle, Montrose	2 July - 31 July excluding Mondays	1:00pm	- 5:00pm
Gallery, Montrose	1 June - 31 August Tuesdays only	1:00pm	- 5:00pm
Hospitalfield Gardens, Westway, Arbroath	14 May - 24 September Saturdays only	2:00pm	- 5:00pm
Pitmuies Gardens, House of Pitmuies, Guthrie	30 January - 13 March & 1 April - 31 October	10:00am	- 5:00pm
The Herbalist's Garden at Logie, Kirriemuir	1 August - 31 August Sundays only	2:00pm	- 5:00pm

Gardens open by arrangement

The Herbalist's Garden at Logie, Kirriemuir	1 June - 31 August	terrill@angusherbalists.co.uk

**PITMUIES GARDENS, HOUSE OF PITMUIES, GUTHRIE
CELEBRATING THEIR 50TH GARDEN OPEN DAY FOR SCOTLAND'S GARDENS IN 2016**

Key to symbols

	New in 2016		Homemade teas		Accommodation
	Teas		Dogs on a lead allowed		Plant stall
	Cream teas		Wheelchair access		Scottish Snowdrop Festival

GARDEN LOCATIONS IN ANGUS & DUNDEE

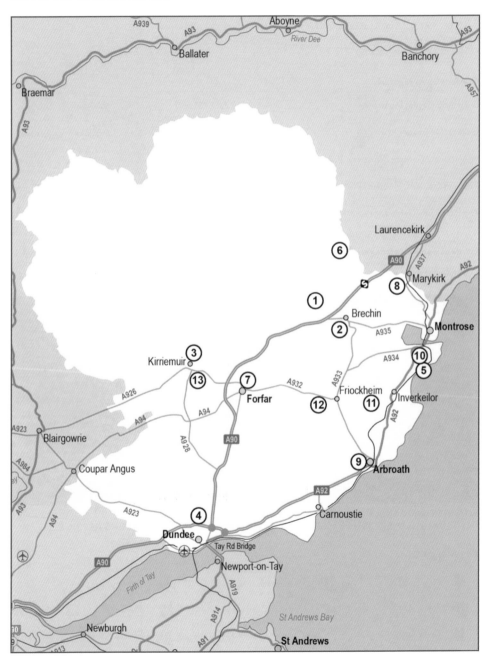

3 BALFOUR COTTAGES
Menmuir DD9 7RN
Dr Alison Goldie and Mark A Hutson T: 01356 660280
E: alisongoldie@btinternet.com www.angusplants.co.uk

Small cottage garden packed with rare and unusual plants. It comprises various 'rooms', containing myriad plants from potted herbs, spring bulbs and alpines in a raised bed, to a 'jungle' with a range of bamboos. Many other interesting plants include primula, hosta, meconopsis, fritillaria, trillium, allium, a large display of bonsai and auriculas.

Other Details: National Plant Collection®: Primula auricula (alpine).

Directions: Leave the A90 two miles south of Brechin and take the road to Menmuir (3½ miles). At the T-junction turn right and it is in the first group of cottages on your left (175 yards).

Disabled Access:
None

Opening Times:
Saturday 7 May
1:00pm - 5:00pm

Admission:
£3.00, accompanied children free

Charities:
Plant Heritage receives 40%, the net remaining to SG Beneficiaries

---

BRECHIN CASTLE
Brechin DD9 6SG
The Earl and Countess of Dalhousie T: 01356 624566
E: mandyferries@dalhousieestates.co.uk www.dalhousieestates.co.uk

The uniquely curving walls of the garden at Brechin Castle are just the first of many delightful surprises in store. The luxurious blend of ancient and modern plantings is the second. Find charm and splendour in the wide gravelled walks, secluded small paths and corners. May sees the rhododendrons and azaleas hit the peak of their flowering to wonderful effect; and with complementary underplanting and a framework of great and beautiful trees sets the collection in the landscape. This is a lovely garden at any time of year and a knockout in the spring.

Other Details: Dogs on leads please.

Directions: A90 southernmost exit to Brechin, one mile past Brechin Castle Centre, Castle gates on right.

Disabled Access:
Partial

Opening Times:
Sunday 1 May
2:00pm - 5:00pm

Admission:
£5.00, OAPs £4.00, accompanied children free

Charities:
Dalhousie Day Care receives 20%, Unicorn Preservation Society receives 20%, the net remaining to SG Beneficiaries

---

DALFRUIN
Kirktonhill Road, Kirriemuir DD8 4HU
Mr and Mrs James A Welsh

A well-stocked connoisseur's garden of about ⅓ acre situated at the end of a short cul-de-sac. There are many less common plants like varieties of Trilliums, Meconopsis (blue poppies), tree peonies (descendants of ones collected by George Sherriff and grown at Ascreavie), Dactylorhiza and Codonopsis. There is a scree and collection of ferns. The vigorous climbing rose Paul's Himalayan Musk grows over a pergola. Interconnected ponds encourage wildlife.

Other Details: Good plant stall with many unusual plants including Trilliums, Meconopsis and tree peonies. Teas served at St Mary's Episcopal Church.

Directions: From centre of Kirriemuir turn left up Roods. Kirktonhill Road is on left near top of hill. Please park on Roods or at St Mary's Episcopal Church. Disabled parking only in Kirktonhill Road.

Disabled Access:
Partial

Opening Times:
Sunday 15 May
2:00pm - 5:00pm

Admission:
£4.00, accompanied children free

Charities:
St Mary's Episcopal Church receives 40%, the net remaining to SG Beneficiaries

DUNDEE & ANGUS COLLEGE GARDENS
Kingsway Campus, Old Glamis Road DD3 8LE
Horticulture Department, D&A College
www.dundeeandangus.ac.uk

The gardens have been developed and re-developed over the past 40 years. Currently the gardens display many different garden rooms along with finished show areas. Other 'rooms' are constantly in a state of construction (and occasional destruction) by our students. This year we are particularly proud of our fruit and vegetable garden, Japanese garden and rock garden which is still under construction. The glass houses and frame yard are always busy with a fine range of bedding plants, alpines and herbaceous plants and a selection of shrubs and trees all of which will be for sale. We always have a few special plants on the go as well.

Other Details: Within the garden you will find lots of busy areas such as the potting shed which is the nerve centre of the garden, the drystane wall site where students learn traditional skills and the covered area, where paving and cement walling are undertaken. You will be able to have a go at some hard landscaping if you wish. Students and staff will be available to help with any questions and demonstrations will go on throughout the day. Tea, coffee and cakes will be available, prepared and served by the college hospitality students.

Directions: Find the college along the Kingsway at the roundabout with Old Glamis Road. National Express buses (18, 19 & 21) run along Old Glamis Road to/from Dundee town centre and stop outside the Campus.

Disabled Access:
Partial

Opening Times:
Saturday 14 May
11:00am - 4:00pm

Admission:
£4.00, accompanied children free

Charities:
Student Foodbank, Dundee & Angus College receives 40%, the net remaining to SG Beneficiaries

DUNNINALD CASTLE
Montrose DD10 9TD
The Stansfeld Family T: 01674 672031
E: visitorinformation@dunninald.com www.dunninald.com

Dunninald Castle is a family home built in 1824, set in policies developed during the 17th and 18th centuries. It offers many attractive features to the visitor including a beech avenue planted around 1670. Snowdrops in spring and bluebells in May carpet the woods and wild garden. At its best in July, the highlight of Dunninald is the walled garden with traditional mixed borders, vegetables, soft fruits, fruit trees and greenhouse.

Other Details: See website for additional opening times. Also open by arrangement for groups.

Directions: Two miles south of Montrose, off A92 Arbroath/Montrose road (Usan turning).

Disabled Access:
Partial

Opening Times:
Sunday 22 May
2:00pm - 5:00pm
for Bluebell Sunday
2 July - 31 July
1:00pm - 5:00pm
excluding Mondays

Admission:
£4.00, accompanied children free

Charities:
Donation to SG Beneficiaries

EDZELL VILLAGE & CASTLE
Edzell DD9 7TT
The Gardeners of Edzell & Historic Scotland

Walk round several fabulous and different gardens in Edzell village including those of Edzell Castle.

Other Details: Strawberry teas will be available, location announced on the day.

Directions: Tickets available in the village, signs will be prominent along the main street (B966) signposted from the A90.

Disabled Access:
Partial

Opening Times:
Sunday 19 June
1:00pm - 5:00pm

Admission:
£4.00, accompanied children free

Charities:
Stracathro Cancer Care Fund UK receives 40%, the net remaining to SG Beneficiaries

FORFAR OPEN GARDEN
36 Lochside Road, Forfar DD8 3JD
Forfar Open Garden Scheme T: 01307 469090
E: craichie@aol.com

This is a brand new therapeutic garden developed by local gardeners banded together in to the charity, Forfar Open Garden Scheme. The quarter acre garden caters for people of all abilities and provides sessions of horticulture therapy in an informal setting. The planting strives for a balance of ornamental, sensory and seasonal productive plants. The garden houses a large greenhouse, polytunnel, and meeting room where the gardeners can mix socially.

Other Details: Conducted tours are available for groups by arrangement.

Directions: Lochside Road is opposite the entrance to Tesco in Forfar. The garden is 200 yards along Lochside Road on the right.

Disabled Access:
Full

Opening Times:
Saturday 2 July
2:00pm - 5:00pm

Admission:
£3.00, accompanied children free

Charities:
Forfar Open Garden Scheme receives 40%, the net remaining to SG Beneficiaries

GALLERY
Montrose DD10 9LA
Mr John Simson T: 01674 840550
E: galleryhf@googlemail.com

The redesign and replanting of this historic garden, featured in the March 2015 edition of *Homes & Gardens*, have preserved and extended its traditional framework of holly, privet and box. A grassed central alley, embellished with circles, links themed gardens, including the recently replanted gold garden and hot border, with the fine collection of old roses and the fountain and pond of the formal white garden. A walk through the woodland garden, home to rare breed sheep, with its extensive border of mixed heathers, leads to the River North Esk. From there rough paths lead both ways along the bank.

Other Details: Teas available only on 28 May and 16 July open days.

Directions: From A90 south of Northwater Bridge take exit to Hillside and next left to Gallery and Marykirk. From A937 west of rail underpass follow signs to Gallery and Northwater Bridge.

Disabled Access:
Partial

Opening Times:
Saturdays
28 May 2:00pm - 5:00pm
16 July 2:00pm - 5:00pm
1 June - 31 August 1:00pm - 5:00pm Tuesdays only

Admission:
£4.00, accompanied children free

Charities:
Practical Action receives 40%, the net remaining to SG Beneficiaries

HOSPITALFIELD GARDENS
Hospitalfield House, Westway, Arbroath DD11 2NH
Hospitalfield Arts
E: info@hospitalfield.org.uk www.hospitalfield.org.uk

Hospitalfield in Arbroath is the historic home of the artist Patrick Allan-Fraser (1813 – 1890). The estate was left in trust to support artists, and became one of Scotland's first Art Schools. Hospitalfield continues to operate an arts programme today with these same aims. The delightful walled garden and surrounding landscapes are beautiful and provide a lovely place to spend the afternoon. Gardens are maintained by an enthusiastic team of staff and volunteers through Garden Club at Hospitalfield.

Other Details: Tea and cake and activities for children are available each Saturday. Hospitalfield House itself is accessible, during seasonal Open Weekends and with guided tours each Wednesday afternoon, in June and September. See website for dates and further information.

Directions: Car - A92 from Dundee. After the Welcome to Arbroath sign turn left at the roundabout onto the Westway. Hospitalfield is 200 yards up the hill.
From Aberdeen take the A90, then A92 or take the slightly longer but very scenic route along the east coast via the A93 and the B974.
Train - Hospitalfield House is 20 minutes walk from Arbroath Station.
Bus - There are regular buses from Dundee and Aberdeen.

Disabled Access:
Partial

Opening Times:
Saturday 9 July
2:00pm - 5:00pm
14 May - 24 September
2:00pm - 5:00pm
Saturdays only

Admission:
£4.00, accompanied children free

Charities:
Donation to SG Beneficiaries

KIRKTON HOUSE
Kirkton of Craig, Montrose DD10 9TB
Campbell Watterson T: 01674 673604
E: campbellkirktonhouse@btinternet.com

A regency manse set in over two acres of garden. The walled garden includes herbaceous borders, a sunken garden, lime allee, statuary and formal rose garden. The wild garden includes a pond and water lilies. There is also a large flock of Jacobs sheep in the adjoining glebe.

Directions: One mile south of Montrose, off A92 at the Balgove turn-off.

Disabled Access:
Partial

Opening Times:
By arrangement
1 May - 30 September

Admission:
£4.00, accompanied children free

Charities:
All proceeds to
SG Beneficiaries

LAWTON HOUSE
Inverkeilor, by Arbroath DD11 4RU
Katie & Simon Dessain

Woodland garden of beech trees carpeted with snowdrops and crocuses in spring, set around a Georgian House. There is also a walled garden planted with fruit trees and vegetables. The property was owned for many years by Elizabeth and Patrick Allan Fraser who built Hospitalfield House in Arbroath.

Directions: Take B965 between Inverkeiler and Friockheim, turn right at sign for Angus Chainsaws. Drive approximately 200 metres, then take second right into drive with green gate.

Disabled Access:
Partial

Opening Times:
Sunday 13 March
2:00pm - 5:00pm
for the Snowdrop Festival

Admission:
£3.00, accompanied children free.

Charities:
Julia Thomson Memorial Trust receives 40%, the net remaining to SG Beneficiaries

---

PITMUIES GARDENS
House of Pitmuies, Guthrie, By Forfar DD8 2SN
Jeanette & Ruaraidh Ogilvie

Two semi-formal walled gardens adjoin the 18th century house and shelter long borders of herbaceous perennials, superb delphiniums, old fashioned roses and pavings with violas and dianthus. Spacious lawns, river and lochside walks are found beneath fine trees. There is a wide variety of shrubs with good autumn colour and an interesting picturesque turreted doocot and 'Gothick' wash house. Myriad spring bulbs include carpets of crocus following the massed snowdrops.

Other Details: Dogs on leads, please.

Directions: A932. Friockheim 1½ miles.

Disabled Access:
Partial

Opening Times:
30 January - 13 March
10:00am - 5:00pm for the Snowdrop Festival
1 April - 31 October
10:00am - 5:00pm

Admission:
£5.00, accompanied children free

Charities:
Donation to SG Beneficiaries

THE HERBALIST'S GARDEN AT LOGIE
Logie House, Kirriemuir DD8 5PN
Terrill and Gavin Dobson
E: terrill@angusherbalists.co.uk www.angusherbalists.co.uk

This garden, featured on *The Beechgrove Garden* 2014, is set amid an 18th century walled garden and large Victorian greenhouse within Logie's organic farm. Featuring more than 150 herbs, the physic garden is divided into eight rectangles including medicinal herbs for different body systems. All the herbs are labelled with a brief description of actions to help novices learn more about this ancient art. The garden also features a herbaceous border and productive fruit and vegetable garden.

Other Details: Groups welcome by arrangement. Homemade teas on 31 July. DIY teas in August when only open on Sundays.

Directions: From the A926 leaving Kirriemuir, fork left at Beechwood Place onto the single track road (or if approaching Kirriemuir take sharp left after Welcome to Kirriemuir sign). Take the first left and follow signs to The Walled Garden.

Disabled Access:
Partial

Opening Times:
Sunday 31 July
2:00pm - 5:00pm
1 - 31 August 2:00pm - 5:00pm Sundays only
By arrangement
1 June - 31 August

Admission:
£4.00, accomp. children free

Charities:
Angus Toy Appeal receives 40%, the net remaining to SG Beneficiaries

FIFE

Scotland's Gardens 2016 Guidebook is sponsored by **INVESTEC WEALTH & INVESTMENT**

District Organiser

Lady Erskine	Cambo House, Kingsbarns KY16 8QD E: fife@scotlandsgardens.org

Area Organisers

Mrs Jeni Auchinleck	2 Castle Street, Crail KY10 3SQ
Mrs Pauline Borthwick	96 Hepburn Gardens, St Andrews KY16 9LP
Mrs Lisa Bremner	Grey Craig House, Bridge Street, Saline KY12 9TS
Mr David Buchanan-Cook	Helensbank, 56 Toll Road, Kincardine FK10 4QZ
Mrs Evelyn Crombie	Keeper's Wood, Over Rankeilour, Cupar KY15 4NQ
Kathryn Jenkins	Newburn House, Drumeldrie, Upper Largo KY8 6JE
Caroline Macpherson	Edenside, Strathmiglo KY14 7PX
Mrs Lindsay Murray	Craigfoodie, Dairsie KY15 4RU
Ms Louise Roger	Chesterhill, Boarhills, St Andrews KY16 8PP
Mrs April Simpson	The Cottage, Boarhills, St Andrews KY16 8PP
Mrs Fay Smith	37 Ninian Fields, Pittenweem, Anstruther KY10 2QU
Mrs Julia Young	South Flisk, Blebo Craigs, Cupar KY15 5UQ

Treasurer

Mrs Sally Lorimore	Willowhill, Forgan, Newport-on-Tay DD6 8RA

Gardens open on a specific date

Lindores House, by Newburgh	Sunday 6 March	11:00am	- 3:00pm
Cambo House	Sunday 17 April	11:00am	- 4:00pm
Rofsie Arts Garden, by Collessie	Sunday 17 April	2:00pm	- 5:00pm
46 South Street, St Andrews	Sunday 24 April	2:00pm	- 5:00pm
The Tower, 1 Northview Terrace, Wormit	Saturday 7 May	12:00pm	- 5:00pm
Kellie Castle Spring Plant Sale, Pittenweem	Sunday 8 May	10:30am	- 4:00pm
St Fort Woodland Garden with Tayfield and Willowhill	Sunday 15 May	1:00pm	- 5:00pm
Kirklands, Saline	Sunday 22 May	2:00pm	- 5:00pm
Lindores House and Garden Cottage, by Newburgh	Sunday 22 May	2:00pm	- 6:00pm
Earlshall Castle, Leuchars	Sunday 29 May	2:00pm	- 5:00pm
Newton Mains and Newton Barns, Auchtermuchty	Saturday 4 June	11:00am	- 4:00pm
Newton Mains and Newton Barns, Auchtermuchty	Sunday 5 June	11:00am	- 4:00pm
Greenhead Farmhouse, Greenhead of Arnot	Sunday 12 June	2:00pm	- 5:00pm

FIFE

Scotland's Gardens 2016 Guidebook is sponsored by INVESTEC WEALTH & INVESTMENT

Blebo Craigs Village Gardens, Cupar	Saturday 18 June	1:00pm	- 4:30pm
Blebo Craigs Village Gardens, Cupar	Sunday 19 June	1:00pm	- 4:30pm
Culross Palace Garden, Culross	Sunday 19 June	12:00pm	- 5:00pm
Earlshall Castle, Leuchars	Sunday 19 June	2:00pm	- 5:00pm
St Monans Village Gardens	Sunday 19 June	2:00pm	- 5:00pm
The Old Farmhouse, Straiton Farm, Balmullo	Sunday 19 June	1:00pm	- 5:00pm
Rofsie Arts Garden, by Collessie	Sunday 26 June	2:00pm	- 5:00pm
The Old Farmhouse, Straiton Farm, Balmullo	Saturday 2 July	1:00pm	- 5:00pm
Boarhills Village Gardens, St Andrews	Sunday 3 July	1:00pm	- 5:00pm
Teasses Gardens, near Ceres	Sunday 10 July	1:00pm	- 5:00pm
Crail: Small Gardens in the Burgh	Saturday 16 July	1:00pm	- 5:00pm
Crail: Small Gardens in the Burgh	Sunday 17 July	1:00pm	- 5:00pm
Falkland Palace and Garden, Falkland, Cupar	Sunday 17 July	12:00pm	- 4:30pm
Balcaskie with Kellie Castle, Pittenweem	Sunday 24 July	12:00am	- 5:00pm
The Tower, 1 Northview Terrace, Wormit	Saturday 30 July	12:00pm	- 5:00pm
The Tower, 1 Northview Terrace, Wormit	Saturday 20 August	12:00pm	- 5:00pm
Craigfoodie, Dairsie	Sunday 4 September	2:00pm	- 5:00pm
Balcarres, Colinsburgh	Sunday 11 September	2:00pm	- 5:00pm
Hill of Tarvit, Cupar	Sunday 2 October	10:30am	- 4:00pm

Gardens open regularly

Willowhill, Forgan, Newport-on-Tay	Saturdays 4 June - 27 Aug	2:00pm	- 7:00pm

Gardens open by arrangement

Barham, Bow of Fife	1 April - 31 July	01337 810227
Helensbank, Kincardine	1 June - 31 July	07739 312912
Logie House, Crossford, Dunfermline	1 April - 31 October	07510 654812
South Flisk, Blebo Craigs, Cupar	15 April - 19 June	01334 850859
The Old Farmhouse, Straiton Farm, Balmullo	On request	01334 870203.
The Tower, 1 Northview Terrace, Wormit	1 April - 30 September	01382 541635 M: 07768 406946
Willowhill, Forgan, Newport-on-Tay	1 May - 31 August	01382 542890
Wormistoune House, Crail	1 April - 30 September	07905 938449

FIFE

Plant sales

Cambo House Spring Plant and Craft Fair, Kingsbarns	Sunday 17 April	11:00am – 4:00pm
Kellie Castle Spring Plant Sale, Pittenweem	Sunday 8 May	10:30am – 4:00pm
Hill of Tarvit Plant Sale and Autumn Fair	Sunday 2 October	10:30am – 4:00pm

Kirklands

Key to symbols

 New in 2016

 Teas

 Cream teas

 Homemade teas

 Dogs on a lead allowed

 Wheelchair access

 Accommodation

 Plant stall

 Scottish Snowdrop Festival

GARDEN LOCATIONS
IN FIFE

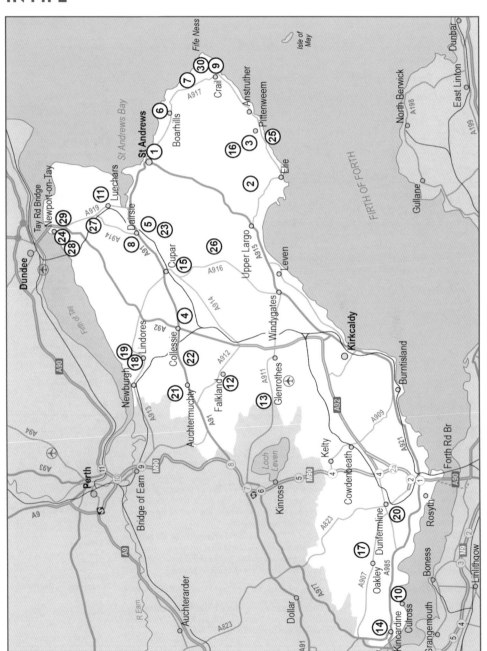

1 46 SOUTH STREET
St Andrews KY16 9JT
Mrs June Baxter T: 01334 474 995

Renowned town garden in Medieval long rig, with orchard, bulbs and many spring flowering shrubs. A historic and unique feature in St Andrews, but also a wonderfully planted space where different styles of planting complement the range of plants used.

Other Details: Teas will be served under cover.

Directions: Entry for the garden off South Street.

Disabled Access:
Partial

Opening Times:
Sunday 24 April
2:00pm - 5:00pm

Admission:
£5.00

Charities:
All Saints' Scottish Episcopal Church St Andrews receives 40%, the net remaining to SG Beneficiaries

2 BALCARRES
Colinsburgh KY9 1HN
The Earl and Countess of Crawford and Balcarres

Superb 19th century formal and extensive woodland gardens with a wide variety of plants. Late summer splendour includes wonderful Eucryphia.

Directions: Half a mile north of Colinsburgh off A942.

Disabled Access:
None

Opening Times:
Sunday 11 September
2:00pm - 5:00pm

Admission:
£5.00, children free

Charities:
Colinsburgh Town Hall Restoration Projects receives 40%, the net remaining to SG Beneficiaries

3 BALCASKIE WITH KELLIE CASTLE
Pittenweem KY10 2RD
The Anstruther Family and The National Trust for Scotland

Balcaskie: In 1905 George Elgood wrote that Balcaskie was 'one of the best and most satisfying gardens in the British Isles'. Over the centuries, the gardens have seen input from Gilpin, Bryce & Nesfield. Today the gardens are at the start of a period of restoration with help from the National Trust for Scotland.
Kellie Castle: This superb garden, around 400 years old, was sympathetically restored by the Lorimer family in the late 19th century. The Arts and Crafts style garden has a selection of old-fashioned roses and herbaceous plants, cultivated organically and hosts an amazing 30 varieties of rhubarb and 75 different types of apple.

Other Details: There will be an exciting mix of artist and craft stalls at Kellie Castle.

Directions: B9171, three miles NNW of Pittenweem. Bus - Flexible from local villages by pre-booking. Access to Balcaskie and Kellie Castle via Kellie Castle only, a free minibus will transport visitors between the gardens.

Disabled Access:
Partial

Opening Times:
Sunday 24 July
12:00am - 5:00pm

Admission:
£8.00 for entrance to both gardens

Charities:
Donation to SG Beneficiaries

BARHAM
Bow of Fife KY15 5RG
Sir Robert & Lady Spencer-Nairn T: 01337 810227

A small woodland garden with snowdrops, spring bulbs, trilliums, rhododendrons and ferns. Also a summer garden with rambler roses, herbaceous borders, island beds and a well stocked vegetable garden.

Other Details: Small nursery of rare and unusual plants grown from seed collected or plants divided from the garden.

Directions: A914 miles west of Cupar.

Disabled Access:
None

Opening Times:
By arrangement
1 April - 31 July

Admission:
£4.00, OAP's £3.00,
children free

Charities:
Pain Association Scotland
receives 40%, the net
remaining to SG Beneficiaries

BLEBO CRAIGS VILLAGE GARDENS
Cupar KY15 5UF
The Gardeners of Blebo Craigs

A selection of the special and varied gardens of Blebo will be open in this lovely Fife village with its wonderful hedgerows, cottages and superb views. A local history trail will also be open bringing the past history of the village to life as you walk around.

Other Details: Wheelchair access is limited but parking is available near the village hall. Disabled toilet in the village hall.

Directions:
From St Andrews - take B939 and after four miles, turn right onto village road.
From Cupar - take B940 to Pitscottie then turn left onto B939 signposted St Andrews. After two miles, turn left at sign into Blebo Craigs.

Disabled Access:
Partial

Opening Times:
Saturday 18 June
1:00pm - 4:30pm
Sunday 19 June
1:00pm - 4:30pm

Admission:
£5.00

Charities:
Blebo Craigs Village Hall
receives 40%, the net
remaining to SG Beneficiaries

BOARHILLS VILLAGE GARDENS
St Andrews KY16 8PP
The Gardeners of Boarhills

Four delightfully varied village gardens exhibiting a range of styles. Colourful, richly planted herbaceous borders at Kenly Green Farm; traditional mixed cottage garden style at The Dirdale with kitchen garden and orchard; spectacular bedding and expertly grown sweet peas at No 5 Old Edinburgh; clever use of different levels and existing built features at The Cottage, which has been completely re-planted in the last 10 years.

Other Details: Teas in the Village Hall

Directions: Enter the Village off the A917. Parking and Plant Stall at Kenly Green Farm.

Disabled Access:
Partial

Opening Times:
Sunday 3 July
1:00pm - 5:00pm

Admission:
£5.00

Charities:
Tayside Children's Hospital
Appeal receives 40%, the net
remaining to SG Beneficiaries

CAMBO HOUSE SPRING PLANT AND CRAFT FAIR
Kingsbarns KY16 8QD
Sir Peter and Lady Erskine T: 01333 450313
E: cambo@camboestate.com www.camboestate.com

Invited nurseries will join Cambo to provide a wide ranging and interesting plant sale. Local craft and food stalls have also been invited. The gardens and woodland walks will be open.

Other Details: National Plant Collection®: Galanthus. Champion Trees: Bundle Beech. 40% of funds raised on this day will go towards the Cambo Stables Project to provide a training and education centre on the estate.

Directions: A917 between Crail and St Andrews.

Disabled Access:
Full

Opening Times:
Plant sale
Sunday 17 April
11:00am - 4:00pm
garden also open

Admission:
£2.50

Charities:
Cambo Stables Project
receives 40%, the net
remaining to SG Beneficiaries

CRAIGFOODIE
Dairsie KY15 4RU
Mr and Mrs James Murray

Restored formal walled garden adjoining 17th century house with extensive range of plants and enjoying fine aspect to the south. Parterre, clock lawn, mixed/ herbaceous borders, shrub roses, terraces with exotic plantings, fruit and vegetable gardens. There is also a tennis lawn, woodland garden and knoll walk.

Other Details: Dogs on leads please.

Directions: On A91 from Cupar to St Andrews turn left at Dairsie School then follow signs.

Disabled Access:
Partial

Opening Times:
Sunday 4 September
2:00pm - 5:00pm

Admission:
£4.00

Charities:
Worldwide Cancer Research
receives 40%, the net
remaining to SG Beneficiaries

CRAIL: SMALL GARDENS IN THE BURGH
KY10 3SQ
The Gardeners of Crail

Three new gardens this year! A number of small gardens in varied styles: cottage, historic, plantsman's and bedding. The stunning coastal location of the gardens presents some challenges for planting but also allows a great range of more tender species to flourish.

Other Details: Tickets and maps available from Mrs Auchinleck, 2 Castle Street, Crail and Ian and Margaret Moonie, 52 Marketgate South, Crail.

Directions: Approach Crail from either St Andrews or Anstruther by A917. Park in the Marketgate.

Disabled Access:
None

Opening Times:
Saturday 16 July
1:00pm - 5:00pm
Sunday 17 July
1:00pm - 5:00pm

Admission:
£5.00

Charities:
Crail Cubs receives 10%, Crail
Preservation Society receives
30%, the net remaining to
SG Beneficiaries

CULROSS PALACE GARDEN

Culross KY12 8JH
The National Trust for Scotland T: 01383 880359
E: larnott@nts.org.uk www.nts.org.uk

Relive the domestic life of the 16th and 17th centuries amid the old buildings and cobbled streets of this Royal Burgh on the River Forth. Explore the recreated 17th Century garden behind the Culross Palace laid out to show the range of plants that were grown for culinary, medicinal and ornamental use. Don't miss the Scot's Dumpy chickens!

Other Details: Fruit and vegetable stalls from produce grown at Culross Palace. Meet the New Head Gardener. Tours with Head Gardener at 12:30pm and 3:30pm. Partial access with difficulties for wheelchair users.

Directions: Off A985, three miles east of Kincardine Bridge, six miles west of Dunfermline. Buses Stagecoach, Stirling to Dunfermline or First, Edinburgh to Dunfermline. Falkirk station twelve miles, Dunfermline station six miles.

Disabled Access:
Partial

Opening Times:
Sunday 19 June
12:00pm - 5:00pm

Admission:
£3.50 garden only admission charge, £6.00 for tour with Head Gardener. N.B. Prices correct at time of going to print.

Charities:
Donation to SG Beneficiaries

EARLSHALL CASTLE
Leuchars KY16 0DP
Paul & Josine Veenhuijzen T: 01334 839205

Extensive and interesting garden designed by Sir Robert Lorimer. Fascinating topiary lawn, for which Earlshall is renowned, rose terrace, croquet lawn with herbaceous borders, shrub border, box garden, orchard, kitchen and herb garden.

Directions: On Earlshall Road, three quarters of a mile east of Leuchars Village (off A919).

Disabled Access:
Partial

Opening Times:
Sunday 29 May
2:00pm - 5:00pm
Sunday 19 June
2:00pm - 5:00pm

Admission:
£5.00, children free

Charities:
RAF Benevolent Fund receives 20% (May), St Athernase Church, Leuchars receives 20% (June), the net remaining to SG Beneficiaries

FALKLAND PALACE AND GARDEN
Falkland, Cupar KY15 7BU
The National Trust for Scotland T: 01337 857397
E: falklandpalace&garden@nts.org.uk www.nts.org.uk

Set in a medieval village, the Royal Palace of Falkland is a superb example of Renaissance architecture. Garden enthusiasts will appreciate the work of Percy Cane, who designed the gardens between 1947 and 1952.

Other Details: Champion Trees: Acer platanoides 'Crimson King'.
The open day, will be dedicated to the herbs we grow in the Palace's physic garden. This garden was inspired by Mary Queen of Scots and planted with 16th century herbs.

Directions: A912, 10 miles from M90, junction 8, 11 miles north of Kirkcaldy. Bus Stagecoach Fife stops in the High Street (100 metres). OS Ref: NO252075.

Disabled Access:
Partial

Opening Times:
Sunday 17 July
12:00pm - 4:30pm

Admission:
Normal NTS admission applies.

Charities:
Donation to SG Beneficiaries

GREENHEAD FARMHOUSE
Greenhead of Arnot KY6 3JQ
Mr and Mrs Malcolm Strang Steel T: 01592 840459
www.fife-bed-breakfast-glenrothes.co.uk

The south facing garden combines a sense of formality in its symmetrical layout, with an informal look of mixed herbaceous borders and a large display of alliums throughout. The west side of the garden has been under considerable change over the last year. There is also a polytunnel which is used to augment the vegetable garden.

Other Details: Dogs on leads.

Directions: A911 between Auchmuir Bridge and Scotlandwell.

Disabled Access:
None

Opening Times:
Sunday 12 June
2:00pm - 5:00pm

Admission:
£4.00

Charities:
Mercy Ships receives 40%, the net remaining to SG Beneficiaries

HELENSBANK
Kincardine FK10 4QZ
David Buchanan-Cook and Adrian Miles T: 07739 312912
E: Helensbank@aol.com

An 18th century walled garden, with main feature a Cedar of Lebanon, reputedly planted in 1750 by the sea captain who built the house. It provides challenges for planting in terms of shade and needle fall. Distinctive garden rooms in part of the garden comprise a perennial blue and white cottage garden, a formal rose garden and an 'Italian' garden with citrus trees in pots. A 'hot' courtyard contains exotics such as bananas, Acacias, Lochromas, Melianthus and Brugmansia. A shaded walk along the bottom of the garden leads to a Japanese pagoda. A large conservatory/greenhouse houses various climbing plants including varieties of Passiflora.

Other Details: Homemade teas available for groups on request.

Directions: On request.

Disabled Access:
None

Opening Times:
By arrangement
1 June - 31 July

Admission:
£4.00

Charities:
Marie Curie receives 40%, the net remaining to SG Beneficiaries

HILL OF TARVIT PLANT SALE AND AUTUMN FAIR
Hill of Tarvit, Cupar KY15 5PB
The National Trust for Scotland/Scotland's Gardens Fife
E: catherine@camboestate.com/hilloftarvit@nts.org.uk www.nts.org.uk

This long established plant sale is a fantastic opportunity to purchase bare root and potted plants from an enormous selection on offer. We also welcome donations of plants prior to the sale and on the day. Bring and buy!

Hill of Tarvit is one of Scotland's finest Edwardian mansion houses. Surrounding the mansion house are spectacular gardens designed by Robert Lorimer, woods, open heath and parkland to explore.

Other Details: House open (reduced entry fee) 1:00pm-5:00pm. Garden Tearoom open 11:00am-5:00pm. The spectacular gardens designed by Robert Lorimer will also be open, normal entrance fee applies. In addition there are woodlands, open heath and parkland to explore.

Directions: Two miles south of Cupar off A916.

Disabled Access:
Partial

Opening Times:
Plant sale Sunday 2 October
10:30am - 4:00pm
Garden also open.

Admission:
Plant sale £2.50, children
under 16 free

Charities:
All proceeds to
SG Beneficiaries

KELLIE CASTLE SPRING PLANT SALE
Pittenweem KY10 2RF
The National Trust for Scotland/Scotland's Gardens Fife
www.scotlandsgardens.org or www.nts.org.uk

Stock up your borders with a wide selection of interesting and unusual plants, grown locally and sourced from private gardens, at Scotland's Gardens Spring Plant Sale held in this this beautiful Arts and Crafts style garden. Enjoy the garden in spring with Clematis montana and apple blossom in flower, red Euphorbia griffithii, forget-me-nots, young vegetables and a great collection of rhubarb.

Directions: Road: B9171, three miles NNW of Pittenweem. Bus - Flexible from local villages by pre-booking.

Disabled Access:
Partial

Opening Times:
Plant sale Sunday 8 May
10:30am - 4:00pm
Garden also open

Admission:
£2.50

Charities:
All proceeds to
SG Beneficiaries

KIRKLANDS
Saline KY12 9TS
Peter & Gill Hart T: 01383 852737
E: gill@i-comment360.com www.kirklandshouseandgarden.co.uk

Kirklands, built in 1832 on the site of an older house, has been the Hart family home for nearly 40 years. Peter and Gill began creating a garden and it is still a work in progress. There are herbaceous borders, a bog garden by the burn, a woodland garden with rhododendrons and a carpet of bluebells, a terraced wall garden with raised beds and espalier fruit trees. Saline Burn divides the garden from ancient woodland and the woodland walk.

Other Details: A tree house for the grandchildren was built last year, as seen on the *The Beechgrove Garden* programme.

Directions: Junction 4, M90, then B914. Parking in the centre of the village, then a short walk to the garden. Limited disabled parking at Kirklands.

Disabled Access:
Partial

Opening Times:
Sunday 22 May
2:00pm - 5:00pm

Admission:
£4.00, children free

Charities:
Saline Environmental Group
receives 40%, the net
remaining to SG Beneficiaries

18 LINDORES HOUSE
By Newburgh KY14 6JD
Mr and Mrs R Turcan

Stunning lochside position with snowdrops, leucojums, aconites and rhododendrons. Woodland walk and amazing 17th century yew believed to be the largest in Fife.

Other Details: Champion Trees: Yew. Plant stall selling snowdrops, leucojum and tender abutilon. Homemade soup and bread available from 11:30am, in the conservatory.

Directions: Off A913 two miles east of Newburgh.

Disabled Access:
Partial

Opening Times:
Sunday 6 March
11:00am - 3:00pm

Admission:
£3.50, children free

Charities:
Newburgh Scout Group
receives 40%, the net
remaining to SG Beneficiaries

19 LINDORES HOUSE AND GARDEN COTTAGE
by Newburgh KY14 6JD
Mr & Mrs R Turcan and Mr & Mrs J Bradburne

Lindores House: Stunning lochside position with a woodland walk and amazing 17th century yew tree believed to be the oldest in Fife. Rhododendrons, trilliums and primulae. Lindores has opened for SG since 2011, see previous entry for further details.
Garden Cottage: This garden has been created from scratch in one year and is opening for SG for the first time.

Other Details: The plant stall will be stocked with a variety of plants from the garden, including trilliums and candelabra primula. Newburgh Scouts are providing the teas.

Directions: Off A913, two miles east of Newburgh.

Disabled Access:
Partial

Opening Times:
Sunday 22 May
2:00pm - 6:00pm

Admission:
£5.00, children free

Charities:
Newburgh Scout Group
receives 20%, Canine
Partners receives 20%,
the net remaining to
SG Beneficiaries

20 LOGIE HOUSE
Crossford, Dunfermline KY12 8QN
**Mrs John Hunt T: Karl 07510 654812
E: sarah@logiehunt.co.uk**

Central to the design of this walled garden is a path through a double mixed border. Long rows of vegetables and fruit also contribute to colour and design when seen from the house and terrace. A long border of repeat flowering roses, and rose and annual beds contribute to an extended season of colour and interest. There is a magnificent and very productive Mackenzie & Moncur greenhouse in excellent condition with fully working vents and original benches and central heating system. The garden is surrounded by a belt of mixed woodland with walks.

Other Details: Group refreshments are available by arrangement. There will be a plant and garden produce stall. Dogs welcome outwith the walled garden.

Directions: M90 exit 1 for Rosyth and Kincardine Bridge (A985). After about two miles turn right to Crossford. At traffic lights, turn right and the drive is on the right at the end of the village main street.

Disabled Access:
Full

Opening Times:
By arrangement
1 April - 31 October - please
note this is for groups only.

Admission:
£5.00

Charities:
Type 1 Juvenile Diabetes
Research Fund receives
40%, the net remaining to
SG Beneficiaries

21 NEWTON MAINS AND NEWTON BARNS
Auchtermuchty KY14 7HR
Ruth and Tony Lear and John and Jess Anderson

Work started on the Newton Mains garden in 2008 with removal of hundreds of self-sown ash saplings and more than a 1000 tons of builder's spoil. Now with a large rockery, borders and lawns the garden merges into the naturalised field.

Newton Barns was created 14 years ago. The borders are planted with choice shrubs, trees and rhododendrons. Central to the garden is a huge rockery and stream. Sweeping lawns and generous borders slope towards Pitmedden Wood. There are breathtaking views across the top of the garden towards the Lomond Hills.

Other Details: Teas and light meals available at the Tannochbrae Tearooms in Auchtermuchty.

Directions: On A91 from Cupar turn right in Auchtermuchty on to B936. Follow Scotland's Gardens signs.

Disabled Access:
None

Opening Times:
Saturday 4 June
11:00am - 4:00pm
Sunday 5 June
11:00am - 4:00pm

Admission:
£5.00, children under 12 free

Charities:
Asbestos Action Tayside receives 40%, the net remaining to SG Beneficiaries

22 ROFSIE ARTS GARDEN
By Collessie KY15 7UZ
Mr and Mrs Andrew and Caroline Thomson
E: caroline.thomson@rofsie-estate.com   www.rofsie-estate.com.

Thought provoking restored 1½ acre walled garden, with themes of family, art and science. Rare plants and daffodils bred by the family's forbears, the Backhouses, form a unique historic collection. The Backhouse Heritage Daffodils are in the process of seeking National Collection status, they caused a sensation in the mid 1800s - mid 1900s and changed daffodil breeding forever. This rare and unique collection of original daffodils bred by three generations of the family are grown in designed beds as a special display, a further 14,000 daffodils grow in the grounds. Graceful 100 metres interrupted rose archway, stunning herbaceous borders, original Victorian Glass House, formal potager, pond, grass labyrinth, new orchard, shade border and sunny lawns. Research of family papers informs plantings and shows close links with Kew Gardens.

Other Details: Help yourself to the homemade teas that will be available. Information area with educational video coming soon. The Backhouse Centre welcomes Academic and Horticultural enquiries, please contact Caroline Thomson. No dogs apart from Guide Dogs.

Directions: Between Auchtermuchty and Collessie on A91. One mile east of Auchtermuchty turn right for Charlottetown, turn first right into Rofsie Estate onto an untarred drive.

Disabled Access:
Partial

Opening Times:
Sunday 17 April
2:00pm - 5:00pm
Sunday 26 June
2:00pm - 5:00pm

Admission:
£4.00

Charities:
Momentum Pathways receives 40%, the net remaining to SG Beneficiaries

23 SOUTH FLISK
Blebo Craigs, Cupar KY15 5UQ
Mr and Mrs George Young T: 01334 850859
E: julia@standrewspottery.co.uk www.standrewspottery.co.uk

A flooded former quarry forms the centrepiece of this enchanting three acre garden. The pond supports toads, frogs, newts, dragonflies and hundreds of golden orfe, water lilies and marginal plants add colour throughout the season. Spectacular views. Boulders, cliffs and many big, mature trees form a backdrop for spring bulbs, rhododendrons, magnolias, azaleas and colourful primulas while the woodland area sports meconopsis, trilliums, podophyllums and beautiful hellebores. At the front of house (a former smiddy) is a charming, mature walled garden with traditional cottage garden planting.

Other Details: Working pottery. Meet George Young and watch him at work.

Directions: Six miles west of St Andrews off the B939 between Strathkinness and Pitscottie. There is a small stone bus shelter opposite the road into the village and a small sign saying Blebo Craigs. Or check out the map on our website.

Disabled Access:
Partial

Opening Times:
By arrangement
15 April - 19 June

Admission:
£5.00, children free

Charities:
RUDA receives 40%, the net remaining to SG Beneficiaries

---

24 ST FORT WOODLAND GARDEN WITH TAYFIELD AND WILLOWHILL
Newport-on-Tay DD6 8RA
Mr & Mrs Andrew Mylius, Mr & Mrs William Berry, Eric Wright & Sally Lorimore

St Fort DD6 8RE: A visit to Ruskins house and woodland garden at Brantwood, was the inspiration for creating a woodland garden here. Paths were formed in a natural and informal way. Azaleas and specimen rhododendrons are the principal plants in the garden as the acid soil within the wood makes them ideal along with ability to withstand browsing from roe deer. The rhododendrons comprise a wide selection of both specimen and hybrids. Most of the azaleas are Azalea ponticum chosen for their excellent scent and good autumn colour. The Northwood is about 30 acres and is home to a colony of red squirrels, some of the paths lead to view points overlooking the fields with the river Tay and Tay Rail Bridge as a backdrop. In addition to over 200 rhododendrons some other plants of interest include Eucryphia, Cerdiphyllum pendulara, tulip tree, various red acers, a wide selection of rowans, liquidambar, metasequoia, magnolias and so on.

Tayfield DD6 8RA: A wide variety of shrubs and fine trees, many to mark celebrations of the family who have lived here for over 200 years. Some trees are of great age and Tayfield has the tallest beech tree recorded in Scotland at 39 metres. A picturesque approach to Tayfield House is enhanced by wonderful large tree rhododendrons in May and views across the Tay all year round. The grounds are wildlife rich and contain two large ponds. Look out for red squirrels which are often seen.

Willowhill DD6 8RA: An evolving three acre garden featured in *Scotland for Gardeners* and *Scotland on Sunday*. The house is surrounded by a series of mixed borders designed with different vibrant colour combinations for effect all season and a vegetable plot. Newly developed area containing borders of bulbs, roses and perennials. A stepped terrace of alpines leads to a wildlife pond in grassland planted with trees, bulbs and herbaceous perennials through which wide sweeping paths are mown.

Other Details: Champion Trees: Beech (at Tayfield). St Fort is approached with a woodland walk of about 400 metres from the car park and garden entrance.

Directions:
St Fort: 1¾ miles south of the Tay Road Bridge off the A92, between the Forgan and Five Roads roundabouts.
Willowhill and Tayfield: 1½ miles south of Tay Road Bridge, take the B995 to Newport off the Forgan roundabout.

Disabled Access:
Partial

Opening Times:
Sunday 15 May
1:00pm - 5:00pm

Admission:
£5.00

Charities:
Forgan Arts Centre receives 40%, the net remaining to SG Beneficiaries

ST MONANS VILLAGE GARDENS
KY10 2BX
The Gardeners of St Monans

Many gardens will be opening, some for the first time, in this picturesque seaside village. Gardens opening include cottage gardens, more formal gardens and many hidden gems. Several unusual plants flourish in this sunny corner of the East Neuk.

Other Details: The medieval church welcomes visitors.

Directions: Tickets can be bought from the Church Hall, Station Road, on entering the village.

Disabled Access:
None

Opening Times:
Sunday 19 June
2:00pm - 5:00pm

Admission:
£4.00

Charities:
Auld Kirk, St Monans receives 40%, the net remaining to SG Beneficiaries

TEASSES GARDENS
Near Ceres KY8 5PG
Sir Fraser and Lady Morrison T: 0796 6529205
E: Craig@Teasses.com

Teasses Gardens have been developed by the present owners for 15 years and now extend to approximately 60 acres. In addition to the restored Victorian walled garden with fruit, vegetables, cut flowers and a large greenhouse, there are formal and informal areas of the garden linked by numerous woodland walks, with several woodland gardens.

Other Details: For further information, contact Mr Craig Cameron, Head Gardener at the telephone number or email listed above.

Directions: Between Ceres and Largo. Enter by Teasses House main gates, three miles from Ceres.

Disabled Access:
Partial

Opening Times:
Sunday 10 July
1:00pm - 5:00pm

Admission:
£5.00

Charities:
Barnardos receives 40%, the net remaining to SG Beneficiaries

THE OLD FARMHOUSE
Straiton Farm, Balmullo KY16 0BN
Mrs Barbara Pickard T: 01334 870203.
E: bmpickard@clara.co.uk

A wonderful profusion of plants: cottage garden favourites including poppies, foxgloves, lupins, Aquilegias, Camassia, and Euphorbias. Also many more unusual varieties of herbaceous and tree peonies, Grevillea, Cornus, Teucrium, Crinodendron, Piptanthus, Hebes etc. A rose garden with 27 varieties of David Austin roses, begun in early 2014, is interplanted with a variety of shrubs and herbaceous plants.

Directions: From Cupar - enter Balmullo via A914 from Dairsie, pass the tel box and shop, leave the village and take the second exit left on a sharp right hand bend. From Dundee - approach Balmullo on A914, go under the railway bridge and take the second right, signposted Lucklawhill. At the T junction, turn right and follow road straight on past the tel box and down the hill to the farm visible in the distance.

Disabled Access:
Full

Opening Times:
Sunday 19 June
1:00pm - 5:00pm
Saturday 2 July
1:00pm - 5:00pm
By arrangement on request

Admission:
£4.00, children free

Charities:
The Rotary Polio Plus Campaign receives 40%, the net remaining to SG Beneficiaries

THE TOWER

1 Northview Terrace, Wormit DD6 8PP
Peter and Angela Davey T: 01382 541635 M: 07768 406946
E: adavey541@btinternet.com

Situated four miles south of Dundee, this one acre Edwardian landscaped garden has panoramic views over the River Tay. Features include a rhododendron walk, rockeries, informal woodland planting schemes with native and exotic plants, offering year round interest. Original raised paths lead to a granite grotto with waterfall pool. Also of interest are raised vegetable beds made from granite sets.

Other Details: Garden is on a hillside with steep paths, therefore unsuited to those with poor mobility. Please contact Mr and Mrs Davey prior to visiting.

Directions: From B946 park on Naughton Road outside Spar shop and walk up path left following signs.

Disabled Access:
None

Opening Times:
Saturdays
7 May 12:00pm - 5:00pm
30 July 12:00pm - 5:00pm
20 August 12:00pm - 5:00pm
By arrangement
1 April - 30 September

Admission:
£3.50

Charities:
Barnados receives 40%, the net remaining to SG Beneficiaries

WILLOWHILL

Forgan, Newport-on-Tay DD6 8RA
Eric Wright and Sally Lorimore T: 01382 542890
E: e.g.wright@dundee.ac.uk   http://willowhillgarden.weebly.com/

An evolving three acre garden featured in *Scotland for Gardeners* and *Scotland on Sunday*. The house is surrounded by a series of mixed borders designed with different vibrant colour combinations for effect all season and a vegetable plot. Newly developed area containing borders of bulbs, roses and perennials. A stepped terrace of alpines leads to a wildlife pond in grassland planted with trees, bulbs and herbaceous perennials through which wide sweeping paths are mown.

Other Details: Also opening on Sunday 17 May with St Fort Woodland Garden and Tayfield.

Directions: 1½ miles south of Tay Road Bridge. Take the B995 to Newport off the Forgan roundabout. Willowhill is the first house on the left hand side next to the Forgan Arts Centre.

Disabled Access:
Partial

Opening Times:
Saturdays
4 June - 27 August
2:00pm - 7:00pm
By arrangement
1 May - 31 August

Admission:
£4.00, season ticket £10.00

Charities:
RIO Community Centre receives 40%, the net remaining to SG Beneficiaries

WORMISTOUNE HOUSE

Crail KY10 3XH
Baron and Lady Wormiston T: Katherine Taylor, Head Gardener 07905 938449
E: ktaylor.home@googlemail.com.

The 17th century tower house and gardens have been painstakingly restored over the last 20 years. The walled garden is a series of 'rooms', including a wildlife meadow, productive potager, intricate formal parterre, magical Griselinia garden, wildlife ponds and rill, and recently planted late-season perennial borders. The garden's backbone is the splendid midsummer herbaceous border peaking in early July. Outside the walled garden, enjoy woodland walks around the newly relandscaped lochan, surrounded by new planting.

Other Details: Owing to building works, Wormistoune will only be open to individuals and groups by arrangement. Please contact us in advance to find out what's looking good in the garden.

Directions: One mile north of Crail on the A917 Crail to St Andrews road.

Disabled Access:
None

Opening Times:
By arrangement
1 April - 30 September

Admission:
£5.00, children free

Charities:
Maggie's Cancer Care Centres receives 40%, the net remaining to SG Beneficiaries

KINCARDINE & DEESIDE

Scotland's Gardens 2016 Guidebook is sponsored by INVESTEC WEALTH & INVESTMENT

District Organisers

Tina Hammond	Sunnybank, 7 Watson Street, Banchory AB31 5UB
Julie Nicol	Bogiesheil, Ballogie, Aboyne AB34 5DU
	E: kincardine@scotlandsgardens.org

Area Organisers

Mrs Andrea Bond	Rosebank, Crathes, Banchory AB31 5JE
Mrs Wendy Buchan	Inneshewen, Dess, Aboyne AB31 5BH
Mr Gavin Farquhar	Ecclesgreig Castle, St Cyrus DD10 0DP
Mrs Helen Jackson	
Mrs Catherine Nichols	Bridge of Canny, Banchory AB31 4AT
Mr and Mrs David Younie	Bealltainn, Ballogie, Aboyne AB34 5DL

Treasurer

Mr A H J Coleman	Templeton House, Arbroath DD11 4QP

Gardens open on a specific date

Crathes Castle Garden, Banchory	Saturday 20 February	10:00am		
Ecclesgreig Castle, St Cyrus	Sunday 28 February	1:00pm	-	4:00pm
Crathes Castle Garden, Banchory	Saturday 16 April	2:00pm		
Inchmarlo House Garden, Inchmarlo, Banchory	Sunday 22 May	1:30pm	-	4:30pm
Drum Castle Garden, Drumoak, by Banchory	Saturday 28 May	11:00am	-	4:00pm
Drum Castle Garden, Drumoak, by Banchory	Sunday 29 May	11:00am	-	4:00pm
Woodend House Garden, Banchory	Sunday 5 June	1:30pm	-	4:30pm
Kincardine, Kincardine O'Neil	Sunday 12 June	1:30pm	-	5:00pm
Ecclesgreig Castle, St Cyrus	Sunday 19 June	1:00pm	-	5:00pm
Finzean House, Finzean, Banchory	Sunday 26 June	2:00pm	-	5:00pm
Drum Castle Garden, Drumoak, by Banchory	Wednesday 6 July	2:00pm		
Douneside House, Tarland	Sunday 10 July	2:00pm	-	5:00pm
Drum Castle Garden, Drumoak, by Banchory	Wednesday 13 July	2:00pm		
Drum Castle Garden, Drumoak, by Banchory	Wednesday 20 July	2:00pm		
Drum Castle Garden, Drumoak, by Banchory	Wednesday 27 July	2:00pm		
Glenbervie House, Drumlithie, Stonehaven	Sunday 7 August	2:00pm	-	5:00pm
Fasque House, Fettercairn, Laurencekirk	Sunday 14 August	2:00pm	-	5:00pm
Tarland Community Garden, Aboyne	Saturday 24 September	2:00pm	-	5:00pm
Drum Castle Garden, Drumoak, by Banchory	Saturday 8 October	11:00am	-	4:00pm
Drum Castle Garden, Drumoak, by Banchory	Sunday 9 October	11:00am	-	4:00pm

KINCARDINE & DEESIDE

Plant sales

Drum Castle Garden, Drumoak, by Banchory	Saturday 8 October	11:00am - 4:00pm
Drum Castle Garden, Drumoak, by Banchory	Sunday 9 October	11:00am - 4:00pm

DOUNESIDE HOUSE, TARLAND
CELEBRATING THEIR 50TH GARDEN OPEN DAY FOR SCOTLAND'S GARDENS IN 2016

Key to symbols

	New in 2016		Homemade teas		Accommodation
	Teas		Dogs on a lead allowed		Plant stall
	Cream teas		Wheelchair access		Scottish Snowdrop Festival

GARDEN LOCATIONS IN
KINCARDINE & DEESIDE

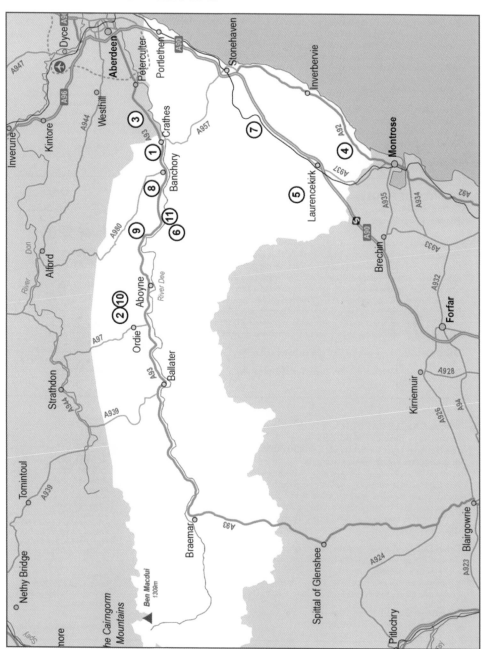

1 CRATHES CASTLE GARDEN
Banchory AB31 5QJ
The National Trust for Scotland T: 01330 844525
E: crathes@nts.org.uk www.nts.org.uk

20 February: Join our expert Head Gardener for a day to learn about the principles of pruning within the beautiful setting of the Crathes Castle gardens. This practical workshop will cover general formative pruning as well as looking at how to prune most roses, trees and shrubs. Price includes a tea/coffee and a light lunch.
16 April: Members of the garden team will lead you through some of the finer points of planning, designing and maintaining a herbaceous border. This practical session will cover general techniques including the division and growing on of your own plants.

Other Details: National Plant Collection®: Dianthus (Malmaison).
Champion Trees: Four champions including Zelkova x verschaffeltii
16 April: Price includes some free plant material. Booking essential via NTS website for both events. Places are limited.

Directions: On A93, 15 miles west of Aberdeen and three miles east of Banchory.

Disabled Access:
Full

Opening Times:
Saturdays
20 February 10:00am
16 April 2:00pm

Admission:
February event: £55.00 (includes lunch).
April event: £20.00.
Admission also applicable to NTS members

Charities:
Donation to SG Beneficiaries

---

2 DOUNESIDE HOUSE
Tarland AB34 4UD
The MacRobert Trust

The MacRobert Trust is very proud that 2016 is Douneside's 50th Gardens Open Day in support of Scotland's Gardens. Douneside is the former home of Lady MacRobert who developed these magnificent gardens in the early to mid-1900s. Ornamental borders and water gardens surround a spectacular infinity lawn overlooking the Deeside hills. A large walled garden supplies vegetables and cut flowers and also houses a large ornamental greenhouse. A new arboretum displays over 130 trees amongst mown grass paths and walking trails behind Douneside offer breathtaking views across the Howe of Cromar and beyond.

Other Details: There will be a local pipe band and raffle.

Directions: B9119 towards Aberdeen. Tarland one mile.

Disabled Access:
Partial

Opening Times:
Sunday 10 July
2:00pm - 5:00pm

Admission:
£4.50, concession
£2.50, children free

Charities:
Perennial receives 40%, the net remaining to SG Beneficiaries

---

3 DRUM CASTLE GARDEN
Drumoak, by Banchory AB31 5EY
The National Trust for Scotland T: 01330 700334
E: drum@nts.org.uk www.nts.org.uk

Join the Head Gardener for a walk through the historic rose garden each Wednesday at 2:00pm in July. The Trust has established a collection of old-fashioned roses which is at its peak for blossom and colour during July. Other areas include a pond and bog garden, wildlife meadow, wildlife garden, a cutting garden and new viewing platform and stumpery.

Other Details: Garden workshops throughout the year - see website for details. Chelsea Fringe weekend is the furthest north venue for harnessing and spreading excitement and energy around gardens and gardening. Plant sales will include home grown herbaceous and bare root plants. Separate garden entry charge for the Chelsea Fringe and plant sales events £4.00, Conc. £2.00 (NTS members free).

Directions: On A93 three miles west of Peterculter. Ten miles west of Aberdeen and eight miles east of Banchory.

Disabled Access:
Partial

Opening Times:
Sat/Sun 28/29 May 11:00am - 4:00pm for Chelsea Fringe
Weds 6, 13, 20, 27 Jul 2:00pm
Plant sale Sat/Sun 8/9 Oct 11:00am - 4:00pm garden also open.

Admission:
Guided walks £5.00 for all participants, advance booking is essential.

Charities:
Donation to SG Beneficiaries

ECCLESGREIG CASTLE
St Cyrus DD10 0DP
Mr Gavin Farquhar T: 01224 214301
E: enquiries@ecclesgreig.com www.ecclesgreig.com

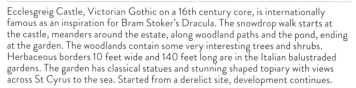

Ecclesgreig Castle, Victorian Gothic on a 16th century core, is internationally famous as an inspiration for Bram Stoker's Dracula. The snowdrop walk starts at the castle, meanders around the estate, along woodland paths and the pond, ending at the garden. The woodlands contain some very interesting trees and shrubs. Herbaceous borders 10 feet wide and 140 feet long are in the Italian balustraded gardens. The garden has classical statues and stunning shaped topiary with views across St Cyrus to the sea. Started from a derelict site, development continues.

Directions: Ecclesgreig will be signposted from the A92 Coast Road and from the A937 Montrose / Laurencekirk Road.

Disabled Access:
Partial

Opening Times:
Sunday 28 February
1:00pm - 4:00pm
Sunday 19 June
1:00pm - 5:00pm

Admission:
£4.00, accompanied children free

Charities:
Scottish Civic Trust receives 20%, Montrose Guides receives 20%, the net remaining to SG Beneficiaries

FASQUE HOUSE
Fettercairn, Laurencekirk AB30 1DN
Mr and Mrs Douglas Dick-Reid
www.fasquehouse.co.uk

Fasque Castle the former family home of William Gladstone four - time PM under Queen Victoria is set deep within its own forested parkland at the end of a drive through a private deer park. The current owners have restored the house to its former glory and the gardens are becoming more stunning each year. Landscaping of the West Garden took place in 2013 with a sunken terrace garden containing a formal pond and a mixture of formal and herbaceous plants. There are some magnificent trees and beautiful long walks in the surrounding woodlands.

Other Details: Self catering accommodation is available. Partial disabled access but please note that there are many gravel paths where pushing a wheelchair is difficult.

Directions: Off B974 Cairn O'Mount road 1¼ miles north of Fettercairn.

Disabled Access:
Partial

Opening Times:
Sunday 14 August
2:00pm - 5:00pm

Admission:
£5.00, children free

Charities:
Fettercairn Community Allotments receives 20%, Home Start Stonehaven receives 20%, the net remaining to SG Beneficiaries

FINZEAN HOUSE
Finzean, Banchory AB31 6NZ
Mr and Mrs Donald Farquharson

Finzean House was the family home of Joseph Farquharson, the Victorian landscape painter, and the garden was the backdrop for several of his paintings. The garden has lovely views over the historic holly hedge to the front of Clachnaben. There is a spring woodland garden, extensive lawns with herbaceous and shrub borders and a working cut flower garden for late summer alongside a recently restored pond area.

Directions: On B976, South Deeside Road, between Banchory and Aboyne

Disabled Access:
Full

Opening Times:
Sunday 26 June
2:00pm - 5:00pm

Admission:
£4.00, OAPs £3.00, children free

Charities:
Forget-Me-Not receives 40%, the net remaining to SG Beneficiaries

GLENBERVIE HOUSE
Drumlithie, Stonehaven AB39 3YA
Mr and Mrs A Macphie

Nucleus of present day house dates from 15th century with additions in 18th and 19th centuries. A traditional, Scottish, walled garden on a slope with roses, herbaceous and annual borders along with fruit and vegetables. One wall is taken up with a Victorian style greenhouse with many species of pot plants and climbers including peach and figs. A woodland garden by a burn is punctuated with many varieties of plants, primula to name but one.

Other Details: Partial disabled access but please note some steep pathways and tree roots can make walking difficult in places. Gravel paths are not suitable for electric wheelchairs. NO DOGS PLEASE.

Directions: Drumlithie one mile. Garden one and a half miles off A90.

Disabled Access:
Partial

Opening Times:
Sunday 7 August
2:00pm - 5:00pm

Admission:
£5.00, children under 12 free

Charities:
Royal National Lifeboat Institute SCO 37736 receives 40%, the net remaining to SG Beneficiaries

INCHMARLO HOUSE GARDEN
Inchmarlo, Banchory AB31 4AL
Skene Enterprises (Aberdeen) Ltd T: 01330 826242
E: info@inchmarlo-retirement.co.uk www.inchmarlo-retirement.co.uk

An ever-changing five acre Woodland Garden, featuring ancient Scots pines, Douglas firs and silver firs, some over 42 metres tall, beeches and rare and unusual trees, including pindrow firs, Pere David's maple, Erman's birch and a mountain snowdrop tree. The Oriental Garden features a Kare Sansui, a dry slate stream designed by Peter Roger, a RHS Chelsea gold medal winner. The Rainbow Garden, within the keyhole-shaped purple Prunus cerasifera hedge, has been designed by Billy Carruthers, an eight times gold medal winner at the RHS Scottish Garden Show.

Directions: From Aberdeen via North Deeside Road on A93, one mile west of Banchory turn right at the main gate to the Inchmarlo Estate.

Disabled Access:
Full

Opening Times:
Sunday 22 May
1:30pm - 4:30pm

Admission:
£5.00, OAP's £4.00, children 14 and under free

Charities:
Alzheimer Scotland receives 20%, Forget Me Not receives 20%, the net remaining to SG Beneficiaries

KINCARDINE
Kincardine O'Neil AB34 5AE
Mr and Mrs Andrew Bradford

A woodland garden with some mature rhododendrons and azaleas and much new planting amongst mature trees. Sculpture by Lyman Whittaker of Utah. Walled garden with a mixture of herbaceous and shrub borders, a sensational laburnum walk, vegetables and fruit trees. Extensive lawns and wildflower meadows and a thought-provoking Planetary Garden. All with a background of stunning views across Royal Deeside and a Victorian castle exhibiting five centuries of architectural styles.

Other Details: Children's treasure trail and excellent plant stall.

Directions: Kincardine O'Neil on A93. Gates and lodge are opposite the village school.

Disabled Access:
Partial

Opening Times:
Sunday 12 June
1:30pm - 5:00pm

Admission:
£5.00, children £2.00
(including entry to the
treasure trail)

Charities:
Children 1st receives 20%,
Kincardine O'Neil Village
Hall receives 20%, the net
remaining to SG Beneficiaries

TARLAND COMMUNITY GARDEN
Aboyne AB34
The Gardeners of Tarland

Tarland Community Gardens opened in 2013 and is a Tarland Development Group project. It provides an inclusive and accessible community growing space for local residents. It has indoor (polytunnel) and outdoor raised beds for rent plus communal planting areas including a soft fruit cage, fruit trees, and a herb garden. The community bee group also manages a hive at the site. It is a place for members to grow produce, learn, share and have fun.

Other Details: Music and homemade teas.

Directions: Take the B9094 from Aboyne or the A96 and B9119 from Aberdeen. Arriving at the village square the gardens will be clearly signposted.

Disabled Access:
Full

Opening Times:
Saturday 24 September
2:00pm - 5:00pm

Admission:
£3.00, children free,
homemade teas £3.00

Charities:
Tarland Community Garden
receives 40%, the net
remaining to SG Beneficiaries

WOODEND HOUSE GARDEN
Banchory AB31 4AY
Mr and Mrs J McHardy

This garden is tucked away in a secluded woodland location. Mature rhododendrons and azaleas with extensive lawns create a stunning backdrop for Woodend House set on the banks of the River Dee. There is a small, walled, cottage garden and a glorious riverside walk amongst the cowslips and wildflowers giving way to ancient and majestic beech trees.

Directions: Four miles west of Banchory on the A93 (Banchory to Aboyne road).

Disabled Access:
Partial

Opening Times:
Sunday 5 June
1:30pm - 4:30pm

Admission:
£4.00

Charities:
Sandpiper Trust receives
40%, the net remaining to
SG Beneficiaries

PERTH & KINROSS

Scotland's Gardens 2016 Guidebook is sponsored by **INVESTEC WEALTH & INVESTMENT**

District Organisers

Mrs Margaret Gimblett	Croftcat Lodge, Grandtully PH15 2QS
Mrs Miranda Landale	Clathic House, by Crieff PH7 4JY
	E: perthkinross@scotlandsgardens.org

Area Organisers

Mrs Sonia Dunphie	Wester Cloquhat, Bridge of Cally, Perthshire PH10 7JP
Miss Henrietta Harland	Easter Carmichael Cottage, Forgandenny Road, Bridge of Earn PH2 9EZ
Mrs Elizabeth Mitchell	Woodlee, 28 St Mary's Drive, Perth PH2 7BY
Mrs Lizzie Montgomery	Burleigh House, Milnathort, Kinross KY13 9SR
Mrs Judy Nichol	Rossie House, Forgandenny PH2 9EH
Miss Judy Norwell	Dura Den, 20 Pitcullen Terrace, Perth PH2 7EQ
Miss Bumble Ogilvy Wedderburn	Garden Cottage, Lude, Blair Atholl PH18 5TR

Treasurer

Mr Michael Tinson	Parkhead House, Parkhead Gardens, Burghmuir Road Perth, PH1 1JF

Gardens open on a specific date

Kilgraston School, Bridge of Earn	Sunday 21 February	1:30pm	-	4:00pm
Megginch Castle, Errol	Sunday 10 April	2:00pm	-	5:00pm
Branklyn Garden, Perth	Sunday 1 May	10:00am	-	4:00pm
Muckhart Village, Dollar	Sunday 22 May	11:00am	-	5:00pm
Rossie House, Forgandenny	Sunday 29 May	2:00pm	-	5:00pm
Bradystone House, Murthly	Thursday 2 June	11:00am	-	4:00pm
Explorers Garden, Pitlochry	Sunday 5 June	10:00am	-	5:00pm
Mill of Forneth, Forneth, Blairgowrie	Sunday 5 June	2:00pm	-	5:00pm
Bradystone House, Murthly	Thursday 9 June	11:00am	-	4:00pm
The Bield at Blackruthven,Tibbermore	Saturday 11 June	2:00pm	-	5:00pm
Bonhard House, Perth	Sunday 12 June	10:00am	-	4:00pm
Glenlyon House, Fortingall	Sunday 12 June	2:00pm	-	5:00pm
Bradystone House, Murthly	Thursday 16 June	11:00am	-	4:00pm
Bradystone House, Murthly	Thursday 23 June	11:00am	-	4:00pm
Blair Castle Gardens, Blair Atholl	Saturday 25 June	9:30am	-	5:30pm
Bradystone House, Murthly	Thursday 30 June	11:00am	-	4:00pm
Wester Cloquhat, Bridge of Cally	Sunday 3 July	2:00pm	-	5:00pm

PERTH & KINROSS

Scotland's Gardens 2016 Guidebook is sponsored by **INVESTEC WEALTH & INVESTMENT**

Bradystone House, Murthly	Thursday 7 July	11:00am	- 4:00pm
Bradystone House, Murthly	Thursday 14 July	11:00am	- 4:00pm
Bradystone House, Murthly	Thursday 21 July	11:00am	- 4:00pm
Bradystone House, Murthly	Thursday 28 July	11:00am	- 4:00pm
Drummond Castle Gardens, Crieff	Sunday 7 August	1:00pm	- 5:00pm
Mount Tabor House, Mount Tabor Road, Perth	Sunday 7 August	12:00pm	- 4:30pm
Wester House of Ross, Comrie	Saturday 24 September	11:00am	- 4:30pm
Wester House of Ross, Comrie	Sunday 25 September	11:00am	- 4:30pm

Gardens open regularly

Ardvorlich, Lochearnhead	1 May - 1 June	9:00am	- Dusk
Blair Castle Gardens, Blair Atholl	25 March - 31 October	9:30am	- 5:30pm
Bolfracks, Aberfeldy	Daily	10:00am	- 6:00pm
Braco Castle, Braco	1 February - 31 October	10:00am	- 5:00pm
Cluny House, Aberfeldy	14 March - 30 October	10:00am	- 6:00pm
	31 October - 13 March	10:00am	- 4:00pm
Drummond Castle Gardens, Crieff	1 May - 31 October	1:00pm	- 6:00pm
Glendoick, by Perth	1 April - 31 May daily	10:00am	- 4:00pm
Glenericht House, Blairgowrie	Daily	9:00am	- Dusk

Gardens open by arrangement

Briglands House, Rumbling Bridge	1 April - 15 June	01577 840205
Briglands House, Rumbling Bridge	1 October - 31 October	01577 840205
Carig Dhubh, Bonskeid	1 May - 30 October	01796 473469
Croftcat Lodge, Grandtully	14 May - 16 October	01887 840288
Delvine, Murthly	15 April - 15 October	01738 710485
Dowhill, Cleish	On request	pippamd@icloud.com
Glenlyon House, Fortingall	On request	01887 830233
Hollytree Lodge, Muckhart, Dollar	25 March - 10 April	0797 337 4687
Hollytree Lodge, Muckhart, Dollar	1 May - 30 June	0797 337 4687
Hollytree Lodge, Muckhart, Dollar	1 September - 31 October	0797 337 4687
Kirkton Craig, Abernyte	3 May - 26 July	01828 686336
Latch House, Abernyte	1 May - 31 August	01828 686816
Little Tombuie, Killiechassie, Aberfeldy	1 May - 31 July	01887 829344
Mill of Forneth, Forneth, Blairgowrie	1 May - 30 September	gaw@gwpc.demon.co.uk
Parkhead House, Burghmuir Road, Perth	1 May - 30 September	01738 625983 M:07769676586

PERTH & KINROSS

Pitcurran House, Abernethy	1 April - 30 September	01738 850933
Pitnacree House , Pitnacree, Ballinluig, Pitlochry	1 May - 31 July	susansherriff@btinternet.com
The Garden at Craigowan, Ballinluig	15 April - 30 June	i.q.jones@btinternet.com
The Steading at Clunie, Newmill of Kinloch, Clunie	8 May - 25 June	01250 884263

Plant sales

Rossie House, Forgandenny	Sunday 29 May	2:00pm - 5:00pm

PLANT SALE, ROSSIE HOUSE
PERTHSHIRE PH2 9EH

2PM TO 5PM
SUNDAY 29 MAY

See page 163 and
www.scotlandsgardens.org
for more details

Key to symbols

	New in 2016		Homemade teas		Accommodation
	Teas		Dogs on a lead allowed		Plant stall
	Cream teas		Wheelchair access		Scottish Snowdrop Festival

GARDEN LOCATIONS IN
PERTH & KINROSS

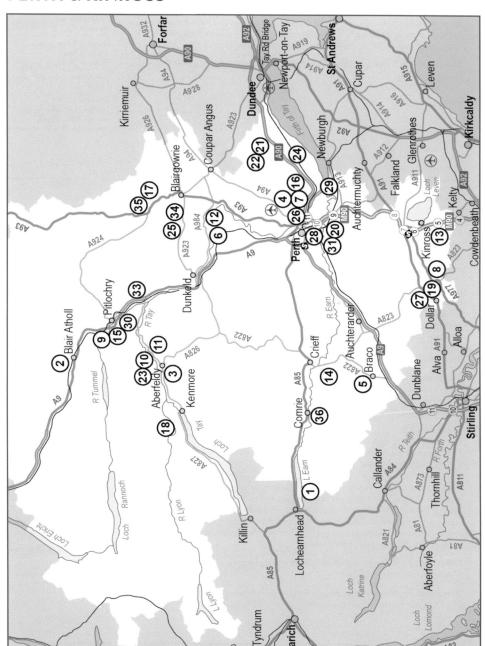

ARDVORLICH
Lochearnhead FK19 8QE
Mr and Mrs Sandy Stewart

Beautiful hill garden featuring over 300 different species and hybrid rhododendrons, grown in a glorious setting of oaks and birches on either side of the Ardvorlich Burn. The ground is quite steep in places and boots are advisable.

Directions: On South Loch Earn Road three miles from Lochearnhead, five miles from St Fillans.

Disabled Access:
None

Opening Times:
1 May - 1 June
9:00am - Dusk

Admission:
£4.00

Charities:
The Gurkha Welfare Trust receives 40%, the net remaining to SG Beneficiaries

---

BLAIR CASTLE GARDENS
Blair Atholl PH18 5TL
Blair Charitable Trust T: 01796 481207
E: office@blair-castle.co.uk www.blair-castle.co.uk

Blair Castle stands as the focal point in a designed landscape of some 2,500 acres within a large and traditional estate. Hercules Garden is a walled enclosure of about nine acres recently restored to its original 18th century form with landscaped ponds, a Chinese bridge, plantings, vegetables and an orchard of more than 100 fruit trees. The glory of this garden in summer is the herbaceous border which runs along the 275 metre south facing wall. A delightful sculpture trail incorporates contemporary and 18th century sculpture as well as eight new works, letter-carving on stone from the Memorial Arts Charity's Art and Memory Collection. Diana's Grove is a magnificent stand of tall trees including Grand Fir, Douglas Fir, Larch and Wellingtonia in just two acres.

Directions: Off A9, follow signs to Blair Castle, Blair Atholl.

Disabled Access:
Partial

Opening Times:
Saturday 25 June
9:30am - 5:30pm
for Scotland's Gardens.
25 March - 31 October
9:30am - 5:30pm

Admission:
£5.90, children £2.70 and families £14.70

Charities:
Donation to SG Beneficiaries

BOLFRACKS
Aberfeldy PH15 2EX
The Douglas Hutchison Trust T: 01887 820344
E: athel@bolfracks.com www.bolfracks.com

Special three acre garden with wonderful views overlooking the Tay Valley. Burn garden with rhododendrons, azaleas, primulas and meconopsis in a woodland garden setting. Walled garden with shrubs, herbaceous borders and rose rooms with old fashioned roses. There is also a beautiful rose and clematis walk. Peony beds are underplanted with tulips and Japanese anemone. The garden has a great selection of bulbs in spring and good autumn colour.

Other Details: Refreshments available for groups by prior arrangement.
Slippery paths in wet weather.

Directions: Two miles west of Aberfeldy on A827. White gates and Lodge are on the left. Look out for the brown tourist signs.

Disabled Access:
None

Opening Times:
Daily
10:00am - 6:00pm

Admission:
£4.50, children under 16 free

Charities:
Donation to SG Beneficiaries

4 BONHARD HOUSE
Perth PH2 7PQ
Stephen and Charlotte Hay T: 01738552471

A marvellous traditional 19th century garden of five acres with mature trees, lawns, rhododendrons, azaleas, hollies, herbaceous borders, ponds and an oak drive lined with primulas and daffodils. There is also a kitchen garden, Pinetum and wooded area.

Other Details: Sensible shoes should be worn.

Directions: From Perth take the A94 north to Scone. Before you reach Scone turn right at the sign to Murrayshall Hotel. Continue for about one mile. The house drive is on the right where the road turns sharp left.

From Balbeggie take A94. Turn left signposted for Bonhard one mile north of Scone and in half a mile turn right. House drive is on the left where the road turns sharp right shortly after Bonhard Nursery.

Disabled Access:
Partial

Opening Times:
Sunday 12 June
10:00am - 4:00pm

Admission:
£4.00

Charities:
Freedom From Fistula Foundation receives 40%, the net remaining to SG Beneficiaries

---

5 BRACO CASTLE
Braco FK15 9LA
Mr and Mrs M van Ballegooijen T: 01786 880437

A 19th century landscaped garden with a plethora of wonderful and interesting trees, shrubs, bulbs and plants. It is an old garden for all seasons that has been extensively expanded over the last 26 years. The partly walled garden is approached on a rhododendron and tree lined path and features an ornamental pond with endless paths taking you to yet another special corner. Spectacular spring bulbs, exuberant shrub and herbaceous borders, and many ornamental trees are all enhanced by spectacular views across the park to the Ochils. Look out for the Embothrium in June, Hoheria in August, Eucryphia in September and an interesting collection of rhododendrons and azaleas with long flowering season.

Other Details: Catering facilities are not available.

Directions: One to one and a half mile drive from gates at north end of Braco Village, just west of bridge on A822.

Disabled Access:
Partial

Opening Times:
1 February - 31 October
10:00am - 5:00pm
Snowdrop Festival
1 February - 13 March
Admission:
£4.00

Charities:
The Woodland Trust receives 40%, the net remaining to SG Beneficiaries

---

6 BRADYSTONE HOUSE
Murthly PH1 4EW
Mrs James Lumsden T: 01738 710308

A true cottage garden converted 20 years ago from derelict farm steadings. It has been beautifully planted to produce an ever changing picture which in summer will take your breath away. Unusual plants complement others in wonderful combinations, and quite often there will be some plants for sale. The small woodland surrounding the garden and interplanted with many interesting shrubs and trees, has now matured, and there is a pretty winding grass walk through the trees. There is also a pond with free roaming ducks and hens. A gem of a garden.

Other Details: Refreshments available by prior arrangement. There is full disabled access, except perhaps the woodland walk which is grassy. Groups welcome.

Directions: From south/north follow A9 to Bankfoot, then sign to Murthly. At crossroads in Murthly take private road to Bradystone.

Disabled Access:
Partial

Opening Times:
Thursdays
2, 9, 16, 23, 30 June and
7, 14, 21, 28 July
11:00am - 4:00pm

Admission:
£5.00

Charities:
Perthshire Abandoned Dogs Society Ltd (PADS) receives 40%, the net remaining to SG Beneficiaries

BRANKLYN GARDEN
116 Dundee Road, Perth PH2 7BB
The National Trust for Scotland T: 01738 625535
E: smcnamara@nts.org.uk www.nts.org.uk

This attractive garden in Perth was once described as "the finest two acres of private garden in the country". It contains an outstanding collection of plants particularly rhododendrons, alpine, herbaceous and peat-loving plants, which attract gardeners and botanists from all over the world.

Other Details: National Plant Collection®: Cassiope, Meconopsis (Himalayan poppy) and Rhododendron subsect. Taliense. Champion Trees: Pinus sylvestris 'Globosa.'
Head Gardener's walk at 2:00pm.

Directions: On A85 Perth/Dundee road.

Disabled Access:
Partial

Opening Times:
Sunday 1 May
10:00am - 4:00pm

Admission:
Normal admission to the garden applies.

Charities:
Donation to SG Beneficiaries

BRIGLANDS HOUSE
Rumbling Bridge KY13 0PS
Mrs Briony Multon T: 01577 840205
E: briony@briglands.com

Lovingly restored by the current owners over the past 35 years, the nine acre, essentially spring garden was originally designed by Sir Robert Lorimer and surrounds the house, remodelled by him in 1898. There are glorious displays of bulbs, rhododendrons, young trees and shrubs, an historic lime walk, newly planted peony garden, topiary, rockery, plus good autumn colour.

Other Details: Rumbling Bridge Nurseries, specialising in unusual alpines, is adjacent to the garden and will open in conjunction with visits.

Directions: On A977 Kinross to Kincardine Bridge road, on the left just beyond Crook of Devon.

Disabled Access:
Partial

Opening Times:
By arrangement
1 April - 15 June
and 1 - 31 October

Admission:
£4.00

Charities:
Local Animal Rescue
Charities receives 40%,
the net remaining to
SG Beneficiaries

CARIG DHUBH
Bonskeid PH16 5NP
Jane and Niall Graham-Campbell T: 01796 473469
E: niallgc@btinternet.com

The garden is comprised of mixed shrubs and herbaceous plants with many species of meconopsis and primulas. It extends to about one acre on the side of a hill with some steep paths and uneven ground. The soil is sand overlying rock - some of which projects through the surface. There are beautiful surrounding country and hill views.

Directions: Take old A9 between Pitlochry and Killiecrankie, turn west on the Tummel Bridge Road B8019, ¾ mile on north side of the road.

Disabled Access:
None

Opening Times:
By arrangement
1 May - 30 October

Admission:
£5.00, children free

Charities:
Poppies Scotland receives
40%, the net remaining to
SG Beneficiaries

CLUNY HOUSE
Aberfeldy PH15 2JT
Mr J and Mrs W Mattingley T: 01887 820795
E: wmattingley@btinternet.com www.clunyhousegardens.com

A wonderful, wild woodland garden overlooking the scenic Strathtay valley. Experience the grandeur of one of Britain's widest trees, the complex leaf variation of the Japanese maple, the beauty of the American trillium or the diversity of Asiatic primulas. There is a good display of snowdrops. Cluny's red squirrels are usually very easily seen. A treasure not to be missed.

Other Details: Open for the Snowdrop Festival 15 February - 13 March. Plant seeds available for sale. Admission free for dates outwith 30 January to 31 October but donations towards squirrel food are welcome.

Directions: Three and a half miles from Aberfeldy on Weem to Strathtay Road.

Disabled Access:
None

Opening Times:
Open all year, 14 Mar - 30 Oct 10:00am - 6:00pm rest of year closes at 4:00pm.

Admission:
30 Jan -13 March £4.00, children £1.00 14 Mar-31 Oct £5.00, children £1.00. Also see Other details opposite

Charities:
Bumblebee Conservation Trust receives 40%, the net remaining to SG Beneficiaries

CROFTCAT LODGE
Grandtully PH15 2QS
Margaret and Iain Gimblett T: 01887 840288
E: iain@gimblettsmill.plus.com

This is a garden for all seasons with colour or interest in almost every month of the year. It is welcoming, inspiring and unusual. It was featured on *The Beechgrove Garden* in 2013 and on Sky television in 2015 when it won an award for the best of three gardens in Scotland, all gardening on difficult sites. Although it extends to over 1 acre now it was largely created and is cared for only by its owners, both now retired. The garden, a series of smaller gardens all linked together, is set on a stony, windy hillside but has panoramic views which have been incorporated into the garden wherever possible. There are lawns, spring and autumn gardens, a small gravel garden, rose terraces, clipped beehive laurels, a collection of clematis, and most lovely of all, a small Japanese water garden with stepping stones and tea pavilion. In 2014 the Japanese garden was extended to include a small wildlife pond with marginal plants, shrub roses and other specimen shrubs and trees, all framing the remains of an old ruined mill and mature ash trees.

Other Details: Wheelchair access is possible to most of the garden with assistance. Margaret and Iain welcome visitors and groups by arrangement. They endeavour to provide tea and home baking whenever possible for all visitors, but, given notice, can provide special afternoon teas for up to six people or a light lunch for up to 20 people.

Directions: From A9 take A827 signposted Aberfeldy. Through Grandtully village and one mile from traffic lights on bridge turn left by cream house set back from road. Croftcat is on left 300 yards up lane.

Disabled Access:
Partial

Opening Times:
By arrangement
14 May - 16 October

Admission:
£5.00 includes tea or coffee

Charities:
Multiple Sclerosis UK receives 40%, the net remaining to SG Beneficiaries

12 DELVINE
Murthly PH1 4LD
Mr and Mrs David Gemmell T: 01738 710485

The gardens at Delvine are situated on Inchtuthil (the island that floods) an old Roman legionary fortress abandoned 85 AD. The old gardens that surrounded the original house were abandoned and are slowly being brought back to life, but these are not what you have come to see. However, if you love something unusual, you must come and see the Millennium Project and Water Gardens set in a beautiful wild and secluded setting, surrounded by fine and very old trees, a little distance from the house. You can wander among collections of different bamboos, shrub roses, birches and other special trees. In the spring you will see swans and geese nesting. There are also peacocks, and if you are really lucky you might be able to see kingfishers, otters and beavers. This is a very special place even in the rain. Boots or waterproof shoes are a must if it is wet.

Directions: On A984, seven miles east of Dunkeld, four miles south west of Blairgowrie.

Disabled Access:
Partial

Opening Times:
By arrangement
15 April - 15 October

Admission:
£5.00, children £0.50

Charities:
ABF Soldiers' Charity receives 40%, the net remaining to SG Beneficiaries

13 DOWHILL
Cleish KY4 0HZ
Mr and Mrs Colin Maitland Dougall
E: pippamd@icloud.com

A garden set off by the background of Benarty Hill and magnificent old trees. Lovely woodland walks to the ruins of Dowhill Castle. There are nine linked ponds. Blue poppies and primulas together with temptingly placed seats make the garden a wonderful place for a picnic in fine weather.

Directions: Three quarters of a mile off M90, exit 5, towards Crook of Devon on the B9097 in the trees.

Disabled Access:
None

Opening Times:
By arrangement on request

Admission:
£4.00

Charities:
Motor Neurone Disease Association receives 40%, the net remaining to SG Beneficiaries

14 DRUMMOND CASTLE GARDENS
Crieff PH7 4HZ
Grimsthorpe & Drummond Castle Trust Ltd
www.drummondcastlegardens.co.uk

The Gardens of Drummond Castle were originally laid out in 1630 by John Drummond, second Earl of Perth. In 1830 the parterre was changed to an Italian style. One of the most interesting features is the multi-faceted sundial designed by John Mylne, Master Mason to Charles I. The formal garden is said to be one of the finest in Europe and is the largest of its type in Scotland.

Other Details: Admission on dates other than Sunday 7 August £5.00, OAPs £4.00, children £2.00, family £12.00.

Directions: Entrance two miles south of Crieff on Muthill road (A822).

Disabled Access:
Partial

Opening Times:
Sun 7 Aug 1:00pm - 5:00pm
1 May - 31 Oct 1pm - 6:00pm

Admission:
Sun 7 Aug £4.00, OAPs £3.00, children £2.00, family £10.00 Also see Other Details opposite

Charities:
British Limbless Ex-Servicemen's Association receives 40% the net remaining to SG Beneficiaries

15 EXPLORERS GARDEN
Pitlochry PH16 5DR
Pitlochry Festival Theatre
www.explorersgarden.com

This 2.4ha (6 acre) woodland garden celebrates the Scottish Plant Hunters who risked their lives in search of new plants. The Explorers Garden is divided into geographic areas, each containing examples of the plants collected from that corner of the globe. Set in beautiful Highland Perthshire countryside, the garden is known for its Meconopsis collection, stunning vistas and interesting sculptures and structures. Each year a photographic exhibition is held in the David Douglas Pavilion.

Directions: A9 to Pitlochry town, follow signs to Pitlochry Festival Theatre.

Disabled Access:
Partial

Opening Times:
Sunday 5 June
10:00am - 5:00pm
Please note the last entry is 4.15pm

Admission:
£4.00 or £5.00 with guided tour

Charities:
Acting for Others receives 40%, the net remaining to SG Beneficiaries

16 GLENDOICK
by Perth PH2 7NS
Peter, Patricia, Kenneth and Jane Cox T: 01738 860205
E: orders@glendoick.com www.glendoick.com

Glendoick is the ideal spring day out with a visit to both the gardens and garden centre in April and May. Glendoick was included in the *Independent on Sunday* survey of Europe's top 50 Gardens and boasts a unique collection of plants from three generations of Cox plant-hunting expeditions in China and the Himalaya. Enjoy one of the finest collections of rhododendrons and azaleas, primulas, meconopsis and other acid-loving plants in the woodland garden, walled garden and the gardens surrounding the house.

Many of the rhododendron and azalea species and hybrids have been introduced from the wild or bred by the Cox family and the gardens boast a huge range of plants from as far afield as Chile, Tasmania and Tibet. Three waterfall viewing platforms have been built in the woodland gardens. You'll find new as yet unnamed hybrids from the Glendoick breeding programme trial beds in the walled garden.

The award-winning Glendoick Garden Centre and Cafe has one of Scotland's best selections of plants including their world-famous rhododendrons and azaleas as well as a gift shop and foodhall.

Other Details: National Plant Collection®: Two collections of Rhododendrons. Rhododendron (Cox hybrids) and Rhododendron sect. Pogonanthum, subsect. Uniflora, subsect. Campylogyna.

Mail Order rhododendrons and azaleas in winter months only.

Refreshments for groups should be pre-booked - for group bookings and refreshments contact Jane Cox by email: jane@glendoick.com.

The woodland garden is not easily accessible to wheelchairs but some of the gardens by the house are. Disabled toilets at the garden centre only.

Peter and Kenneth Cox have written numerous books on rhododendrons and gardens. Kenneth Cox's book *Scotland for Gardeners* describes 500 of Scotland's finest gardens.

Directions: Follow brown signs to Glendoick Garden Centre off A90 Perth - Dundee road. Gardens are ½ mile behind Garden Centre. After buying tickets at the garden centre, please drive up and park at gardens (free parking).

Disabled Access:
None

Opening Times:
1 April - 31 May
10:00am - 4:00pm daily

Admission:
£5.00, school age children free, no dogs.
Tickets must be purchased from the garden centre.

Charities:
Donation to SG Beneficiaries

Glendoick from the air

GLENERICHT HOUSE
Blairgowrie PH10 7JD
Mrs William McCosh T: 01250 872092

Spectacular collection of Victorian planted trees and shrubs which are centred around a Grade 'A' listed suspension bridge (1846). Ninety-two tree varieties, mostly conifers including a top Douglas fir which is 171 feet and still growing, also a collection of younger trees. In May you will be able to view the wonderful daffodils and the rhododendrons in flower.

Directions: Off A93, the Lodge House is five miles north of Blairgowrie on the right hand side A93 from Blairgowrie. Follow avenue to the house.

Disabled Access:
Partial

Opening Times:
Daily
9:00am - 7:00pm or Dusk

Admission:
£4.00

Charities:
SANDS receives 40%,
the net remaining to
SG Beneficiaries

GLENLYON HOUSE
Fortingall PH15 2LN
Mr and Mrs Iain Wotherspoon T: 01887 830233

Interesting garden framed by hedges, with colourful herbaceous borders and fruit trees underplanted with perennials and annuals. There is a kitchen and cutting garden as well as a wildlife pond.

Directions: Take A827 Aberfeldy, B846 Coshieville then turn off for Fortingall and Glen Lyon.

Disabled Access:
Partial

Opening Times:
Sunday 12 June
2:00pm - 5:00pm
By arrangement on request

Admission:
£5.00

Charities:
Fortingall Church receives
40%, the net remaining to
SG Beneficiaries

HOLLYTREE LODGE
Muckhart, Dollar FK14 7JW
Liz and Peter Wyatt T: 0797 337 4687
E: elizwyatt @aol.com

A tranquil garden in the centre of the village of Pool of Muckhart, divided by internal beech hedges into smaller areas. These include a small Japanese garden, spring bulbs naturalised in grass, a mini orchard and wildflowers, a rill, a wildlife pond, mixed herbaceous borders, and various types of roses, all within an acre plot. We have an interesting variety of unusual trees and shrubs including a good collection of rhododendrons and deciduous azaleas, a snow gum, a Metasequoia glyptostroboides, a Persian Ironwood, which colours beautifully in autumn, as do the acers. We have incorporated a tree trail that highlights the more unusual trees which can help guide visitors round the garden.

Our aim is to garden with nature, and organically, complementing our beekeeping interests; the best planting scheme often seems to happen by accident! The opening dates select the passion of the season, so visit us twice and come back in the autumn for free!

We have ongoing projects so come and see what else happens in 2016.

Other Details: Also open on 22 May from 11:00am - 5:00pm as part of the Muckhart Village Open Gardens, see page 161 for more information, or the Scotland's Gardens website.

Directions: Hollytree lodge is off the A91 down the small lane directly opposite the Inn at Muckhart entrance. Parking is available for disabled only, otherwise please park in the village.

Disabled Access:
Full

Opening Times:
By arrangement
25 March - 10 April
1 May - 30 June and
1 September - 31 October

Admission:
£4.00

Charities:
The Coronation Hall, Muckhart. receives 40%, the net remaining to SG Beneficiaries

---

KILGRASTON SCHOOL
Bridge of Earn PH2 9BQ
Kilgraston School T: 01738 815517
E: marketing@kilgraston.com   www.kilgraston.com

Set within the grounds of Kilgraston School, this is a wonderful opportunity to see the snowdrops whilst exploring the woodlands and surroundings of this very unique garden. Statues and sculptures (including work by Hew Lorimer) intermingle with ancient trees, snowdrops and even the resident red squirrels. Spend a Sunday afternoon wandering along wild woodland pathways and through the extensive grounds, and explore the chapel, main hall and artworks within the school.

Other Details: Teas from the school's award-winning catering team are available (indoors, if the weather is against us), alongside a wide range of activities for children.

Directions: Bridge of Earn is three miles south of Perth on the A912. Kilgraston School is well signposted from the main road. Maps are available at *www.kilgraston.com/contact.*

Disabled Access:
Partial

Opening Times:
Sunday 21 February
1:30pm - 4:00pm

Admission:
£4.00

Charities:
The Schools nominated charity will receive 40%, the net remaining to SG Beneficiaries

21 KIRKTON CRAIG
Abernyte PH14 9ST
Heather Berger T: 01828 686336
E: heather@thebergers.org.uk

This ¾ acre walled garden overlooks the Tay in the Braes of the Carse of Gowrie. Mature trees and shrubs and colourful mixed borders with many interesting plants and spring bulbs. The shelter of the high brick walls, generously covered with climbers, allows for the cultivation of plants many of which are borderline hardy and unusual in Eastern Scotland.

Other Details: This garden is only a short distance from Latch House, Abernyte, see entry below, also opening by arrangement. As both are very different from each other, a visit to both would be possible on the same day and is suggested. Small groups are welcome.

Directions: Coming from the A90 Inchture junction, take the B953 to Abernyte village. Opposite the school take a road signposted Church. Kirkton Craig is the second driveway on the left.

Disabled Access:
Full

Opening Times:
By arrangement
3 May - 26 July

Admission:
£5.00, to include tea/coffee/shortbread

Charities:
Crisis receives 40%, the net remaining to SG Beneficiaries

22 LATCH HOUSE
Abernyte Ph14 9SU
Mrs Juliet McSwan T: 01828 686816

Sitting on top of a hill at 600 feet, giving wonderful views over the Tay to Fife. The 1+ acre garden flows round the house with lawns and mixed beds of trees, shrubs and perennials. To the rear, paths run through a wooded area with spring bulbs, rhododendrons and azaleas. Interesting trees, including seven species of rowan. Little rockeries close to the house surround a paved sunken garden and a small, shelved pond where birds love to bathe. Varieties of poppies and trilliums are favourites with the owners. This garden is very close to Kirkton Craig in Abernyte, see entry 21 above. The two gardens are quite different and you might like to visit both on the same day.

Directions: Take the B953 from the A90 Inchture junction. Pass through the village of Abernyte. When the B953 bears to the left - approximately ½ mile from Abernyte, keep to the right and continue up the hill for another ½ mile. Latch House is the first house on the left at the top of the hill.

Disabled Access:
Partial

Opening Times:
By arrangement
1 May - 31 August

Admission:
£5.00, includes tea/coffee

Charities:
Children's Hospice Association Scotland (CHAS) receives 40%, the net remaining to SG Beneficiaries

Cluny House, Lily pyrenaicum

LITTLE TOMBUIE
Killiechassie, Aberfeldy PH15 2JS
Mrs Sally Crystal T: 01887 829344
E: sallycrystal@gmail.com

Perched high up, facing south on the hill overlooking Aberfeldy and the Tay, this is not a garden where everything is finished and perfect. But, if you want to meet a gardener who is diffidently very knowledgeable but warm and welcoming and see a garden which has huge potential, then this is the garden for you. The views alone are worth the journey. Mrs Crystal is not only a compost queen, but builder of dry stone walls, plantswoman and tree planter. Her raised bed vegetable garden would put most of us to shame. The older part of the garden is immaculate with emerald lawns, a wide selection of trees and shrubs and an interesting collection of old stone cheese presses. In the newer part a garden has been carved out from the hill for roses and shrubs with single flowers. In early summer, azaleas and meconopsis are flowering but the autumn colours are wonderful, and you may hear the red deer roaring in the neighbouring fields.

Other Details: This garden is very near to Croftcat Lodge, see garden entry 11, and Pitnacree House gardens, see garden entry 30; they are all very different from each other and so you may like to visit all three of the gardens, perhaps arranged as a combined visit.

Directions: From the A9 take the A827 to Aberfeldy. At the traffic lights turn right and take the B846 crossing the river. Take the first road to the right to Strathtay. The drive to Tombuie is approximately two miles along this road opposite a small graveyard on the right and beside a large copper beech tree.

Disabled Access:
Partial

Opening Times:
By arrangement
1 May - 31 July

Admission:
£4.00

Charities:
Bloodwise receives 40%, the net remaining to SG Beneficiaries

---

MEGGINCH CASTLE
Errol PH2 7SW
Mr Giles Herdman and The Hon. Mrs Drummond-Herdman of Megginch

Romantic fifteenth century turreted castle (not open) with Gothic stable yard and pagoda style doocote. Nineteenth century formal front garden, topiary, ancient yews and a splendid array of daffodils, tulips and rhododendrons. The double walled kitchen garden has a newly planted Cider Apple walk. Scots Dumpy hens roam in the heritage orchard which has been extensively replanted with old Scottish fruit tree varieties.

Directions: Approach from Dundee only, directly off A90, on south side of carriageway half a mile on left after Errol flyover, between lodge gatehouses. It is seven miles from Perth and eight from Dundee.

Disabled Access:
Full

Opening Times:
Sunday 10 April
2:00pm - 5:00pm

Admission:
£4.00, children free

Charities:
Maggie's Cancer Care Centre receives 20%, Dundee and Glencarse Church receives 20%, the net remaining to SG Beneficiaries

25 MILL OF FORNETH
Forneth, Blairgowrie PH10 6SP
Mr and Mrs Graham Wood
E: gaw@gwpc.demon.co.uk

Formerly a watermill, originally laid out in the 1970s by James Aitken, the Scottish landscape designer and naturalist. The sheltered four acre garden has a range of mature trees, including a Himalyan Blue Cedar, large rhododendrons, azaleas and a wide range of shrubs. A 75 metre long mill lade feeds rocky waterfalls and a lily pond. Planting includes established perennials with seasonal colours, many bulbs, primulas and heathers.

Other Details: This garden includes an old watermill with deep and fast flowing water. It is not safe for children under 12. Grassy parking and picnic area available. Take care if weather has been wet and ground is soft!

Directions: Take the A923 Dunkeld to Blairgowrie road. Six miles east of Dunkeld turn south onto a minor road signposted Snaigow and Clunie. Mill of Forneth is the first gate on the left hand side.

Disabled Access:
Partial

Opening Times:
Sunday 5 June 2:00pm - 5:00pm By arrangement 1 May - 30 September

Admission:
£4.00

Charities:
Perth & Kinross District Nurses receives 20%, Blairgowrie Black Watch Army Cadet Force receives 20%, the net remaining to SG Beneficiaries

---

26 MOUNT TABOR HOUSE
Mount Tabor Road, Perth PH2 7DE
Mr and Mrs John McEwan

Mature terraced town garden originally laid out in the late 19th century, but constantly evolving. A sheltered and peaceful garden surrounded by mature trees and hedges with well filled herbaceous borders. There is a cascade of ponds filled with carp and other wildlife and lots of places to sit in the sun and relax.

Other Details: Homemade soups and rolls will be available from 12:00pm until 2:00pm followed by teas and traybakes from 2:00pm until 4:30pm. There will be a plant stall.

Directions: From Dundee Road in Perth at Isle of Skye Hotel, turn right into Manse Road, over mini-roundabout and into Mount Tabor Road.

Disabled Access:
Full

Opening Times:
Sunday 7 August 12:00pm - 4:30pm

Admission:
£3.50

Charities:
The Katie McKerracher Trust receives 40%, the net remaining to SG Beneficiaries

Bolfracks

MUCKHART VILLAGE
Dollar FK14 7JN
The Gardeners of Muckhart Village

Muckhart Primary School Garden:
With a tree worthy of Sherwood Forest this community/school garden is a delight. With flowers, vegetables, fruit trees and a pond it has something for everybody. It has been awarded the best school garden in Clackmannanshire for the past two years.

Mount Stuart House, Glendevon Road (Mr Gordon Smith):
Large rural garden with ongoing development, drystone wall terraces and raised borders, extensive herbaceous and mixed planting areas offset by mature trees, rhododendron and acers; new wetland under construction.

Hollytree Lodge, Pool of Muckhart (Mr and Mrs P Wyatt):
Hollytree Lodge is a tranquil acre in the centre of the village, some unusual trees and shrubs including a good number of rhododendrons and azaleas. Garden is also open by arrangement.

5 Golf View, Pool of Muckhart (Mrs Joy Scott):
This is a wildlife friendly cottage style garden with vegetables and fruit growing alongside the flowers.

Shepherds Cottage, Yetts of Muckhart (Mr and Mrs R Cleworth):
A small pretty cottage garden with shrubs, spring bulbs and mixed herbaceous borders, surrounded by mature trees. Recent addition of a vegetable area with raised beds.

Moss Park Coach House, Rumbling Bridge (Mrs Meriel Cairns):
A small new garden created from a paddock with shrubs and herbaceous flowers, and an attractive pond.

Other Details: Group ticket for entry to all gardens and map, will be available from the village hall, known locally as Coronation Hall. Refreshments at the School and Village Hall. No dogs except guide dogs.

Directions: The adjacent villages are situated on the A91, approximately four miles east of Dollar. Parking is available at Muckhart School Garden, Mount Stuart House and Moss Park Coach House. A shuttle car will be available for those who want it, there is also some parking at various gardens.

Disabled Access:
Partial

Opening Times:
Sunday 22 May
11:00am - 5:00pm

Admission:
£8.00, children free

Charities:
Muckhart Village Hall receives 20%, Muckhart Primary School receives 20%, the net remaining to SG Beneficiaries

PARKHEAD HOUSE
Parkhead Gardens, Burghmuir Road, Perth PH1 1JF
**Mr & Mrs M S Tinson T: 01738 625983 M:07769676586
E: maddy.tinson@gmail.com www.parkheadgardens.com**

Parkhead is an old farmhouse sited within an acre of beautiful gardens. Mature trees include an outstanding 300 year old Spanish chestnut. This hidden gem is a garden for all seasons. Gentle terracing and meandering paths lead you past a large variety of unusual and interesting plants and shrubs. If you seek colour and inspiration come and see this garden.

Other Details: National Plant Collection®: Mylnefield Lilies. This National Collection was originally developed by Dr Christopher North at the Scottish Horticultural Research Institute, Dundee. Mylnefield Lilies flower June and July and are available for sale or order. Homemade teas by request. Variety of plants for sale when available. Individuals and groups welcome.

Directions: Parkhead Gardens is a small lane off the west end of Burghmuir Road in Perth. More detailed directions on request.

Disabled Access:
Partial

Opening Times:
By arrangement
1 May - 30 September
Please call/email before visit. We accept short notice bookings.

Admission:
£4.00

Charities:
Plant Heritage receives 40%, the net remaining to SG Beneficiaries

29 PITCURRAN HOUSE
Abernethy PH2 9LH
The Hon Ranald and Mrs Noel-Paton T: 01738 850933
E: patricianp@pitcurran.com

End of village garden with an interesting combination of trees, shrubs and plants. Behind the house Euphorbia mellifera and melianthus major grown happily amongst hebes and cistus. The garden also includes rhododendrons and azaleas, meconopsis, trilliums, tree peonies, Smilacena racemosa and a good Caragana arborescens 'Lorbergii'.

There is a rose pergola covered in Blush Noisetta, Feicite Perpetue and Paul's Himalayan Musk. A large west facing hydrangea border brightens up the late summer.

Other Details: There will be a few plants for sale.

Directions: SE of Perth. From M90 (exit 9) take A912 towards Glenfarg, go left at roundabout onto A913 to Abernethy. Pitcurran House is at the far eastern end of the village.

Disabled Access:
Partial

Opening Times:
By arrangement
1 April - 30 September

Admission:
£4.00, children free

Charities:
Juvenile Diabetes Research Foundation (JDRF) receives 40% the net remaining to SG Beneficiaries

30 PITNACREE HOUSE
Pitnacree, Ballinluig, Pitlochry PH9 0LW
Mrs Susan Sherriff
E: susansherriff@btinternet.com

Mature grounds surround an 18th century house with fine views south over the Strathtay valley. To the back of the house is a large well maintained walled garden, the main feature of which is a long walk lined with herbaceous planting, roses and tree peonies. Arches and stone sundials draw the eye from one part of the garden to another. Running through the garden is a small burn edged with bog and marginal plants, while to one side of the garden is a formal vegetable parterre. This is a beautiful, peaceful garden, at its best in midsummer and made for slowly meandering through, enjoying the mixture of colours and scents and, on a sunny day, the play of light and shade on the paths.

Other Details: There is disabled access to most parts of the garden although the garden is situated on a gentle slope. This garden is not far from Cluny Gardens and other gardens in Strathtay which open by arrangement and where tea is usually provided. The other gardens are Croftcat Lodge and Little Tombuie , see garden entries 11 and 23 respectively. You might like to combine a visit to the garden at Pitnacree House with another or others on the same day. Each garden is very different from the others. Teas at Pitnacree House only by prior arrangement.

Directions: From The A9 take the A827 towards Aberfeldy. Look out for a sign to the right to the village of Strathtay. The entrance to Pitnacree is approximately ½ to ¾ mile along this narrow road on the right.

Disabled Access:
Partial

Opening Times:
By arrangement
1 May - 31 July

Admission:
£4.00

Charities:
British Heart Foundation receives 20%, MND Scotland receives 20%, the net remaining to SG Beneficiaries

ROSSIE HOUSE
Forgandenny PH2 9EH
Mr and Mrs David B Nichol T: 01738 812265
E: judynichol@rossiehouse.co.uk

This romantic garden has been establishing itself since 1657 when the house was built. The garden is a magical mystery tour of endless paths meandering under magnificent trees, various unusual shrubs with a plethora of woodland bulbs and plants at your feet. You intentionally have to lift the branches of a Hamamelis mollis to find yourself by the pond in an oasis of sculptured beauty. Look up 100 feet to the top of the Abies alba and climb the grass path to the sunken garden and the witches' hut. From snowdrops to hellebores then trillium and bluebells, flowering shrubs, roses and an abundance of water loving plants, this garden's interest goes on through to the magnificent autumn colours. In the height of summer there are more formal gardens close to the house. Sculptures by David Annand and Nigel Ross surprise you on your tour. Look out for the 10 foot tea pot and the yew table ready for the Mad Hatter's tea party!

Directions: Forgandenny is on the B935 between Bridge of Earn and Dunning.

Disabled Access:
Partial

Opening Times:
Plant sale Sunday 29 May
2:00pm - 5:00pm
Garden also open

Admission:
£4.00

Charities:
Sandpiper Trust receives 40%, the net remaining to SG Beneficiaries

THE BIELD AT BLACKRUTHVEN
Blackruthven House, Tibbermore PH1 1PY
The Bield Christian Co Ltd T: 01738 583238
E: info@bieldatblackruthven.org.uk www.bieldatblackruthven.org.uk

The Bield is set in extensive grounds comprising well maintained lawns and clipped hedges, a flower meadow and a large collection of specimen trees. Visitors are encouraged to stroll around the grounds and explore the labyrinth cut into the grass of the old orchard. The main garden is a traditional walled garden containing extensive herbaceous borders, manicured lawns and an organic vegetable plot. The walled garden also contains a wide variety of trained fruit trees, a fruit cage, a glasshouse and a healing garden.

Directions: From Dundee or Edinburgh, follow signs for Glasgow, Stirling Crianlarich which lead onto the Perth bypass. Head west on the A85 signed to Crieff/Crianlarich to West Huntingtower. Turn left at the crossroads to Madderty / Tibbermore. The entrance is on your left after ½ mile and is marked by stone pillars and iron gates. Take a left up the tarmac road passing the gate lodge. Turn right to park at the Steading.

Disabled Access:
Full

Opening Times:
Saturday 11 June
2:00pm - 5:00pm

Admission:
£5.00 includes tea/coffee and home baking

Charities:
Southton Smallholding receives 40%, the net remaining to SG Beneficiaries

33 THE GARDEN AT CRAIGOWAN
Ballinluig PH9 0NE
Ian and Christine Jones
E: i.q.jones@btinternet.com

The Garden at Craigowan is situated on a quiet public road overlooking the Tay and Tummel valleys at an elevation of 600ft. It has had significant redevelopment over the last 25 years and now extends to 5 acres with woodland, lawns and formal herbaceous and planted areas. The plant collection is mainly rhododendrons, magnolia, meconopsis, lilies and other traditional companion plants. There is a good show of meconopsis followed by the giant Himalayan lilies in June. The rhododendron collection comprises species, sourced from Glendoick over nearly 40 years, but more recently there have been additions of good hybrids from the leading English nurseries. The rhododendron and azalea flowering period extends for almost 12 months but the most significant show is from mid April until June. Thereafter the herbaceous borders are of interest and colour until mid October. There is always a frost risk which can wreck rhododendron flowering in the spring but more importantly a good collection of species starting at hardiness category ¾ have grown well and recent losses have been rare. The larger leaf varieties are now starting to flower consistently.

Other Details: Groups are welcome to visit the garden. Tea and coffee by prior arrangement only.

Directions: From north or south A9 to Ballinluig junction. Follow sign for Tulliemet and Dalcapon. Pass the filling station and Red Brolly Cafe. Turn right following the Tulliemet/ Dalcapon sign. This is a steep narrow road so take care. About ½ mile up the road take a left turning with field on either side and Craigowan is the first house on the left about ½ mile along. Park on paviours adjoining house.

Disabled Access:
Partial

Opening Times:
By arrangement
15 April - 30 June

Admission:
£6.00, includes tea

Charities:
LUPUS UK receives 40%, the net remaining to SG Beneficiaries

34 THE STEADING AT CLUNIE
Newmill of Kinloch, Clunie, Blairgowrie PH10 6SG
Jean and Dave Trudgill T: 01250 884263

Newmill policies extend 700 metres along the north bank of the Lunan Burn midway between Lochs Clunie and Marlee. Newmill is at its best in spring and early summer and its main attractions centre around water. They include both garden and wild ponds, the Lunan Burn with a mill lade once converted to trap eels, and a small cottage garden. There is a wooded walk along the lade and Burn, with bridges and some narrow paths, with bluebells and primroses in spring. There is also a wild flower meadow carpeted with cowslips in spring and with several species of wild orchids, including both species of butterfly orchid that usually flower in early to mid-June. Although rarely seen the Lunan Burn is home to otters and beavers and occasional kingfishers and in early June large numbers of roach are sometimes seen spawning.

Directions: Look for a track on a sharp right-hand bend just after a breeze-block wall on the south side of the A923 three miles west of Blairgowrie and 800 metres west of the Kinloch Hotel.

Disabled Access:
None

Opening Times:
By arrangement
8 May - 25 June
for spring flowers and
11 - 19 June for wild orchids

Admission:
£5.00, includes tea/coffee

Charities:
Save the Children receives 40%, the net remaining to SG Beneficiaries

35 WESTER CLOQUHAT
Bridge of Cally PH10 7JP
Brigadier and Mrs Christopher Dunphie

Terraced garden, water garden, lawns, mixed borders with a wide range of shrubs, roses and hebaceous plants. Splendid situation with fine view to the river Ericht.

Directions: Turn off A93 just north of Bridge of Cally and follow signs for ½ mile.

Disabled Access:
None

Opening Times:
Sunday 3 July
2:00pm - 5:00pm

Admission:
£5.00

Charities:
ABF, The Soldiers' Charity receives 40%, the net remaining to SG Beneficiaries

36 WESTER HOUSE OF ROSS
Comrie PH6 2JS
Mrs Sue Young

Wester House of Ross is a four acre garden which has been developed over the last 14 years. We would love to see you and for you to enjoy the start of autumn colours, the asters, crocosmias, hydrangeas, clematis, anemones, geraniums and much more.

Other Details: A large and interesting plant stall. A great tea tent this year with hot soup and rolls and cakes galore.

Directions: On A85 drive westwards through Comrie, past the White Church and at the end of the village take a left turn over a small bridge, signposted Ross. Then take first right, signposted Dalchonzie. After ¼ mile turn left at the three large dustbins and follow signs to parking and the garden.

Disabled Access:
None

Opening Times:
Saturday 24 September
11:00am - 4:30pm
Sunday 25 September
11:00am - 4:30pm

Admission:
£4.00, children free

Charities:
Maggie's Centres receives 40%, the net remaining to SG Beneficiaries

Explorer's Garden, Pitlochry

Each visit you make to one of our gardens in 2016 will raise money for our beneficiary charities:

In addition, funds will be distributed to a charity of the owner's choice.
For the East of Scotland, these include:

Aberdeen Branch MS Society

ABF Soldiers' Charity

Acting for Others

Advocacy Service Aberdeen

Alford Car Transport Service

All Saints' Scottish Episcopal Church

Alzheimer Scotland

Amnesty International

Angus Toy Appeal

Asbestos Action Tayside

Auld Kirk, St Monans

Barnados

Befriend A Child, Aberdeen

Bennachie Guides

Blairgowrie Black Watch
  Army Cadet Force

Blebo Craigs Village Hall

Bloodwise

British Heart Foundation

British Limbless Ex-Servicemen's
  Association

Bumblebee Conservation Trust

Cambo Stables Project

Cancer Research Scotland

Children 1st

CHAS

Colinsburgh Town Hall Restoration
Projects

Crail Cubs

Crail Preservation Society

Crisis

Cruickshank Botanic Gardens Trust

Dalhousie Day Care

Dogs Trust

Dundee and Glencarse Church

Elvanfoot Trust

Fauna and Flora International

Fettercairn Community Allotments

Forfar Open Garden Scheme

Forgan Arts Centre

Forget Me Not

Fortingall Church

Freedom From Fistula Foundation

Friends of Anchor

Home Start Stonehaven

Julia Thomson Memorial Trust

Juvenile Diabetes Research

Kincardine O'Neill Village Hall

Local Animal Rescue Charities

LUPUS UK

Marie Curie

Mercy Ships

Mission to Seafarers

MND Scotland

Momentum Pathways

Montrose Guides

Motor Neurone Disease Association

Muckhart Primary School

Muckhart Village Hall

Multiple Sclerosis UK

Newburgh Scout Group

Pain Association Scotland

Parkinson's UK

Perth & Kinross District Nurses

Perthshire Abandoned Dogs Society

Plant Heritage

Poppies Scotland

Practical Action

RAF Benevolent Fund

RIO Community Centre

RNLI

RUDA

Saline Environmental Group

Sandpiper Trust

SANDS

Save the Children

Scottish Civic Trust

Southton Smallholding

St Athernase Church, Leuchars

St Mary's Episcopal Church

Stracathro Cancer Care Fund UK

Student Foodbank Dundee
  & Angus College

Tarland Community Garden

Tayside Children's Hospital Appeal

The Coronation Hall Muckhart

The Gurkha Welfare Trust

The Katie McKerracher Trust

The Rotary Polio Plus Campaign

The Woodland Trust

Type 1 Juvenile Diabetes Research

Unicorn Preservation Society

Willow Foundation

Worldwide Cancer Research

WEST CENTRAL SCOTLAND

Scotland's Gardens 2016 Guidebook is sponsored by **INVESTEC WEALTH & INVESTMENT**

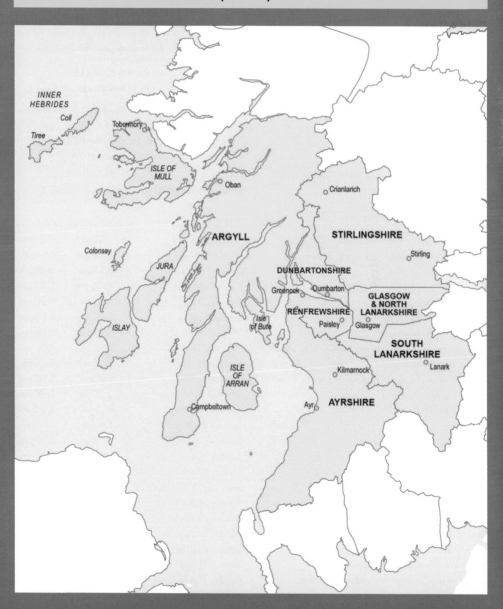

ARGYLL

Scotland's Gardens 2016 Guidebook is sponsored by **INVESTEC WEALTH & INVESTMENT**

District Organiser

Minette Struthers	Ardmaddy Castle, Balvicar, by Oban PA34 4QY E: argyll@scotlandsgardens.org

Area Organisers

Mrs Grace Bergius	Craignish House, Ardfern, by Lochgilphead PA31 8QN
Mrs Mary Lindsay	Dal an Eas, Kilmore, Oban PA34 4XU
Mrs Patricia McArthur	Bute Cottage, Newton, Strachlachan PA27 8DB

Treasurer

Minette Struthers	Ardmaddy Castle, Balvicar, by Oban PA34 4QY

Gardens open on a specific date

Maolachy's Garden, Lochavich, by Taynuilt	Date to be advised	2:00pm	-	6:00pm
Benmore Botanic Garden, Benmore, Dunoon	Sunday 24 April	10:00am	-	6:00pm
Arduaine Garden, Oban	Sunday 8 May	9:30am	-	5:00pm
Braevallich Farm, by Dalmally	Saturday 14 May	11:00am	-	5:30pm
Braevallich Farm, by Dalmally	Sunday 15 May	11:00am	-	5:30pm
Crarae Garden, Inveraray	Sunday 15 May	3:00pm	-	5:00pm
Crarae Garden, Inveraray	Wednesday 18 May	3:00pm	-	5:00pm
Strachur House Flower & Woodland Gardens, Strachur	Saturday 21 May	1:00pm	-	5:00pm
Crarae Garden, Inveraray	Sunday 22 May	3:00pm	-	5:00pm
Strachur House Flower & Woodland Gardens, Strachur	Sunday 22 May	1:00pm	-	5:00pm
Crarae Garden, Inveraray	Wednesday 25 May	3:00pm	-	5:00pm
Knock Cottage, Lochgair	Saturday 28 May	1:30pm	-	5:00pm
Knock Cottage, Lochgair	Sunday 29 May	1:30pm	-	5:00pm
Braevallich Farm, by Dalmally	Saturday 4 June	11:00am	-	5:30pm
Braevallich Farm, by Dalmally	Sunday 5 June	11:00am	-	5:30pm
Torosay Castle Gardens, Craignure, Isle of Mull	Sunday 5 June	10:00am	-	5:00pm
The Shore Villages, by Dunoon	Saturday 25 June	1:00pm	-	5:00pm
The Shore Villages, by Dunoon	Sunday 26 June	1:00pm	-	5:00pm
Caol Ruadh, Colintraive	Saturday 23 July	2:00pm	-	5:00pm
Caol Ruadh, Colintraive	Sunday 24 July	2:00pm	-	5:00pm
Little Kilmory Cottage, Rothesay, Isle of Bute	Saturday 30 July	10:00am	-	5:00pm
Ardchattan Priory, North Connel	Sunday 31 July	12:00pm	-	4:00pm
Little Kilmory Cottage, Rothesay, Isle of Bute	Sunday 31 July	10:00am	-	5:00pm

ARGYLL

Torosay Castle Gardens, Craignure, Isle of Mull	Sunday 7 August	10:00am	5:00pm
Torosay Castle Gardens, Craignure, Isle of Mull	Sunday 2 October	10:00am	5:00pm

Gardens open regularly

Achnacloich, Connel, Oban	25 March - 31 October Saturdays only	10:00am	4:00pm
Ardchattan Priory, North Connel	25 March - 31 October	9:30am	5:30pm
Ardkinglas Woodland Garden, Cairndow	Daily	Dawn	Dusk
Ardmaddy Castle, by Oban	Daily	9:00am	Dusk
Ascog Hall, Ascog, Isle of Bute	1 April - 31 October	10:00am	5:00pm
Barguillean's "Angus Garden", Taynuilt	Daily	9:00am	Dusk
Benmore Botanic Garden, Benmore, Dunoon	1 March - 31 March 1 April - 30 September 1 October - 31 October	10:00am 10:00am 10:00am	5:00pm 6:00pm 5:00pm
Crinan Hotel Garden, Crinan	1 May - 31 August	Dawn	Dusk
Druimneil House, Port Appin	25 March - 31 October	Dawn	Dusk
Fairwinds, 14 George Street, Hunter's Quay, Dunoon	1 April - 31 October	10:00am	6:00pm
Inveraray Castle Gardens, Inveraray	1 April - 31 October	10:00am	5:45pm
Kinlochlaich Gardens, Appin	14 March - 14 October	10:00am	5:00pm
Oakbank, Ardrishaig	1 May - 31 August	10:30am	6:00pm

Gardens open by arrangement

Braevallich Farm, by Dalmally	16 April - 30 June	01866 844246
Eas Mhor, Cnoc-a-Challtuinn, Clachan Seil, Oban	1 May - 31 August	01852 300469
Kinlochlaich Gardens, Appin	15 October - 13 March	07881 525754
Knock Cottage, Lochgair	15 April - 15 June	07554 869239 corranmorhouse@aol.com

Key to symbols

	New in 2016		Homemade teas		Accommodation
	Teas		Dogs on a lead allowed		Plant stall
	Cream teas		Wheelchair access		Scottish Snowdrop Festival

GARDEN LOCATIONS IN ARGYLL

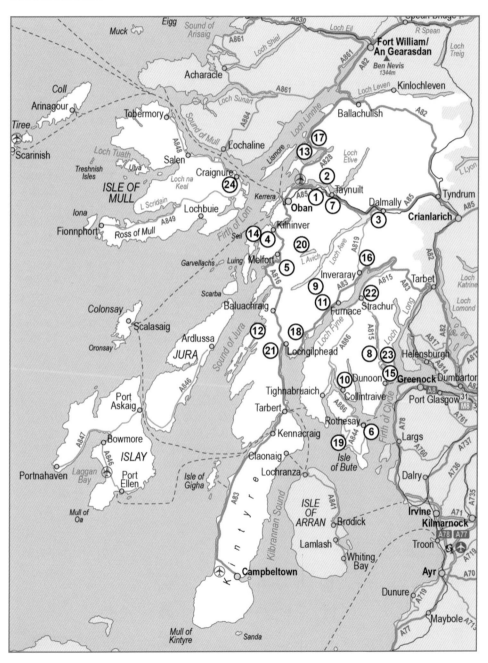

ACHNACLOICH
Connel, Oban PA37 1PR
Mr T E Nelson T: 01631 710796
E: charlie_milne@msn.com

Scottish baronial house by John Starforth of Glasgow. Succession of wonderful bulbs, flowering shrubs, rhododendrons, azaleas, magnolias and primulas. Woodland garden with ponds above Loch Etive. There are good autumn colours.

Directions: On A85 three miles east of Connel. Parking is on the right at the bottom of the drive.

Disabled Access:
Partial

Opening Times:
25 March - 31 October
10:00am - 4:00pm
Saturdays only

Admission:
£4.00

Charities:
All proceeds to
SG Beneficiaries

ARDCHATTAN PRIORY
North Connel PA37 1RQ
Mrs Sarah Troughton T: 01796 481355
E: sh.troughton@virgin.net www.ardchattan.co.uk

Beautifully situated on the north side of Loch Etive. In front of the house there is a rockery, extensive herbaceous and rose borders, with excellent views over the loch. West of the house there are shrub borders and a wild garden, numerous roses and many different varieties of sorbus providing excellent autumn colour. The Priory, founded in 1230, is now a private house. The ruins of the chapel and graveyard are in the care of Historic Scotland and open with the garden.

Other Details: Sunday 31 July Garden Fete - soup lunches, homemade teas, plant and other stalls and other attractions.

Directions: Oban ten miles. From north, turn left off A828 at Barcaldine onto B845 for six miles. From East/Oban on A85, cross Connel Bridge and turn first right, proceed east on Bonawe Road.

Disabled Access:
Partial

Opening Times:
Sunday 31 July
12:00pm - 4:00pm
25 March - 31 October
9:30am - 5:30pm

Admission:
£4.00, children under 16 free

Charities:
Donation to SG Beneficiaries

ARDKINGLAS WOODLAND GARDEN
Cairndow PA26 8BG
Ardkinglas Estate T: 01499 600261
www.ardkinglas.com

In a peaceful setting overlooking Loch Fyne the garden contains one of the finest collections of rhododendrons and conifers in Britain. This includes the mightiest conifer in Europe, a silver fir, as well as many other champion trees. There is also a gazebo with unique "Scriptorium" based around a collection of literary quotes. The garden now has the only Gruffalo trail in Scotland, come and find him! It is a Visit Scotland three star garden.

Other Details: Champion Trees: 'Grand Fir' tallest tree in Britain and other champion trees. Nearby is the Tree Shop, an independent garden centre and café which offers fabulous plants and food.

Directions: Entrance through Cairndow village off A83 Loch Lomond/Inveraray road.

Disabled Access:
Partial

Opening Times:
Daily
Dawn - Dusk

Admission:
£5.00, family ticket £15.00

Charities:
Donation to SG Beneficiaries

ARDMADDY CASTLE
by Oban PA34 4QY
Mr and Mrs Charles Struthers T: 01852 300353
E: ardmaddycastle@btinternet.com www.gardens-of-argyll.co.uk

The gardens, in a most spectacular setting, are shielded by mature woodlands, carpeted with bluebells and daffodils and protected from Atlantic winds by the Castle. The Walled Garden is full of magnificent rhododendrons, an increasing collection of rare and unusual shrubs and plants, the 'Clock Garden' with its cutting flowers, the new crevice garden, fruit and vegetables grown with labour saving formality, all within dwarf box hedging. A woodland walk, with its amazing 60ft hydrangea, leads to the water gardens - in early summer a riot of candelabra primulas, irises, rodgersias and other damp loving plants and grasses. Lovely autumn colour. A garden for all seasons.

Disabled Access:
Full

Opening Times:
Daily
9:00am - Dusk

Admission:
£4.50, children free

Charities:
Donation to SG Beneficiaries

Other Details: Plant stalls and vegetable & summer fruit stalls in season.Toilet suitable for disabled. Six self catering cottages, details at *www.ardmaddy.com*.

Directions: Take A816 south of Oban for eight miles. Turn right B844 to Seil Island/Easdale. Four miles on, take Ardmaddy road for a further two miles.

ARDUAINE GARDEN
Oban PA34 4XQ
The National Trust for Scotland T: 01852 200366
E: arduaine@nts.org.uk http://www.nts.org.uk/property/arduaine-garden

Outstanding 20 acre coastal garden created over 100 years ago on the south facing slope of a promontory separating Asknish Bay from Loch Melfort. This remarkable hidden paradise, protected by tall shelterbelts and influenced favourably by the North Atlantic Drift, grows a wide variety of plants from all over the globe. Internationally known for its rhododendron species collection, the garden also features magnolias, camellias, azaleas and other wonderful trees and shrubs, many being tender and rarely seen. A broad selection of perennials, bulbs, ferns and water plants ensure year-long interest.

Disabled Access:
Partial

Opening Times:
Sunday 8 May
9:30am - 5:00pm

Admission:
Normal admission applies.

Charities:
Donation to SG Beneficiaries

Other Details: Champion Trees: nine including Gevuina avellana. Check our website for event details. Teas available in the local hotel.

Directions: Off A816 Oban-Lochgilphead, sharing an entrance with the Loch Melfort Hotel.

ASCOG HALL
Ascog, Isle of Bute PA20 9EU
Karin Burke T: 01700 503 461
E: karin@ascogfernery.com www.ascogfernery.com

The outstanding feature of this three acre garden is the Victorian Fernery, a sunken structure fed by natural spring waters and housing many fern species, including a 1,000 year old King Fern and thought to be Britain's oldest exotic fern. Rare and exotic species await the visitor wandering the original garden "rooms" while the stables and coach house ruin feed the imagination of long lost times. The garden is generally well labelled and contains a plant hunter's trail.

Disabled Access:
Partial

Opening Times:
1 April - 31 October
10:00am - 5:00pm

Admission:
£5.00 (there are no concessions).

Charities:
Donation to SG Beneficiaries

Other Details: Parking for restricted mobility citizens at top of the drive (close to the house). Personal assistance available for disabled access to Fernery. Guide dogs are permitted. All proceeds are donated to the garden maintenance fund or to charity.

Directions: Three miles south of Rothesay on A844. Close to the picturesque Ascog Bay.

BARGUILLEAN'S "ANGUS GARDEN"
Taynuilt PA35 1HY
The Josephine Marshall Trust T: 01866 822333
E: info@barguillean.co.uk www.barguillean.co.uk

Nine acre woodland garden around an eleven acre loch set in the Glen Lonan Hills. Spring flowering shrubs and bulbs, extensive collection of rhododendron hybrids, deciduous azaleas, conifers and unusual trees. The garden contains a large collection of North American rhododendron hybrids from famous contemporary plant breeders. Some paths can be steep. Three marked walks from 30 minutes to 1½ hours.

Other Details: Self catering accommodation available in seperate comfortable wing of the main house. Coach Tours by appointment.

Directions: Three miles south off A85 Glasgow/Oban road at Taynuilt; road marked Glen Lonan; three miles up single track road; turn right at the sign.

Disabled Access:
None

Opening Times:
Daily
9:00am - Dusk

Admission:
£3.00, children under 14 free

Charities:
Donation to SG Beneficiaries

BENMORE BOTANIC GARDEN
Benmore, Dunoon PA23 8QU
A Regional Garden of the Royal Botanic Garden Edinburgh T: 01369 706261
E: benmore@rbge.org.uk/benmore www.rbge.org.uk

Benmore with its magnificent mountainside setting is a joy to behold. Its 49 hectares/120 acres boast a world-famous collection of plants from regions ranging from the Orient and the Himalaya to North and South America.

Visitors are welcomed by an impressive avenue of giant redwoods, arguably one of the finest entrances to any botanic garden in the world. Established in 1863, these majestic giants now stand over 50 metres high.

Other Details: National Plant Collection®: Abies, South American Temperate Conifers, Picea. Seven miles of trails throughout the Garden lead to beautiful spots such as the restored Victorian Fernery and dramatic viewpoint at 450 feet (140 metres) looking out to the surrounding mountains and Holy Loch. Look out for the traditional Bhutanese and Chilean pavilions as well as the Garden's magnificent Golden Gates. Prices include donation to gardens, for prices without donation see rbge.org.uk.

Directions: Seven miles north of Dunoon or 22 miles south from Glen Kinglass below Rest and Be Thankful pass. Gardens are on the A815.

Disabled Access:
Partial

Opening Times:
Sunday 24 April
10:00am - 6:00pm
for Scotland's Gardens
1 - 31 March
10:00am - 5:00pm
1 April to 30 September
10:00am -6:00pm
1 - 31 October
10:00 am - 5:00pm
Last entry 1 hour before the garden closes.

Admission:
£6.50, concessions £5.50, children under 16 free

Charities:
Donation to SG Beneficiaries

ARGYLL

BRAEVALLICH FARM
by Dalmally PA33 1BU
Mr Philip Bowden-Smith T: 01866 844246
E: philip@brae.co.uk

There are two gardens: one at the farm of approx. 1.5 acres, developed over the last 40 years; its principal features are dwarf rhododendron, azaleas (evergreen and deciduous), large drifts of various primula and meconopsis, and mixed herbaceous shrubs; there is also quite a serious kitchen garden. The second garden, 300m above the farm, at approx. seven acres, was developed over the last 25 years out of a birch and sessile oak wood and is a traditional glen garden with two pretty burns with waterfalls. Many attractive vistas. The plantings are predominantly Rhododendron (120 plus var), deciduous azalea (30 var), camellia, magnolia, eucryphia, and many different shrubs and trees with large drifts of bluebell and other bulbs.

Other Details: Waterproof footwear is recommended.

Directions: Braevallich lies on the SE side of Loch Awe on the B840, fifteen miles from Cladich and seven miles from Ford.

Disabled Access:
None

Opening Times:
Saturday/Sunday 14/15 May
11:00am - 5:30pm
Saturday/Sunday 4/5 June
11:00am - 5:30pm
By arrangement
16 April - 30 June

Admission:
£5.00

Charities:
Mary's Meals receives 40%, the net remaining to SG Beneficiaries

---

CAOL RUADH
Colintraive PA22 3AR
Mr and Mrs C Scotland

Delightful seaside garden on the old B866 shore road looking out over Loch Riddon and the Kyles of Bute in this very beautiful corner of Argyll.

Directions: Turn right off A886 Strachur - Colintraive onto B866 about 2½ miles before Colintraive. From Dunoon take A815 north about 3½ miles, left on to B836 and then left on to A886.

Disabled Access:
None

Opening Times:
Saturday 23 July
2:00pm - 5:00pm
Sunday 24 July
2:00pm - 5:00pm

Admission:
£6.00 includes tea

Charities:
All proceeds to
SG Beneficiaries

CRARAE GARDEN
Inveraray PA32 8YA
The National Trust for Scotland T: 01546 886614
E: mjeffery@nts.org.uk www.nts.org.uk

A rugged woodland garden with a spectacular display of rhododendrons in May and June, a narrow gorge with waterfalls, pools, and varied wildlife from red squirrels and pine martens to otters. Above the garden is the forest garden, a very wild area which was planted in the 1930s as an experiment. This area now has stands of fine tall trees in a unique wild setting and is not open to the public. Select guided tours will take place into this closed part of the property with the new Head Gardener.

Other Details: National Plant Collection®: Nothofagus (Southern Beech). This collection is the most northerly of its type in the UK. Champion Trees: Abies, Acer and Chamaecyparis. Tours cover rough ground, sturdy footwear is required. Waterproofs and midge nets recommended. Disabled access only to part of lower garden. Dogs on leads welcome. wPlant sales, light refreshments and cakes available.

Directions: On A83 ten miles south of Inveraray.

Disabled Access:
Partial

Opening Times:
Sunday 15 May
Wednesday 18 May
Sunday 22 May
Wednesday 25 May
all dates 3:00pm - 5:00pm

Admission:
£15.00 each for tour and is limited to 12.
Advanced booking essential
Ring the property to take part

Charities:
Donation to SG Beneficiaries

CRINAN HOTEL GARDEN
Crinan PA31 8SR
Mr and Mrs N Ryan T: 01546 830261
E: nryan@crinanhotel.com www.crinanhotel.com

Small rock garden with azaleas and rhododendrons created in a steep hillside over a century ago with steps leading to a sheltered, secluded garden with sloping lawns, herbaceous beds and spectacular views of the canal and Crinan Loch.

Other Details: Raffle of painting by Frances Macdonald (Ryan). Tickets at coffee shop, art gallery and hotel. Homemade teas available in the coffee shop.

Directions: Lochgilphead A83, then A816 to Oban, then A841 Cairnbaan to Crinan.

Disabled Access:
None

Opening Times:
1 May - 31 August
Dawn - Dusk

Admission:
By donation

Charities:
Feedback Madagascar receives 40%, the net remaining to SG Beneficiaries

DRUIMNEIL HOUSE
Port Appin PA38 4DQ
Mrs J Glaisher (Gardener: Mr Andrew Ritchie) T: 01631 730228
E: druimneilhouse@btinternet.com

Large garden overlooking Loch Linnhe with many fine varieties of mature trees and rhododendrons and other woodland shrubs. Nearer the house, an impressive bank of deciduous azaleas is underplanted with a block of camassia and a range of other bulbs. A small Victorian walled garden is currently being restored.

Other Details: Teas normally available. Lunch by prior arrangement.

Directions: Turn in for Appin off A828 (Connel/Fort William Road). Two miles, sharp left at Airds Hotel, second house on right.

Disabled Access:
None

Opening Times:
25 March - 31 October
Dawn - Dusk

Admission:
By donation

Charities:
All proceeds to
SG Beneficiaries

EAS MHOR
Cnoc-a-Challtuinn, Clachan Seil, Oban PA34 4TR
Mrs Kimbra Lesley Barrett T: 01852 300 469
E: flora99@maxvall.plus.com

All the usual joys of a west coast garden plus some delightful surprises! A small contemporary garden on a sloping site - the emphasis being on scent and exotic plant material. Unusual and rare blue Borinda bamboos (only recently discovered in China) and bananas. The garden is at its best in mid to late summer when shrub roses and sweet peas fill the air with scent. The delightful sunny deck overlooks stylish white walled ponds with cascading water blades.

Other Details: Cream tea in small artist studio off the deck - enjoy the sound of gentle music. Small groups are welcome.

Directions: At Kilninver turn off A816 from Oban onto B844 signed Easdale and Atlantic Bridge. Over the Bridge onto Seil Island, pass Tigh an Truish pub and turn right after ¼ mile (at bus shelter) up Cnoc-a-Challtuin road. Public car park on the left at the bottom, please park there and walk up the road. Eas Mhor with high deer gates is on right after 2nd speed bump. Please do not block the shared driveway.

Disabled Access:
None

Opening Times:
By arrangement
1 May - 31 August

Admission:
Minimum donation £4.00, refreshments are extra.

Charities:
MS Therapy Centre (Oban) receives 40%, the net remaining to SG Beneficiaries

ARGYLL

15 FAIRWINDS
14 George Street, Hunter's Quay, Dunoon PA23 8JU
Mrs Carol Stewart T: 01369 702666
E: carol.argyll@talk21.com

This mature garden was created in the 1950s from a small orchard. The present owner is constantly trying to add colour and interest for all seasons. Spring brings a flourish of spring flowers, rhododendrons and azaleas. Trees of all kinds display their constantly changing shades throughout the year and in autumn the acers and copper beech are at their very best. Around every corner there is yet another plant of interest, a goldfish pond or a swing.

Other Details: Please call if coming from a distance. Teas available on request.

Directions: On A815. Enter Dunoon on loch side road, turn right up Cammesreinach Brae just before the Royal Marine Hotel opposite West Ferries terminal. The Brae becomes George Street and Fairwinds is on the left.

Disabled Access:
Partial

Opening Times:
1 April - 31 October
10:00am - 6:00pm

Admission:
£2.50, children free

Charities:
The Cowal Hospice receives 40%, the net remaining to SG Beneficiaries

16 INVERARAY CASTLE GARDENS
Inveraray PA32 8XF
The Duke and Duchess of Argyll T: 01499 302203
E: enquiries@inveraray-castle.com www.inveraray-castle.com

Rhododendrons and azaleas abound and flower from April to June. Very fine specimens of Cedrus deodars, Sequoiadendron wellingtonia, Cryptomeria japonica, Taxus baccata and others thrive in the damp climate. The 'Flag-Borders' on each side of the main drive with paths in the shape of Scotland's national flag, the St. Andrew's Cross, are outstanding in spring with Prunus 'Ukon' and 'Subhirtella' and are underplanted with rhododendrons, Eucryphias, shrubs and herbaceous plants giving interest all year. Bluebell Festival during flowering period in May.

Other Details: Guide dogs allowed. Wheelchair users please note there are gravel paths.

Directions: Inveraray is 60 miles north of Glasgow on the banks of Loch Fyne on the A83 with a regular bus service from Glasgow and 15 miles from Dalmally on the A819.

Disabled Access:
Partial

Opening Times:
1 April - 31 October
10:00am - 5:45pm

Admission:
£4.00

Charities:
Donation to SG Beneficiaries

Ascog Hall, Argyll

KINLOCHLAICH GARDENS
Appin PA38 4BD
Mr and Mrs D E Hutchison and Miss F M M Hutchison T: 07881 525754
E: gardens@kinlochlaich-house.co.uk www.kinlochlaichgardencentre.co.uk

Walled garden incorporating the Western Highlands' largest Nursery Garden Centre. Amazing variety of plants growing and for sale. Extensive grounds with woodland walk, spring garden, vegetable gardens and formal garden. Extensive display of rhododendrons, azaleas, trees, shrubs and herbaceous, including many unusuals - Embothrium, Davidia, Stewartia, Magnolia, Eucryphia and Tropaeolum.

Other Details: The gardens surround the historic Kinlochlaich House, which has a tree house, cottages and apartments to let for self catering.

Directions: On the A828 in Appin between Oban, 18 miles to the south, and Fort William, 27 miles to the north. The entrance is next to the Police Station.

Disabled Access:
Partial

Opening Times:
14 March - 14 October
10:00am - 5:00pm
By arrangement
15 October - 13 March
please phone as happy to open!

Admission:
£2.50

Charities:
Appin Village Hall receives 40%, the net remaining to SG Beneficiaries

---

KNOCK COTTAGE
Lochgair PA31 8RZ
Mr and Mrs Hew Service T: 07554 869239
E: corranmorhouse@aol.com

A five acre woodland and water garden centred round a small loch and lily pond. Started in the 1960s most of the garden dates from the creation of the lochan in 1989 and the plantings of the 1990s. Development entered a new phase following the severe storms of 2011/12. Some 80 different rhododendron species and hybrids along with camellias, azaleas and other shrubs are scattered throughout the garden in a natural setting, sheltered by conifers, eucalyptus, birch, rowan, alder and beech

Other Details: Please note there is very limited parking. Waterproof footwear is recommended. Teas will be available on 28/29 May.

Directions: On the A83, from Lochgilphead, ½ mile before the Lochgair Hotel and on the left, and from Inveraray, ½ mile after the Lochgair Hotel and on the right between two sharp bends.

Disabled Access:
Partial

Opening Times:
Sat/Sun 28/29 May
1:30am - 5:00pm
By arrangement
15 April - 15 June

Admission:
£4.00

Charities:
Christchurch Episcopal Church, Lochgilphead receives 20%, RNLI receives 20%, the net remaining to SG Beneficiaries

---

LITTLE KILMORY COTTAGE
Rothesay, Isle of Bute PA20 0QA
Dorothy Cullinane
E: martincullinane@aol.com

A small tranquil cottage garden located on the beautiful unspoilt west side of Bute. Hidden from the road this family garden has been created from practically nothing against many odds. This ever evolving garden contains an eclectic mix of plants, shrubs and trees many of which are grown for their colour and wonderful scent.

Directions: Take the B878 from Rothesay. Turn left on A844 for just over three kilometres and the cottage sits on the shore side of the road.

Disabled Access:
None

Opening Times:
Saturday 30 July
10:00am - 5:00pm
Sunday 31 July
10:00am - 5:00pm

Admission:
£3.00

Charities:
All proceeds to SG Beneficiaries

ARGYLL

MAOLACHY'S GARDEN
Lochavich, by Taynuilt PA35 1HJ
Georgina Dalton T: 01866 844212

Three acres of Woodland Garden with a tumbling burn - created in a small glen over 30 years. At an altitude of 450 feet and two weeks behind the coast we have a shorter growing season. By not struggling to grow tender or late species we can enjoy those that are happy to grow well here and give us all much pleasure. Snowdrops, followed by early rhodies, masses of daffodils in many varieties, bluebells, wild flowers and azaleas, primulas and irises. Herbaceous blooms flower on into summer's greenery. Later flowering shrubs and autumn colours and berries make something to see and enjoy all year. A productive vegetable patch and tunnel feeds the gardener and family!

Other Details: The main path is gravelled, but some others are narrow, steep and not for the faint hearted! Sensible shoes are recommended. The garden steps are being upgraded - please check Scotland's Gardens website for opening weekend.

Directions: A816 to Kilmelford. Turn uphill between the shop and church, signposted Lochavich 6, steep and twisty road with a hairpin bend shortly after leaving the village. Check for passing places. Maolachy Drive is four miles from the village. Cross three county cattle grids; after the 3rd **ignore the forestry tracks** to left and right. Continue downhill towards Loch Avich, and Maolachy is up on the left, first house after Kilmelford. **Ignore satnav.**

Disabled Access:
None

Opening Times:
Dates to be confirmed. Please check SG website for date of opening weekend.
2:00pm - 6:00pm

Admission:
£4.00

Charities:
Hope Kitchen -Oban receives 40%, the net remaining to SG Beneficiaries

---

OAKBANK
Ardrishaig PA30 8EP
Helga Macfarlane T: 01546 603405
E: helgamacfarlane@onetel.com www.gardenatoakbank.blogspot.com

This unusual and delightful garden will appeal to adults and children alike with lots for each to explore, including a secret garden. It extends to some three acres of hillside with a series of paths winding amongst a varied collection of trees, shrubs, bulbs and wild flowers. There are several small ponds, many wonderful wood carvings, an active visiting population of red squirrels and a viewpoint overlooking Loch Fyne to the Isle of Arran.

Directions: On the Tarbert side of Ardrishaig - entry to the garden is at the junction of Tarbert Road (A83) and Oakfield Road and immediately opposite the more southerly Scottish Water lay-by.

Disabled Access:
None

Opening Times:
1 May - 31 August
10:30am - 6:00pm

Admission:
£3.00, children free

Charities:
Diabetes UK receives 40%, the net remaining to SG Beneficiaries

STRACHUR HOUSE FLOWER & WOODLAND GARDENS
Strachur PA27 8BX
Sir Charles and Lady Maclean

Directly behind Strachur House the flower garden is sheltered by magnificent beeches, limes, ancient yews and Japanese maples. There are herbaceous borders, a burnside rhododendron and azalea walk and a rockery. Old fashioned and species roses, lilies, tulips, spring bulbs and Himalayan poppies make a varied display in this informal haven of beauty and tranquillity. The garden gives onto Strachur Park, laid out by General Campbell in 1782, which offers spectacular walks through natural woodland with two hundred-year-old trees, rare shrubs and a lochan rich in native wildlife.

Other Details: Teas available at the Post Office.

Directions: Turn off A815 at Strachur House Farm entrance. Park in farm square.

Disabled Access:
Full

Opening Times:
Saturday 21 May
1:00pm - 5:00pm
Sunday 22 May
1:00pm - 5:00pm

Admission:
£4.00

Charities:
CLASP receives 40%, the net remaining to SG Beneficiaries

THE SHORE VILLAGES
by Dunoon PA23 8SE
The Gardeners of The Shore Villages

19-20 Graham's Point Kilmun (Mr & Mrs A McClintock)
Belhaven, Strone (Mr & Mrs J Hampson)
4 Swedish Houses Ardentinny (E Connell)
5 Swedish Houses Ardentinny (Mr & Mrs B Waldapfel)
Four very different gardens on a seven mile stretch off the A880, overlooking the Holy Loch, the Clyde and Loch Long. Gardening for wildlife, colour combinations and for low maintenance, with terracing, sculpture, wildflower meadows and ponds, herbaceous borders and trees from seed. Some gardens are on steep slopes with limited disabled access.

Other Details: Teas and Plant Stall at Dunclutha, Strone (whose garden will not be open). Tickets, with information sheet, can be purchased at all gardens.

Directions: Approaching Dunoon from the north on the A815, take the left hand turning for Kilmun and follow the yellow arrows.

Disabled Access:
Partial

Opening Times:
Saturday 25 June
1:00pm - 5:00pm
Sunday 26 June
1:00pm - 5:00pm

Admission:
£5.00, accompanied children free

Charities:
All proceeds to
SG Beneficiaries

TOROSAY CASTLE GARDENS
Craignure, Isle of Mull PA65 6AY
Duncan Travers T: 077389 33033
E: d.j.travers@btinternet.com

Magnificent Italianate terraced gardens surrounded by woodland and water gardens in a dramatic setting with borrowed landscapes. Many fine specimens of rare and tender plants, walled gardens with vegetables and spectacular herbaceous borders, extensive collection of hydrangeas. There is a Japanese garden which is under continuous development.

Other Details: The property changed ownership in 2012 and the castle is no longer open to the public.

Directions: One and a half miles from Craignure ferry terminal on A849, in the direction of Fionnphort.

Disabled Access:
Full

Opening Times:
Sunday 5 June
10:00am - 5:00pm
Sunday 7 August
10:00am - 5:00pm
Sunday 2 October
10:00am - 5:00pm

Admission:
£3.00

Charities:
Lochdon School receives 40%, the net remaining to SG Beneficiaries

AYRSHIRE

Scotland's Gardens 2016 Guidebook is sponsored by **INVESTEC WEALTH & INVESTMENT**

District Organiser

Mrs R F Cuninghame	Caprington Castle, Kilmarnock KA2 9AA
	E: ayrshire@scotlandsgardens.org

Area Organisers

Mrs Glen Collins	Grougarbank House, Kilmarnock KA3 6HP
Ms Charlotte Fennell	
Mrs John MacKay	Pierhill, Annbank KA6 5AW
Mrs A J Sandiford	Harrowhill Cottage, Kilmarnock KA3 6HX

Treasurer

Mrs THP Donald	1 Waterslap, Fenwick KA3 6AJ

Gardens open on a specific date

Blair House, Blair Estate, Dalry, Ayrshire	Sunday 14 February	11:00am	-	4:00pm
Craigengillan Estate and Dark Sky Observatory	Sunday 21 February	3:00pm	-	5:30pm
1 Burnside Cottages, Sundrum, Coylton	Sunday 29 May	2.00pm	-	5:00pm
Holmes Farm, Drybridge, by Irvine	Saturday 4 June	1:00pm	-	5:00pm
Holmes Farm, Drybridge, by Irvine	Sunday 5 June	1:00pm	-	5:00pm
Gardening Leave, c/o Gardens Unit, SAC Auchincruive	Sunday 3 July	12:00pm	-	4:00pm
Culzean, Maybole	Tuesday 12 July	2:00pm	-	3:30pm
Cairnhall House, Mauchline Road, Ochiltree	Sunday 24 July	2:00pm	-	5:00pm
Golf Course Road Gardens, Girvan	Sunday 31 July	1:00pm	-	5:00pm
South Logan Farm, Sorn Road, Auchinleck, Ayrshire	Sunday 14 August	2:00pm	-	5:00pm

AYRSHIRE

Gardens open by arrangement

Burnside, Littlemill Road, Drongan	1 April - 14 September	01292 592445
Grougarbank House, Kilmarnock	1 February - 29 February	07881 657479
Grougarbank House, Kilmarnock	16 April - 11 September	07881 657479
High Fulwood, Stewarton	1 May - 31 August	01560 484705

Blair House

Key to symbols

 New in 2016

 Teas

 Cream teas

 Homemade teas

 Dogs on a lead allowed

 Wheelchair access

 Accommodation

 Plant stall

 Scottish Snowdrop Festival

GARDEN LOCATIONS IN AYRSHIRE

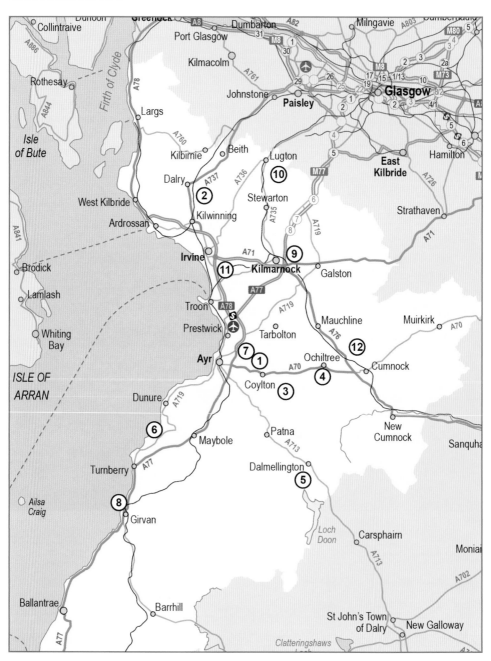

1 BURNSIDE COTTAGES
Sundrum, Coylton KA6 5JX
Carol Freireich T: 07980 164404

A sheltered cottage garden of 1.3 acres. Organically cultivated, native trees and many wild flowers encourage wide varieties of bird and insect life. A stream runs through a small wood, an old orchard with newer plantings of varieties chosen to tolerate northern conditions, a pond, vegetable garden and ornamental plantings all with plenty of places to sit.

Other Details: There will be lovely homemade teas and a plant stall.

Directions: A70 three miles from Ayr signed left at Sundrum Castle Caravan Park. Go up the road for ¾ mile and then left down dirt track where there is limited parking or continue to Coylton first left at Barclauch Drive round to the right, park at Woodhead Road and walk for five minutes to the garden. Look for signposts. Buses 45 or 48 Ayr/Cumnock to foot of Barclaugh Drive and follow signed route.

Disabled Access:
Partial

Opening Times:
Sunday 29 May
2:00pm - 5:00pm

Admission:
£4.00 children under 12 free

Charities:
The Pancreatic Cancer Research Fund receives 40%, the net remaining to SG Beneficiaries

---

2 BLAIR HOUSE, BLAIR ESTATE
Dalry, Ayrshire KA24 4ER
Charles and Sallie Hendry T: 01294 833100
E: enquiries@blairestate.com www.blairestate.com

Blair is a 'Sleeping Beauty' of a garden which is being lovingly restored. There is an atmosphere of a grand 19th century park with masses of changes in mood: sweeping vistas, magnificent trees, shady promenades, and secret groves - everything that is typical of the period.

A start on the Walled Garden has been made with the removal of 600 Christmas trees and we are now starting to compile ideas for future renovation.

In February enjoy beautiful displays of snowdrops. Walks on the Estate will include access to the Private Gardens. Please wear stout footwear.

Blair Estate has not been open to the public since it changed hands four years ago.

Other Details: Within the Undercroft of Blair House, we will be offering a selection of freshly baked produce to include homemade soup, coffee, teas, biscuits and afternoon tea with cakes. There will also be a gift stall.

There is full disabled access for catering and partial disabled access to the garden and grounds.

Directions: From A737 in Dalry, take road signposted to the Station and continue for ½ mile. Access via North Lodge Gates on the right. A one way system will be in place.

Disabled Access:
Partial

Opening Times:
Sunday 14 February
11:00am - 4:00pm
for the Snowdrop Festival

Admission:
£4.00, children free

Charities:
St Margaret's Parish Church, Dalry receives 40%, the net remaining to SG Beneficiaries

AYRSHIRE

BURNSIDE
Littlemill Road, Drongan KA6 7EN
Sue Simpson and George Watt T: 01292 592445

This young 6½ acre garden was started in 2006. There is a wide range of plants from trees to alpines. Features include a 200 yard woodland border along the burn, herbaceous beds, screes, an ericaceous garden, two alpine houses, a collection of alpine troughs and a pond. The informal arboretum is underplanted with groups of daffodils, camassia and fritillaries.

Other Details: Dogs on a lead please. Teas and light refreshments by prior arrangement.

Directions: From A77 Ayr bypass take A70 Cumnock for 5¼ miles, at Coalhall, turn onto B730 Drongan (south) for 2½ miles. Burnside entrance immediately adjacent before black/white parapeted bridge. Ordnance Survey grid reference: NS455162

Disabled Access:
Partial

Opening Times:
By arrangement
1 April - 14 September

Admission:
£4.00, children free

Charities:
Macmillan Nurses receives 40%, the net remaining to SG Beneficiaries

CAIRNHALL HOUSE
Mauchline Road, Ochiltree KA18 2QA
Ian and Sarah Hay

A nature lover's garden created over 10 years from a thistle-filled field into an organic 2 acre garden divided into formal and informal planting areas which include extensive flower beds, a large pond, vegetable plot, grassy meadow, orchard and laburnum tunnel. Something new to see every year.

Other Details: Drop off onto gravel at the house for infirm and wheelchairs.

Directions: From A70 into Ochiltree where road forks to Cumnock, turn left up Mauchline Road. Drive is 150 yards on the left. Please note parking is limited but the cemetery car park nearby is an option. See drop off information above.

Disabled Access:
Partial

Opening Times:
Sunday 24 July
2:00pm - 5:00pm

Admission:
£4.00, children free

Charities:
The Humane Research Trust receives 40%, the net remaining to SG Beneficiaries

CRAIGENGILLAN ESTATE AND DARK SKY OBSERVATORY
Dalmellington KA6 7PZ
Mr Mark Gibson
E: admin@craigengillan.com   http://www.craigengillan.com

Snowdrops and Stars: Craigengillan is peacefully set in a rugged 'Highland' landscape, about 14 miles from the sea. It has a fascinating history and its 3000 acres are recognised by Historic Scotland in their Inventory of Designed Landscapes. The house and stables are listed Category A. The gardens are beautiful and include a sweeping lawn set among time honoured trees. The skies above are among the darkest that most people will ever see. Countless stars, the Milky Way stretching from horizon to horizon, shooting stars, planets, comets and the Northern Lights are all visible.

Other Details: After exploring the snowdrops, visitors will be able to visit the Observatory as it gets dark (approx. 5:30pm). The Resident Astronomer will give a presentation and, if the sky is clear, you will be able to watch the stars at first hand through the powerful telescope. There is full disabled access to the Observatory.

Directions: A713 from Ayr, at the 30mph sign on entering Dalmellington turn right (signposted Craigengillan Stables).
From Carsphairn side, stay on the main road and take first turning on the left after the Jet petrol station.

Disabled Access:
Partial

Opening Times:
Sunday 21 February
3:00pm - 5:30pm
for the Snowdrop Festival
and 5.30pm - 7.00pm
for the Scottish Dark Sky
Observatory Visit.

Admission:
Snowdrops only: £3.00,
children free
Snowdrops & Observatory
Visit: £12.00, children £4.00

Charities:
The Dark Sky Observatory
receives 40%, the net
remaining to SG Beneficiaries

CULZEAN
Maybole KA19 8LE
The National Trust for Scotland T: 0165 588 4400
E: culzean@nts.org.uk   www.nts.org.uk

A major Scottish attraction and a perfect day out for all the family. The 18th century Castle is perched on a cliff high above the Firth of Clyde. The Fountain Garden lies in front of the castle with terraces and herbaceous borders. The large walled garden contains a wide collection of fruit, vegetables and cut flowers plus an extensive vinery and peach house. The 560 acre Country Park offers beaches and rock pools, parklands, woodland walks and the new Adventure Cove.

Other Details: Guided walk on Tuesday 12 July from 2:00pm - 3:30pm, meet at the Walled Garden car park. The walk will take in the Walled Garden plus the Fountain Court. Castle and Estate will be open - see NTS website for details. Dogs are allowed in the park; however only assistance dogs have access to the walled garden and buildings.

Directions: On the A719 twelve miles south of Ayr, four miles west of Maybole. Bus 60 Stagecoach, Ayr/Girvan via Maidens to the entrance. One mile walk downhill from the stop to the Castle/Visitor Centre.

Disabled Access:
Partial

Opening Times:
Tuesday 12 July
2:00pm - 3:30pm

Admission:
Normal admission applies,
guided walk £3.00
(including NTS members)

Charities:
Donation to SG Beneficiaries

GARDENING LEAVE
c/o Gardens Unit, SAC Auchincruive KA6 5HW
Gardening Leave T: 01292 521444
E: admin@gardeningleave.org

Small, walled terrace garden located within the grounds of Auchincruive Estate in Ayrshire run by a charity which provides sessions of horticultural therapy to veterans of the Armed Forces. The garden houses vegetable beds, flower beds and a quiet reflective corner. The charity is also in the process of restoring an 84 metre long Victorian greenhouse known as the Stovehouse. Part of the Stovehouse is open for use.

Other Details: Teas and coffees will be served in the Stovehouse.

Directions: From Whitletts roundabout outside Ayr, follow B743 to Mauchline, bypass the signposted entrance to the Auchincruive Estate SAC. Continue for approximately ¾ mile and take next on right.

Disabled Access:
Partial

Opening Times:
Sunday 3 July
12:00pm - 4:00pm

Admission:
£4.00, children under 12 free

Charities:
Gardening Leave receives 40%, the net remaining to SG Beneficiaries

---

8 ### GOLF COURSE ROAD GARDENS
Girvan KA26 9HZ
The Gardeners of Golf Course Road

The Gardens of Golf Course Road face the Firth of Clyde and Ailsa Craig at one end, and fields and the Isle of Arran at the other. All the gardens suffer from wind and salt spray, however they have a great variety of herbaceous plants and shrubs. In general, the gardens to the front face the sea and therefore take the full brunt of the weather, with the rear gardens in some cases being walled and affording more protection. The soil conditions are light well drained and sandy.

Other Details: Entrance tickets, maps and stickers will be available at each garden. Girvan Golf Clubhouse is hosting the teas for the afternoon. The Clubhouse is in close proximity to the gardens.

Directions: From north - on A77 turn right and follow signs for the Golf Course. **From south** - on A77 come through Girvan, turn left at the lights, then first left and follow signs for the Golf Course.

Disabled Access:
Partial

Opening Times:
Sunday 31 July
1:00pm - 5:00pm

Admission:
£4.00, children under 12 free for entrance to all gardens

Charities:
Friends of Hillcrest receives 20%, CHAS receives 20%, the net remaining to SG Beneficiaries

---

GROUGARBANK HOUSE
Kilmarnock KA3 6HP
Mrs Glen Collins T: 07881 657479

A small garden created over the past eight years which includes borders, trees and shrubs, raised vegetable and fruit beds. A glorious bluebell walk runs down to the River Irvine through mature and newly planted trees. Open in February for snowdrops and then again from mid April through to mid September.

Other Details: Teas/coffees light refreshments to be discussed when booking.

Directions: From A77 take A71 Edinburgh and Hurlford. At Hurlford Roundabout take B7073 (Kilmarnock). From Crookedholm centre turn right up Grougar Road and then at the T junction turn right, go about one mile to the second house on the right. Parking is limited.

Disabled Access:
None

Opening Times:
By arrangement
1 February - 29 February
for the Snowdrop Festival
By arrangement
16 April - 11 September

Admission:
£4.00, children free

Charities:
Marie Curie Ayrshire receives 40%, the net remaining to SG Beneficiaries

HIGH FULWOOD
Stewarton KA3 5JZ
Mr and Mrs Crawford T: 01560 484705

One acre of mature garden, particularly fine in late spring with rhododendrons, azaleas, trillium, hellebore and other spring flowering plants and bulbs. One acre of developing garden with herbaceous borders, vegetable garden and orchard at its best during July and August. Two acres of native broadleaf woodland being created. No neat edges but lots to see at any time.

Directions: From Stewarton Cross take the B760 Old Glasgow Road for one mile - turn onto the road marked to Dunlop, from Glasgow this turning is half a mile past Kingsford. Continue for two miles and turn right at T junction. High Fulwood is a short distance on the right hand side.

Disabled Access:
None

Opening Times:
By arrangement
1 May - 31 August

Admission:
£4.00, children free

Charities:
Hessilhead Wildlife Rescue Trust receives 40%, the net remaining to SG Beneficiaries

HOLMES FARM
Drybridge, by Irvine KA11 5BS
Mr Brian A Young T: 01294 311210
E: hfplants@live.co.uk   www.holmesfarmplants.com

Plantaholic's paradise! A plantsman's garden created by a confirmed plantaholic. An ever evolving selection of perennials, bulbs, alpines and shrubs. Meandering paths guide the eye through plantings predominantly herbaceous, with small trees and shrubs. Some unusual plant collections are housed permanently in polytunnels. The garden opening will hopefully be timed for peak bloom of some of the 400 iris in the garden. Some areas of the garden are currently undergoing a partial replant and redesign. There is a plant nursery with a wide selection of plant treasures from the garden and a gift shop and gallery too!

Directions: Holmes is the only farm between Drybridge and Dreghorn on the B730.

Disabled Access:
None

Opening Times:
Saturday 4 June
1:00pm - 5:00pm
Sunday 5 June
1:00pm - 5:00pm

Admission:
£5.00, children under 12 go free

Charities:
Plant Heritage receives 40%, the net remaining to SG Beneficiaries

SOUTH LOGAN FARM
Sorn Road, Auchinleck, Ayrshire KA5 6NH
Bill and Sue Howat

The holly bush is the only shrub that remains from the original 'garden' of black plastic and tyres (to suppress the weeds) that we 'inherited' when we moved in 19 years ago. The garden has been expanded into the bottom field, an ornamental water feature, small wildlife pond and a mixture of shrubs and herbaceous planting has been added. Our aim was to create a garden that had interest, colour and structure throughout the year, we like to think of it as our garden with '50 shades of green' with plenty of colour throughout the growing season. Perennial planting as well as a cutting patch of annual flowers will be on show, plus lots of garden structures and points of interest.

Other Details: A selection of Sue's wet felt pictures, prints and crafts will be available. (www.etsy.com/sixpennyrose and www.facebook.comsixpennyrose).

Directions: We are situated on the main B706 road running between Auchinleck and Catrine (approximately a mile past Auchinleck Academy). There will be plenty of parking behind the main farmhouse.

Disabled Access:
Full

Opening Times:
Sunday 14 August
2:00pm - 5:00pm

Admission:
£4.00

Charities:
The Scleroderma Society receives 40%, the net remaining to SG Beneficiaries

DUNBARTONSHIRE

Scotland's Gardens 2016 Guidebook is sponsored by **INVESTEC WEALTH & INVESTMENT**

District Organiser

Mrs Tricia Stewart	High Glenan, 24a Queen Street, Helensburgh G84 9LG E: dunbartonshire@scotlandsgardens.org

Area Organisers

Mrs J Goel	33 West Argyle Street, Helensburgh G84 8XR
Mrs M Greenwell	Avalon, Shore Road, Mambeg, Garelochhead G84 0EN
Mrs R Lang	Ardchapel, Shandon, Helensburgh G84 8NP
Mrs R Macaulay	Denehard, Garelochhead G84 0EL
Mrs M Rogers	Station House, Station Road, Tarbet G83 7DA

Treasurer

Mrs K Murray	7 The Birches, Shandon, Helensburgh G84 8HN

West Garemount

DUNBARTONSHIRE

Scotland's Gardens 2016 Guidebook is sponsored by **INVESTEC WEALTH & INVESTMENT**

Gardens open on a specific date

Kilarden, Rosneath	Sunday 17 April	2:00pm	-	5:00pm
Stuckenduff, Shore Road, Shandon	Sunday 15 May	2:00pm	-	5:00pm
Ross Priory, Gartocharn	Sunday 22 May	2:00pm	-	5:00pm
High Glenan and Westburn, Helensburgh	Sunday 29 May	2:00pm	-	5:00pm
Geilston Garden, Main Road, Cardross	Sunday 5 June	1:00pm	-	5:00pm
7 The Birches with West Garemount, Shandon	Sunday 17 July	2:00pm	-	5:00pm
Hill House, Helensburgh	Sunday 28 August	11:00am	-	4:00pm
Glenarn, Rhu, Helensburgh	Sunday 11 September	2:00pm	-	5:00pm

Gardens open regularly

Glenarn, Rhu, Helensburgh	21 March - 21 September	Dawn	-	Dusk

Plant sales

Hill House Plant Sale, Helensburgh	Sunday 28 August	11:00am	-	4:00pm
Glenarn, Rhu, Helensburgh	Sunday 11 September	2:00pm	-	5:00pm

Key to symbols

	New in 2016		Homemade teas		Accommodation
	Teas		Dogs on a lead allowed		Plant stall
	Cream teas		Wheelchair access		Scottish Snowdrop Festival

GARDEN LOCATIONS
IN DUNBARTONSHIRE

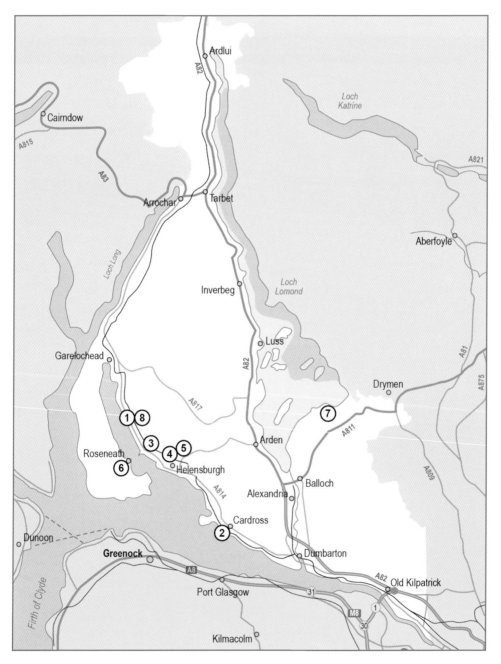

7 THE BIRCHES WITH WEST GAREMOUNT
Shandon, Near Helensburgh G84 8HN
Mrs Kathleen Murray and Maureen & Ian Chatten

7 The Birches: Re-designed and re-planted five years ago, the garden has fine mixed borders, raised beds, gravel garden, rockery, crevice garden and a large greenhouse. A mature Kiftsgate rose stretching the entire length of the garden is a special feature. Colourful containers. A very large plant stall includes perennials propagated from those seen growing in the garden.

West Garemount: This steeply terraced garden with burn running through has many unusual trees and shrubs. Gravel garden and rose arbour. Patios on different levels with fine views over the Gareloch. Very steep steps.

Other Details: Homemade teas at West Garemount.

Directions: Three and three quarter miles north of Helensburgh on A814. Take Ardchapel exit and park on the service road below the houses.

Disabled Access:
Partial

Opening Times:
Sunday 17 July
2:00pm - 5:00pm

Admission:
£3.00, includes entry to both gardens

Charities:
Hessilhead Wildlife Rescue Trust receives 40%, the net remaining to SG Beneficiaries

GEILSTON GARDEN
Main Road, Cardross G82 5HD
The National Trust for Scotland T: 01389 849187
E: afarrell@nts.org.uk www.nts.org.uk

Geilston Garden has many attractive features including the walled garden with the herbaceous border providing summer colour, the tranquil woodland walks and a large working kitchen garden. This is the ideal season for viewing the Siberian Iris in flower along the Geilston Burn and the Japanese Azaleas. During the summer months, July to September, there is a range of fresh fruit and vegetables for sale from the large kitchen garden.

Other Details: There will be a plant stall selling Geilston-grown perennials together with some early produce.

Directions: On the A814, one mile from Cardross towards Helensburgh.

Disabled Access:
Partial

Opening Times:
Sunday 5 June
1:00pm - 5:00pm

Admission:
Usual NTS admission charges apply, children under 12 free

Charities:
Donation to SG Beneficiaries

GLENARN
Glenarn Road, Rhu, Helensburgh G84 8LL
Michael and Sue Thornley T: 01436 820493
E: masthome@btinternet.com www.gardens-of-argyll.co.uk

Glenarn survives as a complete example of a ten acre garden which spans from 1850 to the present day. There are winding paths through glens under a canopy of oak and lime, sunlit open spaces, a vegetable garden with beehives, and a rock garden with views over the Gareloch. It is famous for its collection of rare and tender rhododendrons but horticulturally there is much more besides.

Other Details: Catering for groups by prior arrangement. On Sunday 11 September Glenarn will host a large plant sale with a selection of rhododendrons and magnolias propagated from the collection of special plants. Also unusual shrubs, woodland and rock garden plants including euchryphias, hoherias and acers. Tea and coffee with homemade scones available at the plant sale. Glenarn honey for sale if available.

Directions: On A814, two miles north of Helensburgh, up pier road. Cars to be left at the gate unless passengers are infirm.

Disabled Access:
Partial

Opening Times:
Plant sale Sun 11 Sep 2:00pm - 5:00pm. Garden also open. 21 Mar - 21 Sept Dawn - Dusk

Admission:
Garden entry £4.00
Plant sale entry free

Charities:
Erskine Hospital receives 40% from plant sale, net remaining to SG Beneficiaries. Other dates donation to SG Beneficiaries.

DUNBARTONSHIRE

HIGH GLENAN AND WESTBURN
Helensburgh G84 9LG
Tom & Tricia Stewart and Professor & Mrs Baker

High Glenan 24a Queen Street G84 9LG
A secluded garden with burn and waterside plants, gravel garden, herb and herbaceous borders, kitchen garden with selection of fruit and vegetables. Extensive programme of hard landscaping has been undertaken over the last eight years.

Westburn 50 Campbell Street G84 9NH
A woodland garden of just over 2 acres. The Glennan Burn runs through a woodland of oak and beech trees with bluebells in the springtime. Some of the paths are steep, but there are bridges over the burn and handrails in places. There is also an air raid shelter, and the remains of a kiln where James Ballantyne Hannay manufactured artificial diamonds in the 1800s. A lawn is surrounded by rhododendrons and azaleas, and there is a vegetable garden. Over the years the garden has been enjoyed by children, with lots of room to play and fish in the burn.

Disabled Access:
Partial

Opening Times:
Sunday 29 May
2:00pm - 5:00pm

Admission:
£4.00 includes entry to both gardens, children under 12 free

Charities:
Friends of Hermitage Park receives 40%, the net remaining to SG Beneficiaries

Directions:
High Glenan: The garden is situated in West Helensburgh, approximately ½ mile along Queen Street from its junction with Sinclair Street on the right hand side.

Westburn: Proceed along West Montrose Street from Sinclair Street and take the fourth turn on the right, the entrance of Westburn is 100 yards up Campbell Street on the right hand side.

HILL HOUSE PLANT SALE
Helensburgh G84 9AJ
The National Trust for Scotland/SG T: 01436 673900
E: gsmith@nts.org.uk www.nts.org.uk

The plant sale is held in the garden of The Hill House which has fine views over the Clyde estuary and is considered Charles Rennie Mackintosh's domestic masterpiece. The gardens continue to be restored to the patron's planting scheme with many features that reflect Mackintosh's design. The sale includes a wide selection of nursery grown perennials and locally grown trees, shrubs, herbaceous, alpine and house plants.

Disabled Access:
Full

Opening Times:
Plant sale Sunday 28 August
11:00am - 4:00pm
Garden also open

Admission:
Donations welcomed.

Charities:
All proceeds to
SG Beneficiaries

Other Details: Teas will be served inside Hill House.

Directions: Follow signs to The Hill House.

KILARDEN
Rosneath G84 0PU
Carol Rowe

Sheltered hilly ten acre woodland with notable collection of species and hybrid rhododendrons gathered over a period of fifty years by the late Neil and Joyce Rutherford as seen on the *The Beechgrove Garden*.

Other Details: Homemade teas served in the church hall. The church will be open and there will be organ music to enjoy.

Directions: A quarter of a mile from Rosneath off B833.

Disabled Access:
Partial

Opening Times:
Sunday 17 April
2:00pm - 5:00pm

Admission:
£3.00, children free

Charities:
Friends of St Modan's receives 40%, the net remaining to SG Beneficiaries

---

ROSS PRIORY
Gartocharn G83 8NL
University of Strathclyde

Mansion house with glorious views over Loch Lomond with adjoining garden. Wonderful selection of rhododendrons and azaleas which are the principal plants in the garden, with a varied selection of trees and shrubs throughout. Spectacular spring bulbs, border plantings of herbaceous perennials, shrubs and trees. Extensive walled garden with glasshouses, pergola and ornamental plantings. Play area and putting green beside house.

Other Details: Cream teas are served in the house. Please note that the house is not open to view. Dogs on leads welcome except in the walled garden. Plant stall in the walled garden.

Directions: Gartocharn 1½ miles off A811. The Balloch to Gartocharn bus leaves Balloch at 13.52.

Disabled Access:
Partial

Opening Times:
Sunday 22 May
2:00pm - 5:00pm

Admission:
£5.00, children under 12 free

Charities:
CHAS receives 20%
University of Strathclyde Ross Priory gardens receives 20%, the net remaining to SG Beneficiaries

---

STUCKENDUFF
Shore Road, Shandon G84 8NW
Colin and Louise Burnet

Stuckenduff is a 3.5 acre garden overlooking the Gareloch with mature trees, rhododendrons, azaleas, mixed borders and a magical carpet of bluebells in May. The garden was partially re-landscaped in 2001 when a tennis court was laid alongside the original old walls.

Other Details: Live classical music will be performed during the afternoon.

Directions: Stuckenduff is on Shore Road, off the A814 after Blaidvadach Outdoor Centre opposite the post box.

Disabled Access:
Partial

Opening Times:
Sunday 15 May
2:00pm - 5:00pm

Admission:
£4.00, children under 12 free

Charities:
Music in Hospitals Scotland receives 40%, the net remaining to SG Beneficiaries

GLASGOW & NORTH LANARKSHIRE

Scotland's Gardens 2016 Guidebook is sponsored by **INVESTEC WEALTH & INVESTMENT**

District Organiser

Heidi Stone	15 Dun Park, Kirkintilloch G66 2DU E: glasgow@scotlandsgardens.org

Area Organisers

Mandy Hamilton	Flat 0/1, 12a Belhaven Terrace, Glasgow G12 0TG
Anne Murray	44 Gordon Road, Netherlee G44 3TW

Treasurer

Jim Murray	44 Gordon Road, Netherlee G44 3TW

Gardens open on a specific date

Kew Terrace Secret Gardens, Glasgow	Saturday 11 June	2:00pm	- 5:00pm
Kilsyth Gardens, Allanfauld Road, Kilsyth	Sunday 12 June	2:00pm	- 5:00pm
Crossburn, Stockiemuir Road, Milngavie	Sunday 19 June	2:00pm	- 5:00pm
123 Waterfoot Road, Newton Mearns, Glasgow	Sunday 26 June	2:00pm	- 5:00pm
Strathbungo Gardens	Sunday 3 July	2:00pm	- 5:00pm
Greenbank Garden, Flenders Road, Clarkston	Friday 8 July	6:30pm	
Glasgow Botanic Gardens, Glasgow	Sunday 10 July	2:00pm	- 5:00pm
Auchinstarry Sensory Garden, Kilsyth Marina	Sunday 17 July	2:00pm	- 5:00pm
Kamares, 18 Broom Road, Newton Mearns	Sunday 24 July	2:00pm	- 5:00pm

Gardens open by arrangement

Kilsyth Gardens, Allanfauld Road, Kilsyth	1 April - 30 September	07743 110908

Key to symbols

	New in 2016		Homemade teas		Accommodation
	Teas		Dogs on a lead allowed		Plant stall
	Cream teas		Wheelchair access		Scottish Snowdrop Festival

GARDEN LOCATIONS IN
GLASGOW & NORTH LANARKSHIRE

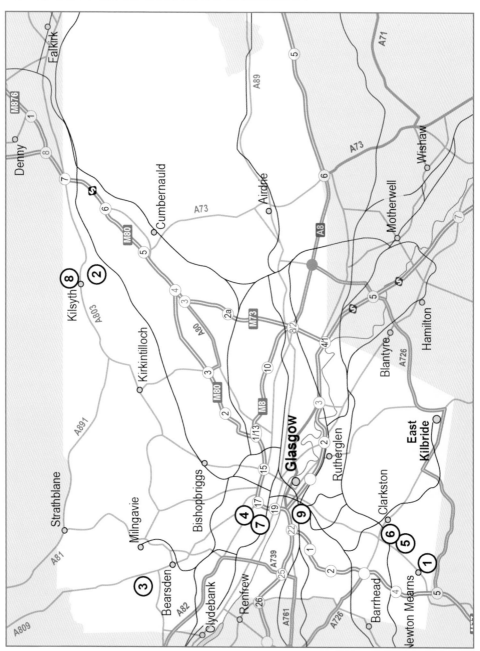

123 WATERFOOT ROAD
Newton Mearns, Glasgow. G77 5JT
Mrs Evi Berlow

From the entrance on Waterfoot Road the garden slopes down towards the house. There is a lawned area and the planting is mostly shrubs, trees and perennials. There is a good view of the garden from a decked terrace near the house. To the back of the house there is a small patio area with colourful potted plants standing on pebbles and slate and sheltered by wall climbing plants.

Other Details: Live piano music.

Directions: From Glasgow on the M77 take exit 3, turn left onto A726. After 1½ miles, take the A77 Ayr Road. Turn left on to Eaglesham Road. Then turn left at the junction and immediately right at the traffic lights on to Waterfoot Road. Local directions- turn left and follow Broom Road East go straight on past Mearns Castle Church continue down the hill to the farm.

Disabled Access:
Partial

Opening Times:
Sunday 26 June
2:00pm - 5:00pm

Admission:
£5.00 including teas, children free

Charities:
Cosgrove Care receives 40%, the net remaining to SG Beneficiaries

AUCHINSTARRY SENSORY GARDEN
Kilsyth Marina G65 9SG
Scottish Waterways Trust T: 07799493936
E: John@scottishwaterwaystrust.org.uk

Auchinstarry is a lovely sensory garden overlooking the marina on the Forth & Clyde Canal at Kilsyth. The gardens have been developed and maintained by volunteers from various groups. There are three living willow arches and many colourful and beautifully scented flowers and plants which are a delight to touch. Lovely seating areas to take in the beautiful views and to watch the activity on the canal.

Other Details: 20 minute boat trips around the marina and canal £5.00

Directions: Entrance on B802, which runs between Croy and Kilsyth. Croy Station is nearby. Bus Stagecoach 349.

Disabled Access:
Partial

Opening Times:
Sunday 17 July
2:00pm - 5:00pm

Admission:
£4.00

Charities:
Scottish Waterways Trust receives 40%, the net remaining to SG Beneficiaries

CROSSBURN
Stockiemuir Road, Milngavie G62 7HJ
Annika Sandell & Robert Johnston and Willie & Pat Anderson T: 0141 955 1789
E: mail@robertjohnston-architects.co.uk

The neighbouring gardens of Annika Sandell and Robert Johnston and Pat & Willie Anderson are set around a listed farm steading and include a host of delights, including a courtyard garden, a fruit and vegetables garden, woodland gardens with rhododendrons, azaleas, meconopsis, primulas, pulmonarias and many other species plants. There are two ponds, one for wildlife, the other a lily pond with a bog garden, blossoming herbaceous borders with daylilies, irises, astrantias, paeonies and some unusual perennial geraniums in abundance with many other goodies.

Directions: From Glasgow take A739 to Bearsden, Drymen Road, turn right on to A809 Stockiemuir Road, signposted Drymen, go straight through Baljaffrey Roundabout, continue to Crossburn Roundabout, take first left road to Douglasmuir Quarry. Glasgow City Bus 15 travels through Mains Estate opposite and First Bus 60A terminates in Mains Estate.

Disabled Access:
None

Opening Times:
Sunday 19 June
2:00pm - 5:00pm

Admission:
£6.00 including teas

Charities:
Allergy UK receives 40%, the net remaining to SG Beneficiaries

Crossburn

GLASGOW BOTANIC GARDENS
730 Great Western Road, Glasgow G12 0UE
Glasgow City Council T: 0141 276 1614

Glasgow Botanic Gardens encompasses 19.4 hectares of gardens and an arboretum. The collections have developed since the establishment of the Botanic Gardens in 1817. The Main Range glasshouses and the world renowned Kibble Palace offer a range of environmental conditions and host plants from around the world. The guided tours, led by senior Gardens staff, will take a look behind the scenes to see the backup collections, propagation facilities and the orchid laboratory. The tour will also include a visit to the Filmy Fern House, rarely seen by the public but not to be missed!

Other Details: National Plant Collection®: 3 Begonia, Dendrobium and Tree Ferns. Free trails and maps available in Kibble Palace. Refreshments at Botanic tea room.

Directions: The Gardens are located at the junction between Byres Road and Great Western Road. Closely located public transport stations include Hillhead (subway) and Partick (railway). Buses 6, 8, 10a and 19 stops nearby.

Disabled Access:
Partial

Opening Times:
Sunday 10 July
2:00pm - 5:00pm

Admission:
£5.00, OAP's £4.00,
children under 12 free

Charities:
The Friends of Glasgow
Botanic Gardens receives
40%, the net remaining to
SG Beneficiaries

GREENBANK GARDEN
Flenders Road, Clarkston G76 8RB
The National Trust for Scotland T: 0141 616 5126
E: dferguson@nts.org.uk www.nts.org.uk

A unique walled garden with plants and designs of particular interest to suburban gardeners. There are also fountains and a woodland walk. For one night only... the critically-acclaimed Pantaloons provide the evening's entertainment with theatre on the lawn. Join the pilgrims in this modern story-telling including puppets, music, rhyme & talking chickens! The show is pure medieval mayhem for the whole family.

Other Details: National Plant Collection®: Bergenia cvs. & spp. The Pantaloons bring Chaucer's Canterbury Tales to Greenbank Garden for a hilarious telling of all 23 tales in 2 hours! There is no disabled access to Greenbank House but full access to the garden.

Directions: Flenders Road, off Mearns Road, Clarkston. Off M77 and A727, follow signs for East Kilbride to Clarkston Toll. Bus 4a, Glasgow to Newton Mearns. Rail - Clarkston station 1¼ miles.

Disabled Access:
Full

Opening Times:
Friday 8 July
6:30pm

Admission:
£12.50 with £1.00 from each
ticket going to SG Charities.

Charities:
Donation to SG Beneficiaries

GLASGOW & NORTH LANARKSHIRE

KAMARES
18 Broom Road, Newton Mearns, Glasgow G77 5DN
Derek and Laura Harrison
E: laurah6367@gmail.com

Sitting in ⅔ acre, Kamares is a hacienda-style house surrounded on all sides by matures trees and a lovely beech hedge. The garden has much of interest including a well-established pond, a collection of acers, well-established and colourful mixed shrub and herbaceous borders, rare US sequoias and a living sculptural arbour. There are also several patio gardens, including a delightful courtyard with rockery. There are many sculptures and other artworks, particularly some fun topiary and cloud pruned pines. The owner is an artist and uses the garden as an alternative canvas.

Other Details: Very well stocked plant stall with established plants grown from the garden.

Directions: From A77 heading south, turn left into Broom Estate and sharp left again into Broom Rd. Kamares is last house on left near top of hill. On road parking is available beyond the house on Broom Rd, Broomcroft Rd, Sandringham Rd and Dunvegan Ave.

Disabled Access:
Full

Opening Times:
Sunday 24 July
2:00pm - 5:00pm

Admission:
£5.00

Charities:
Jewish Care Scotland receives 40%, the net remaining to SG Beneficiaries

KEW TERRACE SECRET GARDENS
Kew Terrace Lane, Glasgow G12 0TE
Professor George G Browning and other Garden Owners

Kew Terrace is one of the grand terraces that line Great Western Road when built in 1845 to 1849, only one of the 20 houses had a mews, the others had back gardens. Over the years the temptation to use them as car storage spaces has been resisted and now there is a series of 'Secret Gardens'. They all enhance green living in a city environment. A walk along the tree lined shrub border owned by Glasgow City at the front of the terrace and which is maintained by the Kew Terrace Association, is an example of what can be done to make the streets of Glasgow green and pleasant. Access to these private gardens is from tree-lined, cobbled Kew Terrace Lane.

Directions: From M8 take junction 17 (A82) and turn right onto Great Western Road. Continue one mile to cross over the Great Western Road/Byres Road junction. Kew Terrace is on the left and access is 250 yards beyond the traffic lights. Car parking may be difficult in the adjacent streets. The Kirklee area on the north side of Great Western Road usually has ample spaces and is a short walk away.

Disabled Access:
None

Opening Times:
Saturday 11 June
2:00pm - 5:00pm

Admission:
£6:00 includes entry to several gardens and homemade teas served from a marquee.

Charities:
Kew on Great Western Road Fund receives 40%, the net remaining to SG Beneficiaries

Blackmill, part of Kilsyth Gardens

KILSYTH GARDENS
Allanfauld Road, Kilsyth G65 9DE
Mr and Mrs A Patrick T: 07743 110908
E: alan.patrick3@googlemail.com

Aeolia:
A third of an acre woodland garden developed since 1960 and designed to have something in flower every month of the year. The garden contains a large variety of mature specimen trees and shrubs, maples, primulas, hardy geraniums and herbaceous plants. Spring bulbs provide early colour and lilies and dahlias provide late season interest. There are a couple of small ponds for wildlife, two greenhouses and a fruit production area. Owners are members of the Scottish Rhododendron Society and have a collection of over 100 specimens, some grown from seed. Areas of the garden are often under development to provide something new to see and provide material for the extensive plant sale, which is all homegrown.

Blackmill:
Across the road from Aeolia, Blackmill is a garden of two parts in that the Garrel Burn runs through the property. On one side is an acre of mature specimen trees, rhododendrons and shrubs on the site of an old waterpowered sickle mill. There is an ornamental pond and a rock pool built into the remains of the mill building. On the other side a further two acres of woodland glen with paths along the Garrel Burn with views to many cascading waterfalls one with a seven metre drop. New is a large area of wildflowers alongside the burn, a Micro Hydro scheme is on view along with many different types of dry stone walls.

Other Details: W.C. available but not suitable for disabled.

Directions: A803 to Kilsyth, through main roundabout. Turn left into Parkburn Road up to the crossroads. Short walk up Allanfauld Road. Buses X86 Glasgow-Falkirk, 24 Stirling-Kilsyth, 89 Glasgow-Kilsyth. The 89 service has a stop at the bottom of Allanfauld Road, a couple of minutes walk from the gardens.

Disabled Access:
Partial

Opening Times:
Sunday 12 June
2:00pm - 5:00pm
By arrangement
1 April - 30 September
Groups welcome.

Admission:
£6.50 includes entry to both gardens and homemade teas.

Charities:
Strathcarron Hospice receives 40%, the net remaining to SG Beneficiaries

STRATHBUNGO GARDENS
G41 2PX
The Gardeners of Strathbungo

An unexpected and interesting terrace cottage style garden in the city, showing what can be turned into a lovely colourful garden for all the occupants of the terrace to enjoy. Just across the road is the second garden, a verdant court garden taking full advantage of the limited light on offer. Streetscaping and innovative container planting are key features of these two distinct urban retreats.

Directions: From the south - take the M74 to junction 1A Polmadie. Turn left onto Polmadie Road, then turn right at next traffic lights onto Calder Street. Proceed to Nithsdale Drive, then turn left into March Street, where ample parking can be found. From the M8, join the M74 and turn right into Polmadie Road at Junction 1A.

Disabled Access:
Partial

Opening Times:
Sunday 3 July
2:00pm - 5:00pm

Admission:
£5.00 including refreshments

Charities:
Association of Local Voluntary Organisations receives 20%, The Divine Innocence Trust receives 20%, the net remaining to SG Beneficiaries

ISLE OF ARRAN

Scotland's Gardens 2016 Guidebook is sponsored by INVESTEC WEALTH & INVESTMENT

District Organiser

Mrs S C Gibbs	Dougarie, Isle of Arran KA27 8EB
	E: isleofarran@scotlandsgardens.org

Treasurer

Mrs E Adam	Bayview, Pirnmill, Isle of Arran KA27 8HP

Gardens open on a specific date

Brodick Castle & Country Park, Brodick	Tuesday 24 May	11:00am - 4:00pm
Brodick Castle & Country Park, Brodick	Thursday 26 May	7:00pm
The Glades, Whiting Bay	Sunday 19 June	2:00pm - 5:00pm
Brodick Castle & Country Park, Brodick	Thursday 30 June	7:00pm
Dougarie	Wednesday 6 July	2:00pm - 5:00pm
Brodick Castle & Country Park, Brodick	Thursday 28 July	7:00pm
Brodick Castle & Country Park, Brodick	Thursday 25 August	7:00pm

Brodick Castle

Key to symbols

New in 2016	Homemade teas	Accommodation
Teas	Dogs on a lead allowed	Plant stall
Cream teas	Wheelchair access	Scottish Snowdrop Festival

BRODICK CASTLE & COUNTRY PARK
Brodick, Isle of Arran KA27 8HY
The National Trust for Scotland T: 01770 302202
E: brodickcastle@nts.org.uk   www.nts.org.uk

At any time of year the gardens are well worth a visit, though especially in spring when the internationally acclaimed rhododendron collection bursts into full bloom. There are exotic plants and shrubs, a walled garden and a woodland garden to be enjoyed by garden enthusiasts, families and children. Venture out into the country park and discover wildflower meadows where Highland cows graze, woodland trails and tumbling waterfalls. There is something for everyone.

Other Details: National Plant Collection®: 3 rhododendrons. Champion Trees: Embothrium coccineum. **26/5** HG tour with Rhododendrons at finest. **30/6 & 28/7** Meet HG see latest in garden. **25/8** Tour walled garden with HG. Evening tours-must book. **24/5** Tearoom open. Dogs on leads welcome outside walled garden.

Directions: Brodick 2 miles. Buses from Brodick Pier to Castle. Regular sailings from Ardrossan and Claonaig (Argyll) call Caledonian MacBrayne, 01475 650100.

Disabled Access:
Partial

Opening Times:
Tues 24 May 11:00am -
4:00pm Tour with new Head
Gardener at 2:00pm and on
Thursdays 26 May,30 June
28 July, 25 August at 7:00pm

Admission:
£7.00 (inc. NTS members)
for tour. Normal Trust
admission applies for garden
and tour on 24 May.

Charities:
Donation to SG Beneficiaries

DOUGARIE
KA27 8EB
Mr and Mrs S C Gibbs
E: office@dougarie.com

Most interesting terraced garden in castellated folly built in 1905 to celebrate the marriage of the 12th Duke of Hamilton's only child to the Duke of Montrose. Good selection of tender and rare shrubs and herbaceous border. Small woodland area with interesting trees including Azara, Abutilon, Eucryphia, Hoheria and Nothofagus.

Other Details: Teas in 19th century boathouse.

Directions: Blackwaterfoot five miles. Regular ferry sailing from Ardrossan and Claonaig (Argyll). Information from Caledonian MacBrayne, Gourock, T: 01475 650100

Disabled Access:
None

Opening Times:
Wednesday 6 July
2:00pm - 5:00pm

Admission:
£3.50

Charities:
Pirnmill Village Association
receives 40%, the net
remaining to SG Beneficiaries

THE GLADES
Whiting Bay KA27 8QS
Mrs Susan Marriott

A recently developed garden with sweeping lawns surrounded by shrubs and herbaceous borders in the heart of Glenashdale. Whispering grasses lead to a rose and laburnum entwined pergola, banked by woodland plants and tree ferns. Spectacular gunnera edge a large spring pond.

Directions: Follow the signs for the Glenashdale Falls leaving the centre of the village at the Coffee Pot. It is a ten minute walk. Parking is available but limited.

Disabled Access:
None

Opening Times:
Sunday 19 June
2:00pm - 5:00pm

Admission:
£3.50

Charities:
Whiting Bay Improvements
and the Village Hall receives
40%, the net remaining to
SG Beneficiaries

RENFREWSHIRE

Scotland's Gardens 2016 Guidebook is sponsored by **INVESTEC WEALTH & INVESTMENT**

District Organisers

Mrs Rosemary Leslie | High Mathernock Farm, Auchentiber Road, Kilmacolm PA13 4SP T:01505 874032

Mrs Alexandra MacMillan | Langside Farm, Kilmacolm, Inverclyde PA13 4SA T: 01475 540423 E: renfrewshire@scotlandsgardens.org

Area Organisers

Mrs Helen Hunter | 2 Bay Street, Fairlie, North Ayrshire KA29 0AL

Mrs B McLean | 49 Middlepenny Road, Langbank, Inverclyde PA14 6XE

Mr J A Wardrop OBE DL | St Kevins, Victoria Road, Paisley PA2 9PT

Treasurer

Mrs Jean Gillan | Bogriggs Cottage, Carlung, West Kilbride KA23 9PS

Gardens open on a specific date

Ardgowan, Inverkip	Sunday 21 February	2:00pm	5:00pm
Highwood, Kilmacolm	Sunday 22 May	2:00pm	5:00pm
Carruth, Bridge of Weir	Sunday 5 June	2:00pm	5:00pm
Newmills Cottage, nr Lochwinnoch/Newton of Belltrees	Sunday 19 June	2:00pm	5:00pm
Gardening Leave, Erskine Hospital, Bishopton	Sunday 26 June	11:00am	3:00pm
Kilbarchan Village Gardens, Kilbarchan	Sunday 21 August	2:00pm	5:00pm

Plant sales

Kilmacolm Plant Sale, Lochwinnoch Road, Kilmacolm	Saturday 23 April	10:00am	12:00pm
Kilmacolm Plant Sale, Lochwinnoch Road, Kilmacolm	Saturday 10 September	10:00am	12:00pm

Key to symbols

 New in 2016

 Teas

 Homemade teas

 Dogs on a lead allowed

 Wheelchair access

 Accommodation

 Plant stall

 Scottish Snowdrop Festival

Cream teas

GARDEN LOCATIONS
IN RENFREWSHIRE

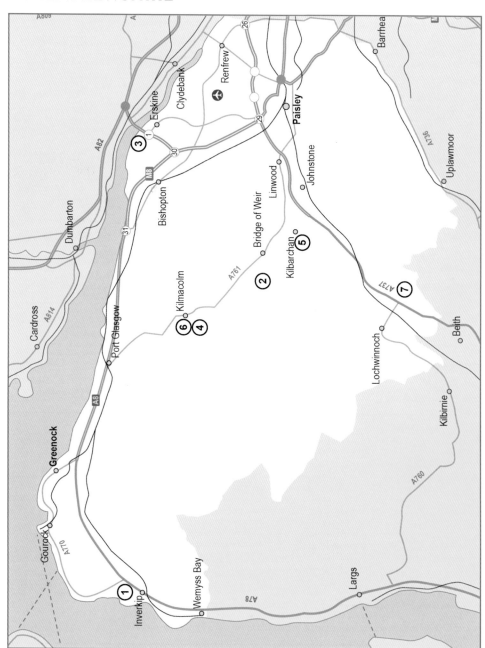

RENFREWSHIRE

ARDGOWAN

Inverkip PA16 0DW
Sir Ludovic Shaw Stewart T: 01475 521656/226
E: info@ardgowan.co.uk

Woodland walks carpeted with masses of snowdrops in a lovely setting overlooking the River Clyde.

Other Details: Snowdrops, both bunches and plants for sale.
If the weather is wet, the paths can be very muddy - sturdy waterproof footwear and clothing should be worn and wheelchair access in the garden is not possible.

Directions: Inverkip 1½ miles. Glasgow/Largs buses to and from Inverkip Village. Please use the main entrance at the roundabout to come in and leave by the Marina entrance to avoid congestion.

Disabled Access:
Partial

Opening Times:
Sunday 21 February
2:00pm - 5:00pm

Admission:
£2.00

Charities:
Greenock Medical Aid
Society receives 40%, the net
remaining to SG Beneficiaries

CARRUTH

Bridge of Weir PA11 3SG
Mr and Mrs Charles Maclean

Over 20 acres of long established rhododendrons, woodland with good bluebells and lawn gardens in lovely landscaped setting. There is also a young arboretum.

Directions: Access from B786 Kilmacolm/Lochwinnoch road. From Bridge of Weir take Torr Road until you get to the B786. Turn right and after approximately 100 yards the garden entrance is on the right. About 3½ miles from Kilmacolm and 5½ miles from Lochwinnoch on B786.

Disabled Access:
Partial

Opening Times:
Sunday 5 June
2:00pm - 5:00pm

Admission:
£4.00

Charities:
Marie Curie Cancer Care
receives 40%, the net
remaining to SG Beneficiaries

GARDENING LEAVE

Old Garden Centre, Erskine Hospital, Bishopton PA7 5PU
Gardening Leave T: 0141 814 4506
www.gardeningleave.org

Large enclosed tarmac garden located on site of the old garden centre at Erskine Hospital. Run by charity Gardening Leave providing sessions of horticultural therapy to serving and ex members of the Armed Forces. A productive garden, housing quirky assortment of raised planters, imaginatively created lawn area, shady wildlife/quiet garden, covered growing areas and other features embracing the up-cycling ethos. Still being developed and evolving. An inspirational and worthwhile charity. Volunteers always welcome (and needed).

Other Details: There will be a stall with gardening goods, jams and pickles made on the premises by veterans. Soup, as well as teas, also available.

Directions: From M8, take exit for Erskine Bridge and turn off to Bishopton. From north, go over Erskine Bridge, take Bishopton turning. Located on south side of Erskine Bridge, enter Erskine Home Estate and follow signs for Gardening Leave.

Disabled Access:
Full

Opening Times:
Sunday 26 June
11:00am - 3:00pm

Admission:
£4.00, children under 16 free

Charities:
Gardening Leave receives
40%, the net remaining to
SG Beneficiaries

HIGHWOOD
Kilmacolm PA13 4TA
Jill Morgan

Woodland walk around 50 acres of beautiful native bluebells in a delightful setting bordering the Green Water River with tumbling waterfalls. Stout waterproof footwear is essential as paths can be muddy. Dogs welcome on a lead. Fantastic opportunities for lovers of wild flowers and photography.

Other Details: Delicious home baked tea and plant sale. Fun duck race on the river for families at 3:30pm with rubber ducks available for purchase on the day.

Directions: Take B786 Lochwinnoch Road out of Kilmacolm and continue for approximately two miles then follow SG signs. From Lochwinnoch take B786 Kilmacolm road for approximately six miles, then follow SG signs.

Disabled Access:
Partial

Opening Times:
Sunday 22 May
2:00pm - 5:00pm

Admission:
Donations welcome

Charities:
Orkidstudio receives
40%, the net remaining to
SG Beneficiaries

KILBARCHAN VILLAGE GARDENS
PA10
Kilbarchan Village Gardeners

Taylor Avenue and Yardshead represent the new and old sides of this traditional weaving village which was used for filming Dr Finlay's Casebook.

No.8 Taylor Avenue
Small garden, well stocked with mature shrubs, herbaceous plants and climbers.

No.12 Taylor Avenue
Established triangular garden, with paths leading to different areas, which have survived the onslaught of children. Deceptively larger than it first appears.

No.14 Taylor Avenue
Large corner site with orchard, fruit and veg plot, lawns with new and established borders with annual, perennials and shrubs providing year round colour.

Yardshead
In contrast, the two gardens in Yardshead in the older part of village, down narrow lane next to Dental Surgery, have a less common format displaying late summer flowering.

Other Details: Afternoon teas and plant sale at 14 Taylor Avenue.

Directions:
From A737, travelling west from M8, take Kilbarchan turning, drive through village up Shuttle street, take second left after Dental Surgery into Taylor Avenue.

From A737, travelling east from Beith, turn off at Howwood through village towards Johnstone, turn left at mini roundabout, pass bus depot and Milliken Park rail station, to second mini roundabout and left into Kilbarchan.

From A761 Bridge of Weir, take Kilbarchan Rd at old railway bridge on edge of village. Uphill past church, past leather works, narrow bridge and over steep hill to Locher Rd Kilbarchan. Taylor Avenue second on right. McGills Bus 38 from Glasgow/Paisley stops just near Taylor Avenue. National cycle route 7 goes through Kilbarchan.

Disabled Access:
Partial

Opening Times:
Sunday 21 August
2:00pm - 5:00pm

Admission:
£4.00

Charities:
St Vincents Hospice receives
20%, Plantlife Scotland
receives 20%, the net
remaining to SG Beneficiaries

RENFREWSHIRE

KILMACOLM PLANT SALE
Outside Kilmacolm Library, Lochwinnoch Road, Kilmacolm PA13 4EL
Scotland's Gardens - Renfrewshire

Spring and end of season plant sales in the centre of Kilmacolm.

Directions: The plant sale will be held at the Cross outside the Library and Cargill Centre.

Disabled Access:
Full

Opening Times:
Saturday 23 April
10:00am - 12:00pm
Saturday 10 September
10:00am - 12:00pm

Admission:
Free, donations welcome

Charities:
Parklea "Branching Out" receives 40%, the net remaining to SG Beneficiaries

NEWMILLS COTTAGE
Nr Lochwinnoch/Newton of Belltrees PA12 4JR
Patricia Allan

Surviving mill in a series of five built in 1864. Well established colourful garden on different levels sloping down to the burn. The garden is divided into different areas with pots and hanging baskets filling areas which cannot be planted. There is also a pond. Steps down the garden are steep but it can be accessed from a gate on the road if needed and can still be seen from the lower level. Lovely colour and planting in a very peaceful setting. The garden has been extended since last opening in 2014.

Directions: Approach from Roadhead roundabout near Lochwinnoch (junction off A760/A737). Take turning by Powerdoors onto Auchengrange Hill. At T junction turn left onto Belltrees Road. Drive for 20 seconds then turn right. Go along the single track road and the garden is on the left after 1 mile.

Disabled Access:
Partial

Opening Times:
Sunday 19 June
2:00pm - 5:00pm

Admission:
£3.00, children under 16 free

Charities:
Kilbarchan Old Library receives 40%, the net remaining to SG Beneficiaries

Ardgowan

SOUTH LANARKSHIRE

Scotland's Gardens 2016 Guidebook is sponsored by **INVESTEC WEALTH & INVESTMENT**

District Organiser

Mrs V C Rogers	1 Snowberry Field, Thankerton ML12 6RJ E: lanarkshire@scotlandsgardens.org

Area Organisers

Mrs M Maxwell Stuart	Baitlaws, Lamington, Biggar ML12 6HR
Janis Sinclair	2 Meadowflatts Cottage, Meadowflatts Road, Thankerton ML12 6NF
David Tattersall	Struan View, Annanside, Moffat DG10 9HB

Treasurer

Mr Gordon Bell	9 Muirkirk Gardens, Strathaven ML10 6FS

Gardens open on a specific date

Cleghorn, Stable House, Cleghorn Farm, Lanark	Sunday 21 February	2:00pm	- 4:00pm
The Castlebank Gardens	Sunday 12 June	1:00pm	- 5:30pm
Dippoolbank Cottage, Carnwath	Sunday 19 June	2:00pm	- 6:00pm
Covington House, Covington Road, Thankerton, Biggar	Saturday 16 July	1:00pm	- 4:30pm
Dippoolbank Cottage, Carnwath	Sunday 17 July	2:00pm	- 6:00pm
Wellbutts, Elsrickle, by Biggar	Sunday 24 July	1:00pm	- 5:00pm
Beeches Cottage Nursery and Smallholding, Lesmahagow	Sunday 31 July	1:30pm	- 5:00pm
The Walled Garden, Shieldhill, Quothquan, Biggar	Sunday 7 August	2:00pm	- 5:00pm
Culter Allers, Coulter, Biggar	Sunday 14 August	2:00pm	- 5:00pm
Old Farm Cottage, The Ladywell, Nemphlar	Saturday 20 August	2:00pm	- 5:00pm

Gardens open by arrangement

Carmichael Mill, Hyndford Bridge, Lanark	Daily	01555 665880
The Scots Mining Company House, Leadhills, Biggar	1 April - 30 September	01659 74235

Key to symbols

	New in 2016		Homemade teas		Accommodation
	Teas		Dogs on a lead allowed		Plant stall
	Cream teas		Wheelchair access		Scottish Snowdrop Festival

GARDEN LOCATIONS IN SOUTH LANARKSHIRE

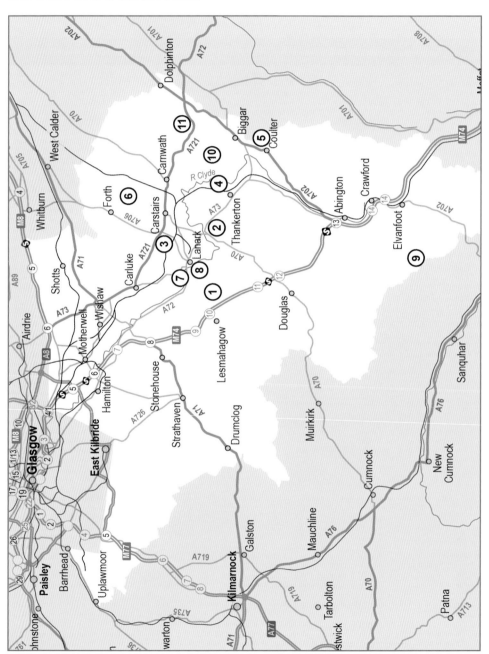

BEECHES COTTAGE NURSERY AND SMALLHOLDING
High Boreland, Near Hawksland, Lesmahagow. ML11 9PY
Steven and Margaret Harrison T: 01555 893369
E: thebeeches.nursery@talktalk.net www.beechescottage.co.uk

Situated at 850 feet Beeches is a working nursery and smallholding started from
a bare field 12 years ago and incorporates stunning herbaceous and mixed borders
planted to provide foliage and flower interest throughout the year. There is a large
fruit and vegetable garden, duckpond, newly planted woodland and other interesting
features which have been built using recycled materials. There are also pens
containing different breeds of ducks, geese and chickens.

Other Details: Dogs on a lead please.

Directions: Leave the M74 at Junction 9 and follow the B7078 looking for the
B7018 (Eastwood Rd), then first right Brocketsbrae Road, then first left Hawksland
Road until a proper crossroads and bear left.

Disabled Access:
Partial

Opening Times:
Sunday 31 July
1:30pm - 5:00pm

Admission:
£4.00

Charities:
Cancer Research UK receives
40%, the net remaining to
SG Beneficiaries

CARMICHAEL MILL
Hyndford Bridge, Lanark ML11 8SJ
Chris, Ken and Gemma Fawell T: 01555 665880
E: ken.fawell@btinternet.com

Riverside gardens surrounding the only remaining workable water powered grain mill
in Clydesdale. Diverse plant habitats from saturated to bone dry allow a vast range
of trees and shrubs, both ornamental and fruit, with a vegetable garden. Herbaceous
perennials, annuals and biennials with ornamental/wildlife pond complementing the
landscape. Also, archaeological remains of medieval grain mills from circa 1200 and
foundry, lint mill and threshing mill activity within the curtilage of the Category B
Listed Building.

Other Details: Admission includes entry to the mill which will be turning, river
levels permitting.

Directions: Just off A73 Lanark to Biggar road ½ mile east of the Hyndford Bridge.

Disabled Access:
Partial

Opening Times:
By arrangement on request

Admission:
£4.00, children over 12
£2.00

Charities:
Donation to SG Beneficiaries

CLEGHORN
Stable House, Cleghorn Farm, Lanark ML11 7RN
Mr and Mrs R Eliot Lockhart T: 01555 663792
E: info@cleghornestategardens.com www.cleghornestategardens.com

18th century garden which is permanently being renovated. There are mature trees
and shrubs, with masses of snowdrops spread around. Enjoy beautiful views to the
south of Tinto Hill and the Cleghorn Glen.

Directions: Cleghorn Farm is situated two miles north of Lanark on the A706.

Disabled Access:
Partial

Opening Times:
Sunday 21 February
2:00pm - 4:00pm

Admission:
By donation

Charities:
Marie Curie receives
40%, the net remaining to
SG Beneficiaries

SOUTH LANARKSHIRE

COVINGTON HOUSE
Covington Road, Thankerton, Biggar ML12 6NE
Angus and Angela Milner-Brown

A three acre old manse garden, including a walled garden, within the historic conservation area of Covington. The garden consists of an ornamental pond, herbaceous borders, species trees and shrubs, as well as a small amount of broadleaf woodland including a fernery. The 18th century walled garden has a potager with vegetables and flowers.

Other Details: Champion Trees: Wellingtonia. A beekeeping display with live observation hive of honey bees at work will be available (weather dependent).

Directions: One mile along Covington Road from Thankerton on the left.

Disabled Access:
Partial

Opening Times:
Saturday 16 July
1:00pm - 4:30pm

Admission:
£4.00

Charities:
Music in Lanark receives 40%, the net remaining to SG Beneficiaries

CULTER ALLERS
Coulter, Biggar ML12 6PZ
The McCosh Family

Culter Allers, a late Victorian baronial house, has maintained its traditional one and a half acre walled kitchen garden, half with fruit and vegetables, the other half with mainly cut flowers and herbaceous borders. The policies of the house include woodland walks and an avenue of 125 year old lime trees leading to the village church.

Directions: In the village of Coulter, three miles south of Biggar on the A702.

Disabled Access:
Partial

Opening Times:
Sunday 14 August
2:00pm - 5:00pm

Admission:
£4.00, children free

Charities:
Coulter Library Trust receives 40%, the net remaining to SG Beneficiaries

DIPPOOLBANK COTTAGE
Carnwath ML11 8LP
Mr Allan Brash

Artist's intriguing cottage garden. Vegetables are grown in small beds. There are herbs, fruit, flowers, pond in woodland area with tree house and summer house. The fernery was completed in 2007. This is an organic garden which was mainly constructed with recycled materials.

Directions: Off B7016 between Forth and Carnwath near the village of Braehead on the Auchengray road. Approximately eight miles from Lanark. Well signposted.

Disabled Access:
None

Opening Times:
Sunday 19 June
2:00pm - 6:00pm
Sunday 17 July
2:00pm - 6:00pm

Admission:
£4.00

Charities:
The Little Haven receives 40%, the net remaining to SG Beneficiaries

---

OLD FARM COTTAGE
Old Farm Cottage, The Ladywell, Nemphlar, Lanark ML11 9GX
Ian and Anne Sinclair T: 01555 663345

This garden has previously opened as part of the Nemphlar Village trail but is opening this year to show the later summer flowering bushes and herbaceous plants. The property was previously a working farm but now is owned by a beekeeper and a gardener. The garden includes mixed borders, a wild flower area, a pond, an apiary and small orchard. The garden is about an acre and has a large grassed area and putting green.

Other Details: Beekeeping demonstrations at 2:30 and 3:30pm and an observation hive will be in situ. Close to the Nemphlar spur of the Clyde Walkway. Visitors are welcome to bring their own picnics. Shelter available if wet. Teepees for the children. Honey and Hive products available. Dogs on a lead please.

Directions: Leave A73 at Cartland Bridge (Lanark to Carluke Road) or A72 (Clyde Valley Road) at Crossford. Both routes well signposted.

Disabled Access:
Partial

Opening Times:
Saturday 20 August
2:00pm - 5:00pm

Admission:
£3.00, children £1.00

Charities:
Kilbryde Hospice receives 40%, the net remaining to SG Beneficiaries

---

THE CASTLEBANK GARDENS
ML11
The Gardeners of Castlebank Gardens T: 01555 662676
E: sylvia_russell@btinternet.com

Centred around the exciting restoration project of Castlebank Park which features a Victorian terrace, fairy dell, bog garden and horticultural centre. This park is being developed by community volunteers. Included is a five acre terraced woodland garden with an impressive collection of azaleas, rhododendrons and heathers. A meandering natural stream provides water features and many winding paths lead down to the river Clyde. Other gardens with seasonal interest to explore.

Other Details: The garden route is quite hilly in places and strong shoes are recommended.

Directions: From Westport in Lanark turn down Friars Lane. Go through main gates of Castlebank Park and park in the main car park where tickets and maps will be issued.

Disabled Access:
Partial

Opening Times:
Sunday 12 June
1:00pm - 5:30pm

Admission:
£5.00, children free

Charities:
Lanark Community Development Trust receives 40% Charity donations will be used for the restoration of Castlebank Gardens, the net remaining to SG Beneficiaries

SOUTH LANARKSHIRE

9 THE SCOTS MINING COMPANY HOUSE

Leadhills, Biggar ML12 6XS
Charlie and Greta Clark T: 01659 74235
E: clarkc@sky.com

Disabled Access:
Partial

Opening Times:
By arrangement
1 April - 30 September

Admission:
£3.00

Charities:
Scots Mining Company
Trust receives 40%, the net
remaining to SG Beneficiaries

The site is about 400 metres above sea level, which is high for a cultivated garden. The surrounding landscape is open moorland with sheep grazing. The garden is largely enclosed by dense planting, but the various walks allow views through the trees into the surrounding countryside. Historic Scotland in its register of *Gardens and designed landscapes* describe the garden as "An outstanding example of a virtually unaltered, small, 18th century garden layout connected with James Stirling, the developer of the profitable Leadhills mining enterprise, and possibly William Adam." Say goodbye to spring walking among what must be some of the last daffodils of the year.

Other Details: Homemade teas available by prior request.

Directions: On Main Street, Leadhills (B797) six miles from M74 Junction 13 (Abington). Gate in Station Road.

10 THE WALLED GARDEN, SHIELDHILL

Quothquan, Biggar ML12 6NA
Mr and Mrs Gordon T: 01899 221961

Disabled Access:
Partial

Opening Times:
Sunday 7 August
2:00pm - 5:00pm

Admission:
£4.00

Charities:
Medicins sans Frontieres
receives 40%, the net
remaining to SG Beneficiaries

This 200 year old walled garden has been completely redesigned and planted in 2014/15 and is still a work in progress. It has been designed as a contemporary take on a traditional walled garden and incorporates a modern rill, perennial borders, a sunken sitting area and fruit and vegetable growing areas. It is surrounded by a mature woodland walk.

Directions: Turn off the B7016 between Biggar and Carnwath towards Quothquan. After about a mile, look for signs and turn right at the lodge.

11 WELLBUTTS

Elsrickle, by Biggar ML12 6QZ
Mr and Mrs N Slater

Disabled Access:
None

Opening Times:
Sunday 24 July
1:00pm - 5:00pm

Admission:
£4.00

Charities:
Macmillan Cancer Support
receives 40%, the net
remaining to SG Beneficiaries

Started in 2000 from a bare brown site around a renovated croft cottage, with additional field ground obtained in 2005, the garden is now approximately two acres. Due to the exposed and elevated (960 feet) position the ongoing priority is hedge and shrub planting to give some protection for the many and varied herbaceous borders, two large ponds and 'boggery'.

Other Details: Strawberry cream teas will be available.

Directions: Parking on the main road (A721) then walk to the garden (approximately 200 yards).

STIRLINGSHIRE

Scotland's Gardens 2016 Guidebook is sponsored by **INVESTEC WEALTH & INVESTMENT**

District Organiser

Mandy Readman	Hutchison Farm, Auchinlay Road, Dunblane FK15 9JS E: stirlingshire@scotlandsgardens.org

Area Organisers

Gillie Drapper	Kilewnan Cottage, Fintry G63 0YH
Maurie Jessett	The Walled Garden, Lanrick, Doune FK16 6HJ
Rosemary Leckie	Auchengarroch, 16 Chalton Rd, Bridge of Allan FK9 4DX
Iain Morrison	Clifford House, Balkerach Street, Doune FK16 6DE
Douglas Ramsay	The Tors, 2 Slamannan Road, Falkirk FK1 5LG
Fiona Wallace	Nether Spittalton, Coldoch, Blair Drummond FK9 4XD
Gillie Welstead	Ballingrew, Thornhill FK8 3QD
Clare Young	Merlo, Buchanan Castle Estate, Drymen G63 0HX

Treasurer

Rachel Nunn	9 Cauldhame Crescent, Cambusbarron FK7 9NH

Gardens open on a specific date

West Plean House, Denny Road, by Stirling	Sunday 28 February	1:00pm	- 4:00pm
Tamano, by Braco	Wednesday 2 March	2:00pm	- 4:30pm
Tamano, by Braco	Wednesday 9 March	2:00pm	- 4:30pm
The Pass House, Kilmahog, Callander	Sunday 24 April	2:00pm	- 5:00pm
Dun Dubh, Kinlochard Road, Aberfoyle	Sunday 15 May	2:00pm	- 5:00pm
Milseybank, Bridge of Allan	Sunday 22 May	2:00pm	- 5:00pm
Kippenrait with St Blanes House, Sheriffmuir, Dunblane	Sunday 29 May	2:00pm	- 5:00pm
Gartmore Village with the Walled Garden	Sunday 5 June	2:00pm	- 5:00pm
Park House, Blair Drummond	Sunday 19 June	1:00pm	- 5:00pm
Tillicoultry Allotments, Tillicoultry	Sunday 19 June	12:00pm	- 4:30pm
Thorntree, Arnprior	Sunday 26 June	2:00pm	- 5:00pm
Bridgend of Teith, Doune	Sunday 24 July	2:00pm	- 5:00pm
The Tors, 2 Slamannan Road, Falkirk	Sunday 31 July	2:00pm	- 5:30pm
Kilbryde Castle, Dunblane	Sunday 18 September	2:00pm	- 5:00pm
Little Broich, Kippen	Sunday 2 October	2:00pm	- 5:00pm
Harvest Lunch at Easter Culmore, Kippen	Sunday 9 October	12:30pm	

STIRLINGSHIRE

Gardens open regularly

Gargunnock House Garden, Gargunnock	1 February - 13 March Daily	11:00am	- 3:00pm
	16 Apr - 30 Sep (weekdays)	11:00am	- 3:30pm

Gardens open by arrangement

Arndean, by Dollar	16 May - 17 June	01259 743525
Duntreath Castle, Blanefield	1 Feb - 30 November	01360 770215
Gardener's Cottage Walled Garden, Killearn,	1 May - 31 October	01360 551682
Kilbryde Castle, Dunblane	1 April - 30 September	01786 824897
Manorcroft, Manor Loan, Blairlogie	1 May - 15 July	01259 761318
Milseybank, Bridge of Allan	1 April - 31 May	01786 833866
Plaka, 5 Pendreich Road, Bridge of Allan,	1 June - 30 September	01786 832287
Rowberrow, 18 Castle Road, Dollar	1 February - 31 December	01259 742584
The Linns, Sheriffmuir, Dunblane	15 February - 30 September	01786 822295
The Steading at Dollar, Yetts O'Muckhart	1 April - 15 October	01259 781559
The Tors, 2 Slamannan Road, Falkirk	1 May - 30 September	01324 620877
Thorntree, Arnprior	1 April - 15 October	01786 870710

Plant sales

Gartmore Village Plant Sale, Gartmore	Saturday 7 May	10:00am - 12:30pm

Key to symbols

	New in 2016		Homemade teas		Accommodation
	Teas		Dogs on a lead allowed		Plant stall
	Cream teas		Wheelchair access		Scottish Snowdrop Festival

GARDEN LOCATIONS
IN STIRLINGSHIRE

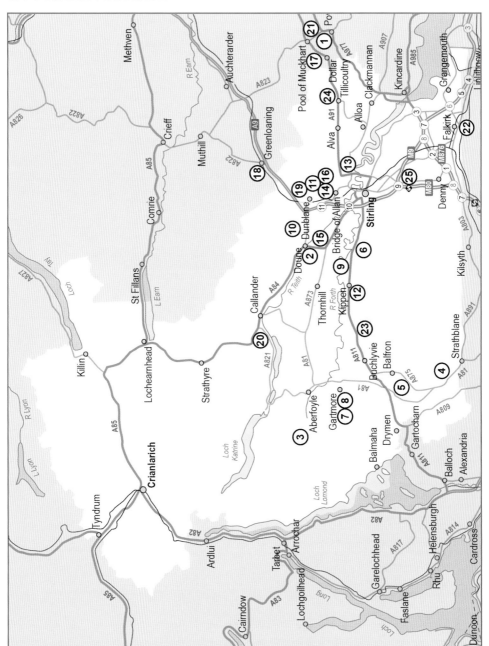

STIRLINGSHIRE

1 ARNDEAN
by Dollar FK14 7NH
Johnny and Katie Stewart T: 01259 743525
E: johnny@arndean.co.uk

This is a beautiful mature garden extending to 15 acres including the woodland walk. There is a formal herbaceous part, a small vegetable garden and orchard. In addition, there are flowering shrubs, abundant and striking rhododendrons and azaleas as well as many fine specimen trees. There is a tree house for children.

Other Details: Groups are welcome.

Directions: Arndean is well sign posted off the A977.

Disabled Access:
Full

Opening Times:
By arrangement
16 May - 17 June

Admission:
£5.00, children free

Charities:
Marie Curie Cancer Care
receives 40%, the net
remaining to SG Beneficiaries

2 BRIDGEND OF TEITH
Doune FK16 6AD
Colin and Caroline Stroyan T: 01786 841494
E: c.j.stroyan@btinternet.com

An oasis of calm above the Teith just south of Doune. Protected by glorious hedges including a 100 year old yew hedge. The shrubs and perennials are many and varied including an abutilon, a yellow weigela and unusual roses. There is also a lovely kitchen garden.

Other Details: Cream teas and music in St Modoc's Church. No dogs.

Directions: On the A84 just south of the Teith Bridge at the junction with the B8032. Follow the Garden Open signs. Disabled parking only at the house. Other parking opposite at the Chain Gate Lodge.

Disabled Access:
Partial

Opening Times:
Sunday 24 July
2:00pm - 5:00pm

Admission:
£4.00, accompanied children
free

Charities:
Crossroads Caring Scotland
(West Stirling Branch)
receives 40%, the net
remaining to SG Beneficiaries

3 DUN DUBH
Kinlochard Road, Aberfoyle FK8 3TJ
Callum Pirnie, Head Gardener T: 01877 382698
E: callumpirnie@gmail.com

A late Victorian garden of 6 acres undergoing restoration and development. Set on a series of terrace slopes running down to Loch Ard with superb views to Ben Lomond. There is an enclosed, colour themed formal garden on 3 terraces and a new Victorian style glasshouse overlooking a terraced kitchen and fruit garden. The paved terrace overlooks a newly developed rock garden & crag while the lower walk gives views across the Loch. A developing woodland garden leads to a formal late summer herbaceous border and terraced heather garden. Featured on *The Beechgrove Garden* May 2014 & *Scottish Field* in Nov 2014.

Other Details: Disabled badge holders parking. Free transport to/from Aberfoyle car park. Parking on road outside garden is dangerous & will be stopped. Guide dogs only.

Directions: Follow signs to car park in centre of Aberfoyle, look for the Garden Open signs. Minibus from Tourist Office bus stop. Turn around time about 15 minutes.

Disabled Access:
Partial

Opening Times:
Sunday 15 May
2:00pm - 5:00pm

Admission:
£4.00, children free

Charities:
Help for Heroes receives
40%, the net remaining to
SG Beneficiaries

DUNTREATH CASTLE
Blanefield G63 9AJ
Sir Archibald & Lady Edmonstone T: 01360 770215
E: juliet@edmonstone.com www.duntreathcastle.co.uk

Extensive gardens with mature and new plantings. Ornamental landscaped lake and bog garden. Sweeping lawns below formal fountain and rose parterre with herbaceous border leading up to an attractive waterfall garden with shrubs and spring plantings. Stunning display of snowdrops along the side of former drive. There is a woodland walk and a 15th century keep and chapel.

Other Details: Groups are welcome.

Directions: A81 north of Glasgow between Blanefield and Killearn.

Disabled Access:
Full

Opening Times:
By arrangement
1 February - 30 November

Admission:
£4.00, children free

Charities:
All proceeds to
SG Beneficiaries

GARDENER'S COTTAGE WALLED GARDEN
Ballochruin Road, Killearn, G63 9QB
Derek and Morna Knottenbelt T: 01360 551682
E: mornaknottenbelt@hotmail.com

Present owners acquired the garden in 2013 & planted large herbaceous borders with box hedging, roses & many unusual plants. There is a White garden, an orchard, vegetable area, long shrub border and an alpine border. The Victorian Fernery has peach & pear trees, vegetables & Salvias. Long season of interest; peonies, bulbs in spring, roses and herbaceous flowers in summer, many autumn flowers. The garden is surrounded by mature conifers of the Designed Landscape of Carbeth.

Other Details: Won the Hidden Gardens of Killearn trophy in 2014 and 2015.

Directions: From A811 from Stirling take turning to Balfron A875 go right through village towards Killearn, over bridge take next turning to right signposted Balfron Station. Entrance to drive second on left. From A81 from Milngavie, drive through Killearn & after ½ mile take next turning to left signposted Balfron Station. Avoid relying on Satnav with our postcode as it takes you to the wrong place.

Disabled Access:
Partial

Opening Times:
By arrangement
1 May - 31 October

Admission:
£5.00 includes garden tour and tea/coffee and scones. Groups welcome

Charities:
British Horse Society Scotland receives 40%, the net remaining to SG Beneficiaries

---

GARGUNNOCK HOUSE GARDEN
Gargunnock FK8 3AZ
The Gargunnock Trustees T: 01786 860392
E: gargunnockgardens@btinternet.com

Large mature garden with walled garden, well established house garden, woodland walks with species & hybrid rhododendrons, massed plantings of azaleas and wonderful specimen trees. Snowdrops in Feb/Mar, over 40 varieties of daffodils in April and glorious Azaleas and Rhododendrons in May. Late season colours from the wonderful trees along the drive. The 3 acre walled garden is being fully restored with perennial borders, cut flower beds, kitchen garden & newly planted orchard. Look inside gardeners' polytunnels; on guided tours they can explain their propagation methods. Picnic benches & seating in walled garden. New arboretum being planted in late 2015.

Other Details: Guided tours available for parties with refreshments; arrange using email above. Please note Gargunnock House will not be open. Plant Stalls at rear of Gargunnock House and in Walled Garden (Rhododendron, azaleas and shrubs)

Directions: Five miles west of Stirling on A811, follow the Scotland's Gardens signs.

Disabled Access:
Full

Opening Times:
1 Feb - 13 Mar 11:00am -
3:00pm for Snowdrop Festival
16 April - 30 September
11:00am - 3:30pm Mon - Fri

Admission:
£4.00, children free.
Honesty Box at the car park.

Charities:
Children's Hospice Association receives 20%, Gargunnock Community Trust receives 20%, the net remaining to SG Beneficiaries

STIRLINGSHIRE

7 GARTMORE VILLAGE PLANT SALE

The Village Hall, Main Street, Gartmore FK8 3RN
E: jo@oldmansegartmore.co.uk

Big plant sale to include plants from Gargunnock House Gardens and other sources. There will be demonstrations in the Hall of how to present produce for Horticultural Shows. It is the 100th anniversary of the Gartmore Horticultural Society, they also hosted *Gardener's Question Time* in September 2015.

Other Details: Please note this is a Saturday! Teas/coffees and homebaking in the Hall.

Directions: Gartmore Village is accessed via a loop road off the A81.

Disabled Access:
Full

Opening Times:
Plant sale Saturday 7 May
10:00am - 12:30pm

Admission:
£3.00, accompanied children free

Charities:
Crossroads Caring Scotland (West Stirling Branch) receives 40%, the net remaining to SG Beneficiaries

8 GARTMORE VILLAGE WITH THE WALLED GARDEN GARTMORE HOUSE

Main Street, Gartmore FK8 3RW
The Gardeners of Gartmore
E: ant@vinbay.co.uk

Several (at least six) attractive and interesting small gardens will be open in and around this beautiful peaceful village with splendid views. It is the 100th anniversary of the Gartmore Horticultural Society, they also hosted *Gardener's Question Time* in September 2015. More details on gardens on the SG website nearer the time.

Other Details: Soup and sandwiches will be served in The Walled Garden (Green Routes) at Gartmore House from 12:30pm. Cream teas and plant stall at the Village Hall. Map and entry ticket to all gardens can be purchased at any of the open gardens. Look for the yellow Garden Open signs.

Directions: Gartmore Village is on a small loop road off the A81 Glasgow - Aberfoyle Road which is well signposted. It is about four miles from Aberfoyle. The Walled Garden, Gartmore House will be signed from the A81.

Disabled Access:
Partial

Opening Times:
Sunday 5 June
2:00pm - 5:00pm

Admission:
£5.00, children free

Charities:
Crossroads Caring Scotland (West Stirling Branch) receives 20%, Green Routes receives 20%, the net remaining to SG Beneficiaries

9 HARVEST LUNCH AT EASTER CULMORE

Kippen, Stirlingshire FK8 8BQ
Neil and Mary Kenyon T: Iain Morrison 01786 841007
E: mor990@aol.com

Neil and Mary Kenyon are very kindly hosting this event in their Barn. There will be a short talk, music, a raffle and autumn floral displays by Fiona Wallace.

Other Details: Tickets available from Iain Morrison T: 01786 841007 or E: mor990@aol.com.

Directions: Easter Culmore is on the Dumbarton road at Kippen. At the sign for Glinns Road turn left. SG signs will be displayed.

Disabled Access:
Partial

Opening Times:
Sunday 9 October
12:30pm

Admission:
£20.00 to include lunch and a glass of wine

Charities:
SSAFA, the Armed Forces Charity receives 40%, the net remaining to SG Beneficiaries

KILBRYDE CASTLE
Dunblane FK15 9NF
Sir James and Lady Campbell T: 01786 824897
E: kilbryde1@aol.com www.kilbrydecastle.com

The Kilbryde Castle gardens cover some 12 acres and are situated above the Ardoch Burn and below the castle. The gardens are split into 3 parts: formal, woodland and wild. Natural planting (azaleas, rhododendrons, camellias and magnolias) is found in the woodland garden. There are glorious spring bulbs and autumn colour provided by clematis and acers.

Other Details: Cream teas available on 18 September only.

Directions: Three miles from Dunblane and Doune, off the A820 between Dunblane and Doune. On Scotland's Gardens' day the garden is signposted from A820.

Disabled Access:
Partial

Opening Times:
Sunday 18 September
2:00pm - 5:00pm
By arrangement
1 April - 30 September

Admission:
£4.00, children free

Charities:
Leighton Library receives 40%, the net remaining to SG Beneficiaries

---

KIPPENRAIT WITH ST BLANES HOUSE
Sheriffmuir, Dunblane FK15 0LP
Richard & Merete Stirling-Aird and Guy & Maud Crawford

Kippenrait FK15 0LP T: 01786 826888 E: merete@kippendavie.com. Created over 12 years, the garden has great views over Carse of Stirling, east to Dumyat & to mountains in west. Delightful 2½ acres of bulbs, rhododendrons, azaleas & other spring flowering shrubs, primulas & specimen trees. Small orchard & water feature.

St Blanes House FK15 0ER T: 01786 823310 E: maud.crawford@btinternet.com Opened as part of Dunblane Gardens in 2010. Well established two acre garden with a wide variety of trees, rhodendrons, azaleas and other shrubs and herbaceous perennials. There is a short walk through a wooded area.

Other Details: Paths may be slippery. Teas at Kippenrait. Plant stall at St Blanes.

Directions: For Kippenrait turn up Glen Road from Fourways roundabout Dunblane. After ¾ mile, turn left signposted Sheriffmuir, and after about ¼ mile turn right onto drive. St Blanes House is almost directly opposite Dunblane Library.

Disabled Access:
Partial

Opening Times:
Sunday 29 May
2:00pm - 5:00pm

Admission:
£5.00 for both gardens, accomp. children free

Charities:
Forth Driving Group RDA receives 40%, the net remaining to SG Beneficiaries

---

LITTLE BROICH
Kippen FK8 3DT
John Smith T: 01786 870275

A tree lover's heaven! A hidden arboretum of about eight acres, planted over the last twenty years, with an extensive collection of native and non-native conifers and broad-leaf specimens. Fern leaf oaks, Hungarian oaks, Cercidiphyllum and Glyptostrobus amongst many others around wide, slightly sloping grass paths (can be slippery when wet). Stunning views across the Carse of Stirling and the autumn colours should be outstanding. The garden featured in an October 2014 issue of *Scotland on Sunday* and on *The Beechgrove Garden*.

Other Details: No dogs except guide dogs.

Directions: Will be signposted off the B8037. Parking on the road, disabled badge holders can park at the bottom of the lane.

Disabled Access:
Partial

Opening Times:
Sunday 2 October
2:00pm - 5:00pm

Admission:
£4.00, children free

Charities:
Strathcarron Hospice receives 40%, the net remaining to SG Beneficiaries

13 MANORCROFT

Manor Loan, Blairlogie FK9 5PJ
Brian and Susan Jamieson T: 01259 761318
E: bj5.manorcroft@btinternet.com

An opportunity to visit a delightful garden. An informal garden of about ⅓ acre surrounded by a woodland area which was originally developed to provide shelter, but is now a feature itself. The underplanting is fascinating and includes rhododendrons, azaleas, Scottish fruit trees, spring bulbs, trilliums, hostas and ferns; there is a surprise around every corner. There is a superb selection of roses, including a Himalayan musk rose and a productive vegetable garden.

Other Details: When you phone to make an appointment you can book teas as well! Garden groups welcome. Please note parking is limited.

Directions: In the centre of Blairlogie follow the signs for the Farm Shop/Coffee Bothy and it is the first driveway on the right.

Disabled Access:
Full

Opening Times:
By arrangement
1 May - 15 July

Admission:
£4.00, children free

Charities:
Strathcarron Hospice receives 40%, the net remaining to SG Beneficiaries

---

14 MILSEYBANK

Bridge of Allan FK9 4NB
Murray and Sheila Airth T: 01786 833866
E: smairth@hotmail.com

Wonderful and interesting sloping garden with outstanding views, terraced for ease of access. Woodland with bluebells, rhododendrons, magnolias and camellias, and many other unusual plants, including a big variety of meconopsis. This is a true plantsman's garden.

Other Details: Teas at Lecropt Kirk Hall on 22 May only. Plant stall at Milseybank. Disabled parking only at the house, otherwise at the Kirk Hall or the Station Car Park.

Directions: Situated on A9, one mile from junction 11, M9 and a ¼ mile from Bridge of Allan. Milseybank is at the top of the lane at Lecropt Nursery, 250 yards from Bridge of Allan train station.

Disabled Access:
Full

Opening Times:
Sunday 22 May
2:00pm - 5:00pm
By arrangement
1 April - 31 May

Admission:
£4.00, accompanied children free

Charities:
Strathcarron Hospice receives 40%, the net remaining to SG Beneficiaries

15 **PARK HOUSE**
Blair Drummond FK9 4UP
Jamie and Sue Muir T: 01786 841799
E: jamie@blairdrummond.com

Mature three acre garden with herbaceous borders, lawns, vegetable and wild gardens. Extensive woodland walks lead to Camphill Blair Drummond.

Other Details: Homemade teas at Camphill. There will also be a plant stall.

Directions: Six miles NW of Stirling on A84. One mile after the Safari Park entrance turn right at sign to caravan park and continue up hill (speed bumps!) Go left at grass triangle and Park House is behind the hedge.

Disabled Access:
Full

Opening Times:
Sunday 19 June
1:00pm - 5:00pm

Admission:
£5.00, children free

Charities:
Camphill Blair Drummond receives 40%, the net remaining to SG Beneficiaries

---

16 **PLAKA**
5 Pendreich Road, Bridge of Allan, FK9 4LY
Malcolm & Ann Shaw T: 01786 832287
E: annshaw@mac.com

Plaka has previously opened with Bridge of Allan Gardens, it is half an acre of semi-terraced garden divided into outdoor rooms with wild spaces. There are beautiful rhododendrons, perennials, a water feature and two ponds. Also to be found in the garden are some interesting sculptures and stonework.

Other Details: Teas/coffees may be available, please check when you get in touch.

Directions: Turn into Blairforkie Drive in Bridge of Allan and follow the signs for the Golf Club. Plaka is on the left about 100 metres before the Golf Club.

Disabled Access:
Partial

Opening Times:
By arrangement
1 June - 30 September

Admission:
£3.00, accompanied children free

Charities:
Strathcarron Hospice receives 40%, the net remaining to SG Beneficiaries

---

17 **ROWBERROW**
18 Castle Road, Dollar FK14 7BE
Bill and Rosemary Jarvis T: 01259 742584
E: rjarvis1000@hotmail.com

On the way up to Castle Campbell overlooking Dollar Glen, this colourful garden has several mixed shrub and herbaceous borders, a wildlife pond, two rockeries, alpine troughs, fruit and vegetable gardens, and a mini-orchard. The owner is a plantaholic and likes to collect unusual specimens. Rowberrow was featured on the *Beechgrove Garden* in summer 2011.

Directions: Pass along the burn side in Dollar, turn right at T junction, follow signs for Castle Campbell and Dollar Glen. Park at the bottom of Castle Road or in the Quarry car park just up from the house.

Disabled Access:
Partial

Opening Times:
By arrangement
1 February - 31 December

Admission:
£4.00, children free

Charities:
Hillfoot Harmony Barbershop Singers receives 40%, the net remaining to SG Beneficiaries

18 TAMANO
By Braco FK15 9LP
Douglas and Tina Lindsay T: 01786 880271

A very informal woodland and wildlife garden with beautiful views. The garden has evolved, and is still evolving from a bare hillside 600 feet above sea level over the last 30 years. It is mainly planted with trees and shrubs, including a large number of rowans. There is a wildlife pond, stream and bog garden. Snowdrops and other early spring bulbs should be at their peak. A lovely courtyard area completes a wonderful experience. Featured in *Scotland on Sunday* in October 2014.

Other Details: Paths are grass and can be slippery and not all are suitable for wheelchairs.

Directions: Tamano is about 1½ miles north of Kinbuck. Coming from south to north on A9 turn on to B8033 from Dunblane to Kinbuck and go through Kinbuck towards Braco. From north to south turn off at the Greenloaning and Braco sign, turn left in Braco following signs for Kinbuck.

Disabled Access:
Partial

Opening Times:
Wednesday 2 March
2:00pm - 4:30pm
Wednesday 9 March
2:00pm - 4:30pm

Admission:
£3.00, children free

Charities:
Cancer Research receives 40%, the net remaining to SG Beneficiaries

19 THE LINNS
Sheriffmuir, Dunblane FK15 0LP
Drs Evelyn and Lewis Stevens T: 01786 822295
E: evelyn@thelinns.org.uk

A plantsman's garden of 3½ acres of mature woodland created from scratch since 1984 at west end of Ochils. It shows what is possible in what would otherwise be a windswept and bleak location. The layout of trees including beautiful species such as Cercidiphyllum japonicum, Acer griseum and Betula albosinensis, rhododendrons, hedges and walls, has created a wide variety of interesting and attractive garden spaces, giving a sense of exploration and surprise. From early Jan onwards it delights with drifts of near 100 forms of special snowdrops, a variety of large hellebores and dainty winter aconites. Then come corydalis, trilliums, erythroniums, daffodils etc. In summer a superb collection of Meconopsis and a woodland meander through many other well-loved perennials.

Other Details: No dogs except guide dogs. Plants may be on sale. Groups welcome. Phone or email for appointment.

Directions: Sheriffmuir by Dunblane.

Disabled Access:
Partial

Opening Times:
By arrangement
15 February - 30 September
includes the Snowdrop
Festival from 15 February -
13 March

Admission:
£4.00, children free

Charities:
Sophie North Charitable Trust receives 40%, the net remaining to SG Beneficiaries

The Pass House

THE PASS HOUSE
Kilmahog, Callander FK17 8HD
Dr and Mrs D Carfrae

Well planted, medium-sized garden with steep banks down to a swift river. The garden paths are not steep. There are lovely displays of camellias, magnolias, rhododendrons, azaleas, alpines and shrubs. The Scotland's Gardens plaque awarded for 25 years of opening is on display.

Other Details: Tea/coffee and a biscuit for a donation if the weather is fine.

Directions: Two miles from Callander on A84 to Lochearnhead.

Disabled Access:
None

Opening Times:
Sunday 24 April
2:00pm - 5:00pm

Admission:
£4.00, children free

Charities:
Crossroads Caring
Scotland(West Stirling
Branch) receives 40%,
the net remaining to
SG Beneficiaries

THE STEADING AT DOLLAR
Yetts O'Muckhart, by Dollar FK14 7JT
Fiona and David Chapman T: 01259 781559
E: david.fiona.chapman@gmail.com

Now 20 years old, this south-facing rural garden, situated at the foot of the Ochil Hills, continues to develop and rejuvenate. Curvaceous paths meander through a variety of terraced beds and ponds planted with a wide range of seasonal plants and species trees to give all year colour and interest.

Other Details: No dogs except guide dogs.

Directions: Situated at the Yetts o' Muckhart junction on the A823/A91 Dunfermline/Crieff road.

Disabled Access:
None

Opening Times:
By arrangement
1 April - 15 October

Admission:
£4.00, children free

Charities:
Muckhart Parish Church
receives 20%, Friendship
Club receives 20%, the net
remaining to SG Beneficiaries

THE TORS
2 Slamannan Road, Falkirk FK1 5LG
Dr and Mrs D M Ramsay T: 01324 620877
E: dmramsay28@yahoo.co.uk

An award winning Victorian garden of just over one acre with a secret woodland garden to the side and small orchard and wild area to the rear. Many unusual maple trees and rhododendrons are the main interest of this garden and there are several wildlife ponds and water features. Featured on the *Beechgrove Garden* for autumn colour in Sept 2010, but the best time to see garden is at end of July or the beginning of August. The *Scotland on Sunday* featured the house and garden in an article with many lovely photographs in September 2015.

Other Details: No dogs - except guide dogs.

Directions: The B803 to the south of Falkirk leads to Glenbrae Road. Turn right at the traffic lights into Slamannan Road and The Tors is a Victorian building immediately on the left. The Tors is within 200 yards of Falkirk High Station.

Disabled Access:
Partial

Opening Times:
Sunday 31 July
2:00pm - 5:30pm
By arrangement
1 May - 30 September

Admission:
£4.00

Charities:
Strathcarron Hospice receives
40%, the net remaining to
SG Beneficiaries

23 THORNTREE

Arnprior FK8 3EY
Mark and Carol Seymour T: 01786 870710
E: info@thorntreebarn.co.uk www.thorntreebarn.co.uk

Charming country garden with flower beds around a courtyard. The garden includes an Apple walk, Saltire garden and new Meconopsis bed. There are also lovely views from Ben Lomond to Ben Ledi. A bank of primroses greets you as you drive up to the courtyard at the end of April and the beginning of May.

Other Details: Plants are for sale throughout the year. No dogs except guide dogs. On 26 June, there may be coffee/tea and a biscuit for a donation if the weather is fine.

Directions: A811. In Arnprior take Fintry Road, Thorntree is second on the right.

Disabled Access:
Full

Opening Times:
Sunday 26 June
2:00pm - 5:00pm
By arrangement
1 April - 15 October

Admission:
£4.00, children free

Charities:
Forth Driving Group RDA receives 40%, the net remaining to SG Beneficiaries

24 TILLICOULTRY ALLOTMENTS

East Chapelle Crescent, Tillicoultry FK13 6NL
Tillicoultry Allotments Association
E: alandidcock@yahoo.co.uk

Set up 12 years ago the Allotments consist of more than 40 plots, mostly organic, in a sheltered site where hedges have been planted to form the boundaries. Within the plots a huge variety in planting of vegetables, fruit and flowers can be found. There is also a communal area and greenhouses, an impressive composting system and an area used by Alloa Academy. The site won the Community Shield for the best communal area for the last two years and individual plot holders have won prizes for their plots and produce.

Other Details: There will be a big plant stall, homemade teas, produce stall and tombola.

Directions: Turn down Bank Street, beside the Clydesdale Bank and continue on to Chapelle Crescent.

Disabled Access:
Full

Opening Times:
Sunday 19 June
12:00pm - 4:30pm

Admission:
£2.50, accompanied children free

Charities:
Strathcarron Hospice receives 20%, Tillicoultry Allotments Association receives 20%, the net remaining to SG Beneficiaries

25 WEST PLEAN HOUSE

Denny Road, by Stirling FK7 8HA
Tony and Moira Stewart T: 01786 812208
E: moira@westpleanhouse.com www.westpleanhouse.com

Beautiful woodland walks with snowdrops in February and March. This well established garden includes the site of an Iron Age homestead and panoramic views over seven counties. There are woodlands with mature rhododendrons, specimen trees, extensive lawns, shrubs and a walled garden with a wide variety of vegetables. Includes woodland walk with planting of azaleas and rhododendrons.

Other Details: On 28 February tea or coffee available by donation.

Directions: Leave all routes at Junction 9 roundabout where M9/M80 converge. Take the A872 for Denny, go less than a mile, turn left at the house sign and immediately after lodge cottage. Carry on up the drive.

Disabled Access:
Full

Opening Times:
Sunday 28 February
1:00pm - 4:00pm for the Snowdrop Festival

Admission:
£4.00, children free

Charities:
Scottish Motor Neurone Disease Association receives 40%, the net remaining to SG Beneficiaries

Each visit you make to one of our gardens in 2016 will raise money for our beneficiary charities:

In addition, funds will be distributed to a charity of the owner's choice. For West Central Scotland, these include:

Allergy UK

Appin Village Hall

Association of Local Voluntary Organisations

Break the Silence

British Horse Society Scotland

Camphill Blair Drummond

Children's Hospice Association

Christchurch Episcopal Church

CLASP

Cosgrove Care

Coulter Library Trust

Crossroads Caring Scotland

Diabetes UK

Erskine Hospital

Feedback Madagascar

Forth Driving Group RDA

Friends of Hermitage Park

Friends of Hillcrest

Friends of St Modan's

Friendship Club

Gardening Leave

Gargunnock Community Trust

Girl Guiding North Ayrshire

Green Routes

Greenock Medical Aid Society

Help for Heroes

Hessilhead Wildlife Rescue Trust

Hillfoot Harmony Barbershop Singers

Hope Kitchen -Oban

Jewish Care Scotland

Kew on Great Western Road Fund

Kilbarchan Old Library

Kilbryde Hospice

Lanark Community Development Trust

Leighton Library

Lochdon School

Macmillan Cancer Support

Marie Curie Cancer Care

Mary's Meals

Medicins sans Frontieres

MS Therapy Centre (Oban)

Muckhart Parish Church

Music in Hospitals Scotland

Music in Lanark

Orkidstudio

Pirnmill Village Association

Plant Heritage

Plantlife Scotland

Scots Mining Company Trust

Scottish Motor Neurone Disease Association

Scottish Waterways Trust

Sophie North Charitable Trust

SSAFA, the Armed Forces Charity

St Margaret's Parish Church, Dalry

St Vincents Hospice

The Cowal Hospice

The Dark Sky Observatory

The Divine Innocence Trust

The Friends of Glasgow Botanic Gardens

The Humane Research Trust

The Little Haven

The Scleroderma Society

Tillicoultry Allotments Association

Whiting Bay Improvements

SOUTH WEST SCOTLAND

Scotland's Gardens 2016 Guidebook is sponsored by **INVESTEC WEALTH & INVESTMENT**

DUMFRIESSHIRE

Scotland's Gardens 2016 Guidebook is sponsored by **INVESTEC WEALTH & INVESTMENT**

District Organiser

Mrs Sarah Landale	Dalswinton House, Dalswinton, Auldgirth DG2 0XZ E: dumfriesshire@scotlandsgardens.org

Area Organisers

Mrs Fiona Bell-Irving	Bankside, Kettleholm, Lockerbie DG11 1BY
Mrs Liz Mitchell	Drumpark, Irongray, Dumfriesshire DG2 9TX

Treasurer

Mr Harold Jack	The Clachan, Newtonairds DG2 0JL

Gardens open on a specific date

Craig, Langholm	Sunday 21 February	12:00pm	4:00pm
Barjarg Tower, Auldgirth	Wednesday 24 February	10:00am	4:00pm
Barjarg Tower, Auldgirth	Thursday 25 February	2:00pm	5:00pm
Barjarg Tower, Auldgirth	Saturday 27 February	10:00am	4:00pm
Barjarg Tower, Auldgirth	Wed/Thu 13/14 April	10:00am	4:00pm
Barjarg Tower, Auldgirth	Saturday 16 April	10:00am	4:00pm
Dalswinton House, Dalswinton	Sunday 17 April	2:00pm	5:00pm
Portrack House, Holywood	Sunday 1 May	12:00pm	5:00pm
Drumpark, Irongray	Saturday 14 May	11:00am	5:00pm
Capenoch, Penpont, Thornhill	Sunday 15 May	2:00pm	5:00pm
The Crichton Rock Garden & Arboretum	Sun 22 May	12:00pm	4:00pm
Dalswinton House, Dalswinton	Sunday 29 May	2:00pm	5:00pm
Amisfield Tower, Amisfield	Sunday 5 June	1:00pm	5:00pm
The Old Mill, Keir Mill, Thornhill	Sunday 12 June	2:00pm	5:00pm
Dunesslin, Dunscore	Saturday 18 June	10:00am	5:00pm
Cowhill Tower, Holywood	Sunday 19 June	2:00pm	5:00pm
Newtonairds Lodge, Newtonairds	Sunday 26 June	2:00pm	5:00pm
The Gardens of Middleshaw, Lockerbie	Sunday 26 June	2:00pm	5:00pm
Dalgonar, Dunscore, Dumfries	Sunday 3 July	2:00pm	5:00pm

Key to symbols

	New in 2016		Homemade teas		Accommodation
	Teas		Dogs on a lead allowed		Plant stall
	Cream teas		Wheelchair access		Scottish Snowdrop Festival

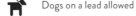

GARDEN LOCATIONS
IN DUMFRIESSHIRE

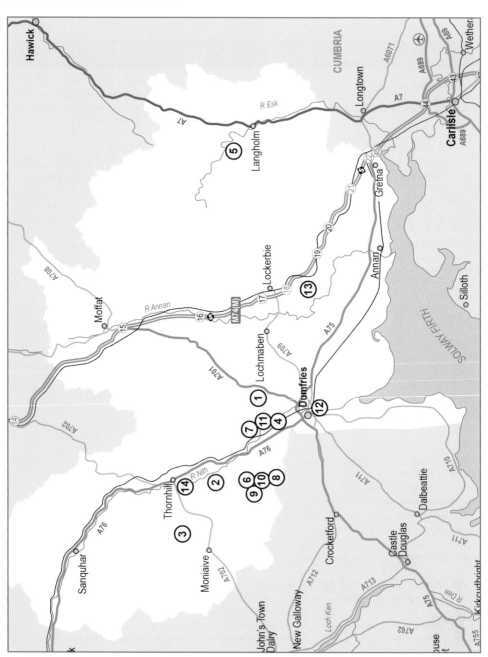

AMISFIELD TOWER
Amisfield DG1 3PA
Mrs Jane Johnstone
E: amisfield@hotmail.com

Large walled garden and greenhouses run by Coverglen Support Services for Adults with Learning Difficulties. Extensive policies around the house and border tower offer a good and interesting walk.

Other Details: Dogs are welcome but must be kept on a lead.

Directions: Take A701 from Dumfries towards Moffat. In Amisfield Village, after five miles, turn left at the crossroads towards Auldgirth and Duncow. Go straight over the next crossroads. Keep left and house is one mile further on on the right.

Disabled Access:
Partial

Opening Times:
Sunday 5 June
1:00pm - 5:00pm

Admission:
£4.00, children £0.50

Charities:
Coverglen Support Services
receives 40%, the net
remaining to SG Beneficiaries

BARJARG TOWER
Auldgirth DG2 0TN
Mary and Archie Donaldson T: 01848 331545

Barjarg Tower lies on a gentle slope enjoying the lovely views of the surrounding Lowther hills. The original Tower House dates back to the late 16th century but has had various cleverly designed additions over the years. The gardens have undergone considerable development since they were last opened to the public, though the carpets of snowdrops in the surrounding woods and the swathes of daffodils that line the driveway remain a tribute to the care of earlier generations.

Other Details: Morning coffee and afternoon teas are available in Auldgirth and Penpont tearooms. Both are equidistant at some four miles from Barjarg. Wear Wellies or strong shoes for your visit.

Directions: Situated on the C125 half way between Auldgirth and Penpont. Driving from Auldgirth, the stone, arched entrance is on the left hand side with Barjarg engraved on sandstone.

Disabled Access:
Partial

Opening Times:
Wed/Thu 24/25 February
Saturday 27 February
10:00am - 4:00pm
for the Snowdrop Festival
Wed/Thu 13/14 April
Saturday 16 April
10:00am - 4:00pm
for daffodils

Admission:
Honesty box for donations.
As a guide a minimum of
£3.00 per person would be
most welcome.

Charities:
Alzheimer's Research receives
40%, the net remaining to
SG Beneficiaries

CAPENOCH
Penpont, Thornhill DG3 4TZ
Mr and Mrs Robert Gladstone

There are rare trees throughout the grounds and the main garden is the remnant of the garden laid out in Victorian times. There is a pretty little raised knot garden called the Italian garden and a lovely old Victorian conservatory. Parking is available at the house but you may prefer to park in Penpont Village and walk up the drive to Capenoch as there are lovely bluebells and wild flowers in the oak woods on either side of the drive.

Other Details: There is a good variety of plants for sale in the old Walled Garden where Morag has the garden centre. This year homemade teas will be available in the Conservatory.

Directions: Take the A702 west from Thornhill, drive through Penpont and the entrance to the house is at the lodge on the left hand side, just at the speed restriction sign.

Disabled Access:
Partial

Opening Times:
Sunday 15 May
2:00pm - 5:00pm
for Bluebells

Admission:
£4.00, children £0.50

Charities:
The Jo Walters Trust receives 40%, the net remaining to SG Beneficiaries

---

COWHILL TOWER
Holywood DG2 0RL
Mr and Mrs P Weatherall T: 01387 720304

This is an interesting walled garden. There are topiary animals, birds and figures and a beautiful woodland walk. Splendid views can be seen from the lawn right down the Nith valley. There are also a variety of statues from the Far East.

Directions: Holywood one and a half miles off A76, five miles north of Dumfries.

Disabled Access:
Partial

Opening Times:
Sunday 19 June
2:00pm - 5:00pm

Admission:
£5.00, children £1.00

Charities:
Maggie's Cancer Caring Centres receives 40%, the net remaining to SG Beneficiaries

---

CRAIG
Langholm DG13 0NZ
Mr and Mrs Neil Ewart T: 013873 70230
E: nmlewart@googlemail.com

Craig snowdrops have evolved over the last 30 or so years. Round the house and policies a large variety have been planted with a varied flowering season stretching from the start of January until April and peaking mid-February. Large drifts of Leucojum Vernum (Winter Snowflake) have started to naturalise here and along the riverbank a variety of snowdrops, swept down by the river, have naturalised in the adjacent woodland, known as the Snowdrop Walk.

Other Details: Each walk takes about 20 minutes. Wellies are essential. Wheelchair access down by the river is not possible but easier around the house.
Teas will be available in the nearby Bentpath Village Hall from 2:00pm - 4:00pm.

Directions: Craig is three miles from Langholm on the B709 towards Eskdalemuir. The Village Hall is at Bentpath, one mile further towards Eskdalemuir.

Disabled Access:
Partial

Opening Times:
Sunday 21 February
12:00pm - 4:00pm for the Snowdrop Festival

Admission:
£4.00, children £0.50

Charities:
Kirkandrews Church receives 40%, the net remaining to SG Beneficiaries

DALGONAR
Dunscore, Dumfries DG2 0SS
Judge and Mrs William Crawford T: 01387 820339

There are well-wooded policies with woodland paths and a traditional , very well maintained walled garden containing an unusual and beautiful sundial.

Directions: Half a mile northwest of Dunscore, Dumfriesshire on the B729 road to Moniaive. Entrance through black gates on north side of the road.

Disabled Access:
Partial

Opening Times:
Sunday 3 July
2:00pm - 5:00pm

Admission:
£5.00, children under 16 free

Charities:
Dunscore Church receives 20%, Compassion in World Farming receives 20%, the net remaining to SG Beneficiaries

DALSWINTON HOUSE
Dalswinton DG2 0XZ
Mr and Mrs Peter Landale T: 01387 740220

Late 18th century house sits on top of a hill surrounded by herbaceous beds and well established shrubs, including rhododendrons and azaleas overlooking the loch. Attractive walks through woods and around the loch. It was here that the first steamboat in Britain made its maiden voyage in 1788 and there is a life-size model beside the water to commemorate this. Over the past year, there has been much clearing and development work around the loch, opening up the views considerably.

Other Details: There has recently been a new walk created through the woods at the back of the Walled Garden which leads to the village. For the daffodil opening, teas will be served in the newly refurbished village hall half way along the walk. Wear wellies.

Directions: Seven miles north of Dumfries off A76. Parking is available at the village hall.

Disabled Access:
Partial

Opening Times:
Sunday 17 April 2:00pm - 5:00pm for daffodils
Sunday 29 May
2:00pm - 5:00pm

Admission:
£5.00, children under 16 free

Charities:
Marie Curie Cancer receives 40% (April), Kirkmahoe Parish Church receives 40% (May), the net remaining to SG Beneficiaries

DUMFRIESSHIRE

DRUMPARK
Irongray DG2 9TX
Mr and Mrs Iain Mitchell T: 01387 820323

Well contoured woodland garden and extensive policies with mature azaleas, rhododendrons and rare shrubs among impressive specimen trees. Water garden with primulas and meconopsis. Victorian walled garden with fruit trees and garden produce. There is also a beautiful herbaceous border. All set in a natural bowl providing attractive vistas.

Other Details: The nearest place for teas and refreshments is either at the Auldgirth Tearoom or into Dumfries both equidistant at about five miles away.

Directions: From Dumfries bypass, head north on A76 for ½ mile, turn left at the signpost to Lochside Industrial Estates and immediately right onto Irongray Road; continue for five miles; gates in sandstone wall on left (½ mile after Routin' Brig).

Disabled Access:
Partial

Opening Times:
Saturday 14 May
11:00am - 5:00pm

Admission:
£5.00, children free

Charities:
Loch Arthur Community
(Camphill Trust) receives
40%, the net remaining to
SG Beneficiaries

DUNESSLIN
Dunscore DG2 0UR
Iain and Zara Milligan T: 01387 820345

Set in the hills with good views, the principal garden consists of a series of connecting rooms filled with herbaceous plants. There is a substantial rock garden with alpines and unusual plants and a hill walk to view three cairns by Andy Goldsworthy.

Directions: From Dunscore, follow the road to Corsock. Approximately 1½ miles further on, turn right at the post box, still on the road to Corsock and at small crossroads ½ mile on, turn left.

Disabled Access:
None

Opening Times:
Saturday 18 June
10:00am - 5:00pm

Admission:
£5.00, children under 16 free

Charities:
Alzheimer Scotland receives
40%, the net remaining to
SG Beneficiaries

NEWTONAIRDS LODGE
Newtonairds DG2 0JL
Mr and Mrs J Coutts
www.newtonairds-hostasandgarden.co.uk

An interesting 1.2 acre plantsman's garden punctuated with topiary, trees and shrubs, surrounding a 19th century listed baronial lodge. The National Collection is integrated with a further 150 other hosta varieties on a natural terraced wooded bank.

Other Details: National Plant Collection®: Hosta Plantaginea hybrids and cultivars. The plants, of which there is a great variety, are of exceptional quality and all grown and brought on in situ at Newtonairds Lodge.

Directions: From Dumfries take A76 north. At Holywood take B729 (Dunscore). After one mile turn left (Morrinton). After three miles red sandstone lodge is on right, behind black iron railings.

Disabled Access:
Partial

Opening Times:
Sunday 26 June
2:00pm - 5:00pm

Admission:
£4.00

Charities:
Peter Pan Moat Brae Trust
receives 40%, the net
remaining to SG Beneficiaries

PORTRACK HOUSE
Holywood DG2 0RW
Charles Jencks
www.charlesjencks.com

Original 18th century manor house with Victorian addition; octagonal folly library. Twisted undulating landforms and terraces designed by Charles Jencks as "The Garden of Cosmic Speculation"; lakes designed by Maggie Keswick; rhododendrons, large new greenhouse in a geometric kitchen garden of the Six Senses; Glengower Hill plantation and view; woodland walks with Nonsense Building (architect: James Stirling); Universe cascade and rail garden of the Scottish Worthies; interesting sculpture including that of DNA and newly completed Comet Bridge.

Other Details: Payment at the gate only, there are no pre-sale tickets available. Parking is provided in fields next to the garden. You will be directed to a space by the attendants. Buses can be accommodated. There will be a pipe band playing on the day.

Directions: Holywood one and a half miles off A76, five miles north of Dumfries.

Disabled Access:
Partial

Opening Times:
Sunday 1 May
12:00pm - 5:00pm

Admission:
£7.00

Charities:
Maggie's Cancer Caring Centres receives 40%, the net remaining to SG Beneficiaries

THE CRICHTON ROCK GARDEN AND ARBORETUM

The Crichton University Campus, Bankend Road DG1 4ZL

The Crichton E: elainecarruthers@easterbrookhall.co.uk

Over 100 acres of mature landscaped parkland in Dumfries makes up these famous grounds. The Rock Garden and Arboretum dating from the early 1900s house many unusual and striking plants. The extensive grounds offer enjoyable walking trails with stunning views of the surrounding countryside.

Other Details: Refreshments will be available in the Easterbrook Hall located at the centre of the Campus. A heritage walking route leaflet of the Crichton Estate will be available on arrival and will include directions of where to go.

Directions: Follow the B725 South out of Dumfries or, more easily, follow the signs for the hospital. Drive past the hospital on the right and continue on to the roundabout at the Easterbrook Hall Entrance.

Disabled Access:
Partial

Opening Times:
Sunday 22 May
12:00pm - 4:00pm

Admission:
£5.00, children free

Charities:
The Crichton Trust receives 40%, the net remaining to SG Beneficiaries

THE GARDENS OF MIDDLESHAW

Kettleholm, Lockerbie DG11 1BY

The Gardeners of Middleshaw T: 01576 510210

Middleshaw Gardens are a collection of rural gardens in many different styles in the Annandale Valley and are located within a short walking distance of the River Milk, a tributary of the River Annan. As a group they offer a variety of shrubs, borders, perennials and annuals, an impressive vegetable garden and fruit.

Half a mile away, White Hill DG11 1AL is also open as part of Middleshaw Gardens. It is best to drive to this garden and it will be well signposted on the day. There are azaleas, rhododendrons, a pond with a range of water-loving plants and great walks.

Directions: Middleshaw is to the west off the B723, four miles south of Lockerbie; one mile south of Kettleholm and six miles north of Annan. Proceed to Mrs Bell-Irving, Bankside, Kettleholm, Lockerbie DG11 1BY which will be signposted off the B723.

Disabled Access:
Partial

Opening Times:
Sunday 26 June
2:00pm - 5:00pm

Admission:
£4.00, children under 12 free

Charities:
Palliative Care Unit, Dumfries Hospital receives 20%, Alzheimer Scotland, Dumfries Branch receives 20%, the net remaining to SG Beneficiaries

THE OLD MILL

Keir Mill, Thornhill DG3 4DF

Mr Robin and Mrs Margaret Thomson

This is a maturing garden of shrubs and azaleas with beautiful herbaceous borders. There is also a naturalised pond and riverside boundary.

Directions: Situated in the village of Keir Mill on C125, one mile from Penpont on the Auldgirth road. There is car parking at the Village Hall.

Disabled Access:
Partial

Opening Times:
Sunday 12 June
2:00pm - 5:00pm

Admission:
£6.00 which includes homemade tea.

Charities:
Caerlaverock - Wildfowl and Wetlands Trust receives 40%, the net remaining to SG Beneficiaries

KIRKCUDBRIGHTSHIRE

Scotland's Gardens 2016 Guidebook is sponsored by **INVESTEC WEALTH & INVESTMENT**

District Organiser

Julian and Theodora Stanning

Seabank, Merse Road, Rockcliffe DG5 4QH
E: kirkcudbrightshire@scotlandsgardens.org

Area Organisers

Mr Hedley Foster	Deer Park, Fleet Forest, Gatehouse of Fleet DG7 2DN
Mrs Sheila McEwan	The Mill House, Gelston, Castle Douglas DG7 1SH
Mrs Lesley Pepper	Anwoth Old Schoolhouse, Gatehouse of Fleet DG7 2EF
Mrs C V Scott	14 Castle Street, Kirkcudbright DG6 4JA
Mrs Audrey Slee	Holmview, New Galloway, Castle Douglas DG7 3RN
Mr George Thomas	Savat, Meikle Richorn, Dalbeattie DG5 4QT

Treasurer

Mr Duncan Lofts

Balcary Tower, Auchencairn, Castle Douglas DG7 1QZ

Mill House at Gelston

KIRKCUDBRIGHTSHIRE

Gardens open on a specific date

Danevale Park, Crossmichael	Date to be confirmed	2:00pm	- 4:30pm
3 Millhall, Shore Road, Kirkcudbright	Sunday 17 April	2:00pm	- 5:00pm
Threave Garden, Castle Douglas	Sunday 8 May	10:00am	- 5:00pm
Corsock House, Corsock, Castle Douglas	Sunday 29 May	2:00pm	- 5:00pm
Cally Gardens, Gatehouse of Fleet	Sunday 5 June	10:00am	- 5:30pm
Broughton House Garden, Kirkcudbright	Thursday 9 June	6:00pm	- 9:00pm
Seabank, The Merse, Rockcliffe	Sunday 19 June	2:00pm	- 5:00pm
Glenlivet with The Limes, Kirkcudbright	Sunday 26 June	1:00pm	- 5:00pm
Southwick House, Southwick	Sunday 3 July	2:00pm	- 5:00pm
Crofts, Kirkpatrick Durham, Castle Douglas	Sunday 24 July	2:00pm	- 5:00pm
Cally Gardens, Gatehouse of Fleet	Sunday 7 August	10:00am	- 5:30pm
Threave Garden, Castle Douglas	Sunday 7 August	10:00am	- 5:00pm
3 Millhall, Shore Road, Kirkcudbright	Sunday 18 September	2:00pm	- 5:00pm

Gardens open by arrangement

Anwoth Old Schoolhouse, Anwoth, Gatehouse of Fleet	15 February - 15 November	01557 814444
Brooklands, Crocketford	1 February - 1 October	01556 690685
Corsock House, Corsock, Castle Douglas	1 April - 30 June	01644 440250
Stockarton, Kirkcudbright	1 April - 31 July	01557 330430
The Mill House at Gelston, Gelston	12 July - 13 September	01556 503955

Key to symbols

 New in 2016

 Homemade teas

 Accommodation

 Teas

 Dogs on a lead allowed

 Plant stall

 Cream teas

 Wheelchair access

 Scottish Snowdrop Festival

GARDEN LOCATIONS
IN KIRKCUDBRIGHTSHIRE

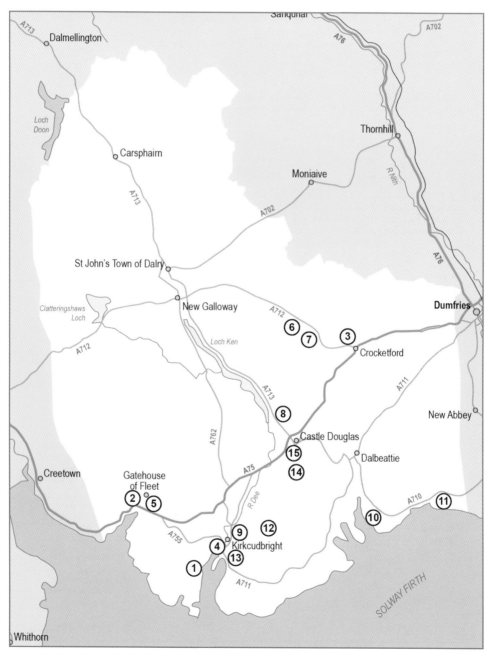

KIRKCUDBRIGHTSHIRE

1 3 MILLHALL
Shore Road, Kirkcudbright DG6 4TQ
Mr Alan Shamash

Impressive five acre garden with a large collection of mature shrubs, including rhododendron species, many camellias, perennials, hydrangeas and rare Southern Hemisphere plants. The garden is on a steep hillside running along the rocky shore of the Dee Estuary in Kirkcudbright Bay, close to the beach at the Dhoon and three miles from Kirkcudbright.

Directions: On the B727 between Kirkcudbright and Gatehouse of Fleet three miles off the A75 route Carlisle to Stranraer. Parking at The Dhoon public car park by the beach, with a five to ten minute walk to the house.

Disabled Access:
None

Opening Times:
Suns 17 April & 18 September
2:00pm - 5:00pm

Admission:
£4.00, children free

Charities:
The Kirkcudbright Hospital League of Friends receives 20% (April) Alzheimer's Research UK receives 20% (Sept), the net remaining to SG Beneficiaries

2 ANWOTH OLD SCHOOLHOUSE
Anwoth, Gatehouse of Fleet DG7 2EF
Mr & Mrs Pepper T: 01557 814444
E: lesley.pepper@btinternet.com

Two acres of delightful cottage style gardens behind the old schoolhouse and cottage in a picturesque setting opposite Anwoth old church (in ruins) and graveyard. Winding paths alongside burn, informally planted with unusual woodland perennials and shrubs. Wildlife pond, fish pond, rock garden, wildflower area and viewpoint, vegetable garden.

Directions: Driving west on the A75, take the Anwoth turnoff about half a mile after Gatehouse of Fleet. Anwoth Church is about half a mile along the road and Anwoth Old Schoolhouse is a little further along, opposite Anwoth Old Church (in ruins).

Disabled Access:
None

Opening Times:
By arrangement
15 February - 15 November

Admission:
£3.00

Charities:
Dogs for the Disabled receives 40%, the net remaining to SG Beneficiaries

3 BROOKLANDS
Crocketford DG2 8QH
Mr and Mrs Robert Herries T: Head Gardener John Geddes 01556 690685

Large old walled garden, richly planted with a wide variety of perennials, including many unusual species, soft fruit and vegetables. Mature woodland garden full of rhododendrons and carpeted with snowdrops in February and daffodils in spring.

Directions: Turn off the A712 Crocketford to New Galloway Road one mile outside Crocketford at the Gothic gatehouse (on the right travelling north).

Disabled Access:
Partial

Opening Times:
By arrangement
1 February - 1 October
Groups only

Admission:
£4.00

Charities:
All proceeds to
SG Beneficiaries

BROUGHTON HOUSE GARDEN
12 High Street, Kirkcudbright DG6 4JX
The National Trust for Scotland T: 01557 330437
E: broughtonhouse@nts.org.uk www.nts.org.uk

Broughton House Garden is a fascinating townhouse garden that belonged to
E A Hornel - artist, collector and one of the 'Glasgow boys'. Full of colour, mostly
herbaceous, old apple trees, greenhouse with old pelargonium varieties, fruit and
vegetable garden.

Other Details: Broughton House Garden by starlight. This event will offer
visitors an evening of live music, garden walks with our new Head Gardener and
refreshments (included in the entry price). It is a chance to see the garden in a
different light!

Directions: Off A711/A755 on Kirkcudbright High Street. Stagecoach buses 500/
X75 and 501 from Dumfries and Castle Douglas. By bike, NCN 7. Nearest train
station Dumfries, then taxi/bus to Kirkcudbright.

Disabled Access:
Partial

Opening Times:
Thursday 9 June
6:00pm - 9:00pm

Admission:
£4.00 includes refreshments

Charities:
Donation to SG Beneficiaries

CALLY GARDENS
Gatehouse of Fleet DG7 2DJ
Mr Michael Wickenden T: 01557 815029
E: info@callygardens.co.uk www.callygardens.co.uk

A specialist nursery in a densely planted 2.7 acre 18th century walled garden with
old vinery and bothy, all surrounded by the Cally Oak Woods. Our collection of
3,500 varieties of plants can be seen and a selection will be available pot-grown.
Excellent range of rare herbaceous perennials.

Other Details: The telephone at Cally Gardens is a recorded message only.

Directions: From Dumfries take the Gatehouse turning off A75 and turn
left through the Cally Palace Hotel gateway from where the gardens are well
signposted.

Disabled Access:
Full

Opening Times:
Sunday 5 June
10:00am - 5:30pm
Sunday 7 August
10:00am - 5:30pm

Admission:
£2.50

Charities:
ROKPA Tibetan Charity
receives 40%, the net
remaining to SG Beneficiaries

CORSOCK HOUSE
Corsock, Castle Douglas DG7 3DJ
The Ingall Family T: 01644 440250

Corsock includes an amazing variety of types of designed landscape, from a strictly
formal walled garden, through richly planted woodlands full of different vistas,
artfully designed water features and surprises to manicured lawns showing off
the Bryce baronial mansion. This is an Arcadian garden with pools and temples,
described by Ken Cox as 'the most photogenic woodland garden in Scotland.'

Directions: Off A75 Dumfries fourteen miles, Castle Douglas ten miles, Corsock
village ½ mile on A712.

Disabled Access:
Partial

Opening Times:
Sunday 29 May
2:00pm - 5:00pm
By arrangement
1 April - 30 June

Admission:
£4.00

Charities:
Corsock and Kirkpatrick
Durham Church receives
40%, the net remaining to
SG Beneficiaries

KIRKCUDBRIGHTSHIRE

7 CROFTS
Kirkpatrick Durham, Castle Douglas DG7 3HX
Mrs Andrew Dalton T: 01556 650235
E: jenniedalton@mac.com

Victorian country house garden with mature trees, a walled garden with fruit and vegetables and glasshouses, hydrangea garden and a pretty water garden. Delightful woodland walk, colourfully planted with bog plants, with stream running through.

Directions: A75 to Crocketford, then three miles on A712 to Corsock and New Galloway.

Disabled Access:
Partial

Opening Times:
Sunday 24 July
2:00pm - 5:00pm

Admission:
£4.00

Charities:
Kirkpatrick Durham Church receives 40%, the net remaining to SG Beneficiaries

8 DANEVALE PARK
Crossmichael DG7 2LP
Mrs M R C Gillespie T: 01556 670223
E: danevale@tiscali.co.uk

First opening for snowdrops in 1951 these mature grounds have a wonderful display of snowdrops as well as aconites and many other wild flowers.

Walks through the woods and alongside the River Dee, followed by an old fashioned afternoon tea in the house can make this a memorable day!

Other Details: In 2013 Mrs Gillespie was awarded the *Diana Macnab Award* for outstanding service to Scotland's Gardens.

Directions: On the A75 two miles from Castle Douglas and one mile short of Crossmichael.

Disabled Access:
Partial

Opening Times:
Date for the snowdrop opening to be advised, see SG website for details

Admission:
£2.50

Charities:
Poppy Scotland receives 40%, the net remaining to SG Beneficiaries

9 GLENLIVET WITH THE LIMES
Tongland Road, Kirkcudbright DG6 4UR
Alec and Doreen Blackadder T: 01557 332333
E: alec@alecblackadder.wanadoo.co.uk

This new town garden of half an acre on the edge of Kirkcudbright has been developed by the owners from scratch over the past seven years. It has a remarkably mature appearance already and is packed with colour and a huge variety of thriving plants, shrubs and trees, all carefully tended. There are two small ponds connected by a rill, with fountains at each end, herbaceous beds, gravel beds and a variety of statuary and garden structures. The garden is in a lovely position overlooking the River Dee. For details about The Limes please see garden entry 13.

Directions: Coming in to Kirkcudbright via the A711 and Tongland Bridge, on the outskirts of the town pass the Arden House hotel on the left. Glenlivet is about half a mile further on the right. It is exactly half a mile from the town centre crossroads on the Tongland Road. Parking is on the main road.

Disabled Access:
Partial

Opening Times:
Sunday 26 June
1:00pm - 5:00pm

Admission:
£5.00 includes entry to both gardens

Charities:
Friends of Kirkcudbright Swimming Pool receives 40%, the net remaining to SG Beneficiaries

SEABANK
The Merse, Rockcliffe DG5 4QH
Julian and Theodora Stanning T: 01556 630244

The one and a half acre gardens extend to the high water mark with fine views across the Urr Estuary, Rough Island and beyond. Herbaceous borders surround the house and there is a new walled garden for fruit and vegetables. A plantswoman's garden with a range of interesting and unusual plants.

Directions: Park in the public car park at Rockcliffe. Walk down the road about fifty metres towards the sea and turn left along The Merse, a private road. Seabank is the sixth house on the left.

Disabled Access:
Partial

Opening Times:
Sunday 19 June
2:00pm - 5:00pm

Admission:
£3.50

Charities:
Marie Curie (DG5 Fundraising Group) receives 40%, the net remaining to SG Beneficiaries

---

 SOUTHWICK HOUSE
Southwick DG2 8AH
Mr and Mrs R H L Thomas

The extensive gardens at Southwick House comprise three main areas. The first is a traditional formal walled garden with potager and large glasshouse producing a range of fruit, vegetables and cutting flowers. Adjacent to this is a hedged formal garden with herbaceous, shrub and rose beds centred around a lily pond, with roses predominating as an interesting feature. Outwith the formal gardens there is a large water garden with two connected ponds with trees, shrubs and lawns running alongside the Southwick Burn.

Directions: On A710 near Caulkerbush. Dalbeattie seven miles, Dumfries seventeen miles.

Disabled Access:
Partial

Opening Times:
Sunday 3 July
2:00pm - 5:00pm

Admission:
£4.00

Charities:
Friends of Loch Arthur Community receives 40%, the net remaining to SG Beneficiaries

---

 STOCKARTON
Kirkcudbright DG6 4XS
Lt. Col. and Mrs Richard Cliff T: 01557 330430

This charming garden was started in 1994. The aim has been to create small informal gardens around a Galloway farmhouse, leading down to a lochan, where there are a number of unusual small trees and shrubs. In 1996 a small arboretum of oak was planted, including some very rare ones, as a shelter belt.

Directions: On B727 Kirkcudbright to Gelston Road. Kirkcudbright three miles, Castle Douglas seven miles.

Disabled Access:
Partial

Opening Times:
By arrangement
1 April - 31 July

Admission:
£3.00

Charities:
Friends of Loch Arthur Community receives 40%, the net remaining to SG Beneficiaries

13 THE LIMES WITH GLENLIVET
Kirkcudbright DG6 4XD
Mr and Mrs McHale

Seven years ago this one and a quarter acre garden was mainly lawn, a few mature trees and some shrubs. There is now a large rock garden, gravel garden, mixed perennial and shrub borders and three woodland areas. The McHales grow most of their own fruit and vegetables. The greenhouse is used for propagating and protecting tender plants in winter, and tomatoes are grown in summer. Many new introductions are grown from seed, obtained from the seed exchanges of specialist plant groups. For details about Glenlivet please see garden entry 9.

Directions: In Kirkcudbright go straight along St Mary Street towards Dundrennan. The Limes is on the right, about ½ mile from the town centre crossroads, on the edge of the town (i.e. ½ mile in the opposite direction from Glenlivet).

Disabled Access:
Partial

Opening Times:
Sunday 26 June
1:00pm - 5:00pm

Admission:
£5.00 includes entry to both gardens

Charities:
Friends of Kirkcudbright Swimming Pool receives 40%, the net remaining to SG Beneficiaries

---

14 THE MILL HOUSE AT GELSTON
Gelston DG7 1SH
Malcolm and Sheila McEwan T: 01556 503955
E: sheilamcewan@yahoo.co.uk

Large cottage garden on several levels surrounding former Mill House, with adjacent stream and path along former mill lade. The garden is owned by a retired wildlife ranger who has recently planted swathes of colourful perennials especially to attract wildlife. It is now a haven for insects, butterflies and birds. Some of the conifers, planted by the previous owner, remain; in addition, large numbers of flowering plants, shrubs and trees have been planted during the past six years, giving this garden, which was previously opened by the former owner, a new emphasis and layout.

Directions: Travelling west along the A75, take the turnoff for Castle Douglas at the second Castle Douglas roundabout, then follow signs for Gelston. The Mill House is the last/first house in the village within the 30mph limit.

Disabled Access:
Partial

Opening Times:
By arrangement
12 July - 13 September

Admission:
£3.00

Charities:
The South of Scotland Wild Life Hospital receives 40%, the net remaining to SG Beneficiaries

---

15 THREAVE GARDEN
Castle Douglas DG7 1RX
The National Trust for Scotland T: 01556 502575
E: rapolley@nts.org.uk www.nts.org.uk

Home of the Trust's School of Heritage Gardening. Spectacular daffodils in spring, colourful herbaceous borders in summer, striking autumn trees, interesting water features and a heather garden. There is also a working walled garden. For more information on the Scotland's Gardens event, please contact the property or visit *www.nts.org.uk/events/*.

Other Details: Champion Trees: Acer platanoides 'Princeton Gold'. National Vegetable Society workshops on growing vegetables on 8 May. Music in the Garden on 7 August. Cafe open daily. Plants and garden produce for sale. Self-catering accommodation available.

Directions: Off A75, one mile west of Castle Douglas. Whilst dogs are welcome on the wider Threave estate, only asssistance dogs are permitted in the garden.

Disabled Access:
Full

Opening Times:
Sunday 8 May
10:00am - 5:00pm
Sunday 7 August
10:00am - 5:00pm

Admission:
Normal NTS admission applies

Charities:
Donation to SG Beneficiaries

WIGTOWNSHIRE

Scotland's Gardens 2016 Guidebook is sponsored by INVESTEC WEALTH & INVESTMENT

District Organiser

Mrs Ann Watson	Doonholm, Cairnryan Road, Stranraer DG9 8AT
	E: wigtownshire@scotlandsgardens.org

Area Organisers

Mrs Eileen Davie	Whitehills House, Minnigaff, Newton Stewart DG8 6SL
Mr Giles Davies	Elmlea Plants, Minnigaff, Newton Stewart DG8 6PX
Mrs Andrew Gladstone	Craichlaw, Kirkcowan, Newton Stewart DG8 0DQ
Mrs Shona Greenhorn	Burbainie, Westwood Avenue, Stranraer DG9 8BT
Mrs Janet Hannay	Cuddyfield, Carsluith DG8 7DS
Mrs Enid Innes	Crinan, Creetown, Newton Stewart DG8 7EP
Mrs Annmaree Mitchell	Cottage 2, Little Float, Sandhead DG9 9LD
Mrs Vicky Roberts	Logan House Gardens, by Stranraer DG9 9ND

Treasurer

Mr George Fleming	Ardgour, Stoneykirk, Stranraer DG9 9DL

Gardens open on a specific date

Logan Botanic Garden, by Stranraer	Sunday 7 February	10:00am - 4:00pm
Dunskey Gardens and Maze, Portpatrick	Saturday 13 February	10:00am - 4:00pm
Dunskey Gardens and Maze, Portpatrick	Sunday 14 February	10:00am - 4:00pm
Logan Botanic Garden, by Stranraer	Sunday 14 February	10:00am - 4:00pm
Dunskey Gardens and Maze, Portpatrick	Saturday 20 February	10:00am - 4:00pm
Dunskey Gardens and Maze, Portpatrick	Sunday 21 February	10:00am - 4:00pm
Logan Botanic Garden, by Stranraer	Sunday 21 February	10:00am - 4:00pm
Logan Botanic Garden, by Stranraer	Sunday 28 February	10:00am - 4:00pm
Claymoddie Garden, Newton Stewart	Sunday 24 April	11:00am - 5:00pm
Logan House Gardens, by Stranraer	Sunday 15 May	1:00pm - 4:30pm
Logan Botanic Garden, by Stranraer	Sunday 22 May	10:00am - 5:00pm
Woodfall Gardens, Glasserton	Sunday 19 June	10:30am - 4:30pm
Ardoch with Damnaglaur House , Stranraer	Sunday 3 July	1:00pm - 5:00pm
Woodfall Gardens, Glasserton	Sunday 10 July	10:30am - 4:30pm
Hill Cottage, Portlogan, Stranraer	Sunday 24 July	1:00pm - 4:00pm

WIGTOWNSHIRE

Gardens open regularly

Claymoddie Garden, Newton Stewart	1 April - 30 September 1 October - 31 March	10:00am - 5:00pm Daylight hours
Dunskey Gardens and Maze, Portpatrick	25 March - 30 September	10:00am - 5:00pm
Glenwhan Gardens, Dunragit, by Stranraer	1 April - 31 October	10:00am - 5:00pm
Logan Botanic Garden, by Stranraer	15 March - 31 October	10:00am - 5:00pm
Logan House Gardens, by Stranraer	1 March - 30 September	10:00am - 5:00pm

Gardens open by arrangement

Dunskey Gardens and Maze, Portpatrick	22 February - 24 March	07899 092070
Woodfall Gardens, Glasserton	On request	woodfallgardens@btinternet.com

Claymoddie

Key to symbols

	New in 2016		Homemade teas		Accommodation
	Teas		Dogs on a lead allowed		Plant stall
	Cream teas		Wheelchair access		Scottish Snowdrop Festival

GARDEN LOCATIONS
IN WIGTOWNSHIRE

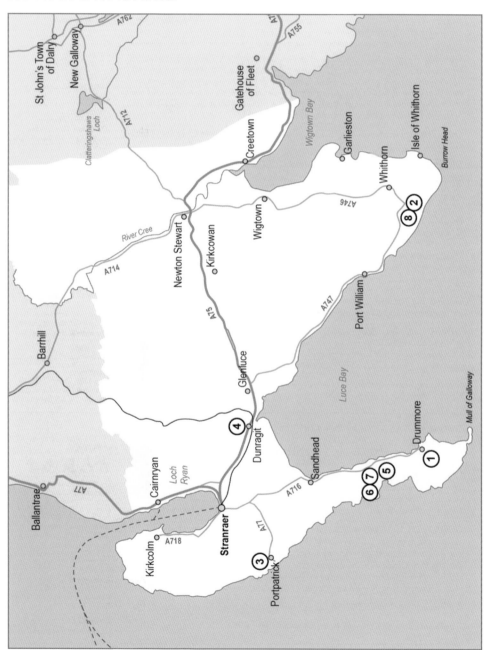

ARDOCH WITH DAMNAGLAUR HOUSE
Drummore, Stranraer DG9 9QN
Joy Hadley and Frances Collins T: Frances Collins 01776 840636
E: chunky.collins@btinternet.com

Disabled Access:
Partial

Opening Times:
Sunday 3 July
1:00pm - 5:00pm

Admission:
£4.00 (includes both
gardens)

Charities:
Various local charities
will receive 40%, the net
remaining to SG Beneficiaries

Ardoch: A rural garden of approx. two acres with a burn along one side. Under restoration after years of neglect. A large reinstated lawn area with many new areas: a rockery, heather bed, a new courtyard area, and large greenhouse with a succulent bed.

Damnaglaur House: A well-established garden. Landscaping & planting started in 1991, but is a work in progress, around a 200 year old stone house. Full of trees, shrubs and herbaceous plants, it gives colour year round, with gravel paths giving access even on wet days. Wind-defeating shrubs form a micro-climate in which tender & unusual plants thrive, while making a series of interlinked areas & providing glimpses through one area to the next. Stunning views over Luce Bay & Galloway Hills.

Other Details: Locally made crafts and plants. Teas nearby at Gallie Craig at the Mull of Galloway.

Directions: 100 yards north of Junction of B7041/B7065.

CLAYMODDIE GARDEN
Whithorn, Newton Stewart DG8 8LX
Mrs Mary Nicholson T: 01988 500422
E: mary.claymoddie@aol.co.uk www.claymoddiegarden.com

Disabled Access:
Partial

Opening Times:
Sunday 24 April
11:00am - 5:00pm
for Scotland's Gardens
1 April - 30 September
10:00am - 5:00pm rest of
year open during daylight hrs.

Admission:
24 April £5.00 per person.

Charities:
Macmillan Cancer Support
receives 40%, the net
remaining to SG Beneficiaries

This romantic five acre garden, designed and developed by the owner, an avid landscaper and plantsman, reflects 50 years of dedicated work. It provides timeless, intimate settings, shady and sunny, for a vast range of plants from both hemispheres, all helped by the proximity of the Gulf Stream. A burn feeds a large pond which, along with the variety of plants and a backdrop of mature woodland provides the perfect habitat for wildlife, in particular birds. There are changes in levels, but mostly accessible to wheelchairs.

Other Details: On 24 April only, light lunch/afternoon tea price £2.50. Groups welcome all year by arrangement. Guided tours also available by prior arrangement. Very good nursery with wide range of plants propagated from Claymoddie Garden, open daily. On other days no tearoom; Whithorn has several cafes.

Directions: From Whithorn: A746 for 2 miles to Glasserton crossroads, then right onto B7004. After 300 yards turn right up farm road signed Claymoddie.

DUNSKEY GARDENS AND MAZE
Portpatrick, Stranraer DG9 8TJ
Mr and Mrs Edward Orr Ewing T: 01776 810211
E: gardens@dunskey.com www.dunskey.com

Disabled Access:
Partial

Opening Times:
Sat/Sun 13/14 & 20/21 Feb
10am - 4pm (snowdrops)
25 Mar - 30 Sept 10am - 5pm
By arrangement
22 February - 24 March

Admission:
Snowdrops £4.00, under
16 £0.50, families £12.00.
Admission for other dates see
Other details

Charities:
Donation to SG Beneficiaries

Welcoming walled and woodland gardens with snowdrop walks. Forty-three named varieties of snowdrops including: Galanthus 'Dunskey Talia', Galanthus 'Fred's Giant', Galanthus 'Robin Hood', Galanthus 'Sickle'. Featured on *Beechgrove Garden* in 2013.

Other Details: National Plant Collection®: Clianthus, Sutherlandia and Nicotiana Gardener led strolls at 2:00pm on 14/21 Feb. Weds at 11:00am in summer. Designated dog walk, shaded parking for dog owners, dogs allowed on snowdrop walks but not in gardens. Picnic tables. Disabled loos and mobility scooter. Children's games and tree identification. Plant for sale all raised at Dunskey. Tearoom with soups and homemade food. 4-star gardens. See website for details and in extreme weather conditions.

Admission: Apr - Oct £5.50, conc £5.00, under16 £2.00, reduction for groups.

Directions: One mile from Portpatrick on B738 off A77.

GLENWHAN GARDENS

Dunragit, by Stranraer DG9 8PH
Mr and Mrs W Knott T: 07787 990702
E: www.glenwhangardens.co.uk

Glenwhan Garden has been described as one of the most beautiful gardens in
Scotland, situated at 300 feet, overlooking Luce Bay and the Mull of Galloway,
with clear views to the Isle of Man. Thirty-five years ago there was wild moorland,
but with dedication and vision, you can now see glorious collections of plants
from around the world. There is colour in all seasons and the winding paths, well
placed seats, and varied sculptures, focusing around small lakes, add to the tranquil
atmosphere. There is a 17 acre moorland wildflower walk, the chance to see red
squirrels and a well marked Tree Trail.

Other Details: Thriving plant nursery & tearoom with delicious home produce. Parties
catered for with notice. Although disabled access is partial, it is available in most parts.

Directions: Seven miles east of Stranraer, one mile off A75 at Dunragit (follow
brown VisitScotland signs).

Disabled Access:
Partial

Opening Times:
1 April - 31 October
10:00am - 5:00pm

Admission:
£5.00, season ticket £15.00,
family ticket £12.00 (up to
three children)

Charities:
Donation to SG Beneficiaries

HILL COTTAGE

Portlogan, Stranraer DG9 9NT
Mrs Mary Shaw

Hill Cottage is a half-acre cottage garden sitting amongst glorious scenery with
marvellous views over hills and down to the coast. Mainly a cottage garden with a
large natural rockery, small pond and vegetable plot.

Directions: Turn left from Port Logan, left again onto Killumpha Road about
quarter of a mile and it is the second cottage on the right.

Disabled Access:
Full

Opening Times:
Sunday 24 July
1:00pm - 4:00pm

Admission:
£4.00 (includes teas)

Charities:
Macmillan Nurses receives
40%, the net remaining to
SG Beneficiaries

LOGAN BOTANIC GARDEN

Port Logan, by Stranraer DG9 9ND
A Regional Garden of the Royal Botanic Garden Edinburgh T: 01776 860231
www.rbge.org.uk/logan

Logan is unrivalled as the country's most exotic garden. With a mild climate
washed by the Gulf Stream, a remarkable collection of bizarre and beautiful
plants, especially from the southern hemisphere, flourish out of doors. Enjoy the
colourful walled garden with its magnificent tree ferns, palms and borders along
with the contrasting woodland garden with its unworldly gunnera bog. The Logan
Conservatory which houses a special collection of tender South African species.

Other Details: National Plant Collection®: Gunnera/Leptospermum/Griselinia.
Champion Trees: Polylepis/Eucalyptus. Home baking, botanic shop, Discovery
Centre, audio tours and Logan Exhibition studio. Last entry one hour before closing.
Admission includes donation to garden; for prices without donation see rbge.org.uk.

Directions: 10 miles south of Stranraer on A716 then 2½ miles from Ardwell Village.

Disabled Access:
Full

Opening Times:
Suns 7/14/21/28 Feb 10am -
4pm for Snowdrop Festival
Sun 22 May 10am -5pm
15 March - 31 Oct 10 - 5pm

Admission:
£6.50, conc. £5.50, u16 free

Charities:
RBGE receives 40%, the net
remaining to SG Beneficiaries

WIGTOWNSHIRE

LOGAN HOUSE GARDENS
Port Logan, by Stranraer DG9 9ND
Mr and Mrs Andrew Roberts

The Queen Anne house is surrounded by sweeping lawns and a truly spectacular woodland garden. Rare and exotic plants together with champion trees and fine species of rhododendrons provide an excellent habitat for an interesting variety of wildlife.

Other Details: Champion Trees: seven UK and eleven Scottish Champions. Soup and rolls available from 1:00pm with teas served later in the afternoon. Lunches, teas and plant stall on 15 May opening only.

LOGAN HOUSE GARDENS ARE CELEBRATING THEIR 75TH GARDEN OPEN DAY FOR SCOTLAND'S GARDENS IN 2016

Directions: On A716 thirteen miles south of Stranraer, 2½ miles from Ardwell village.

Disabled Access:
Partial

Opening Times:
Sunday 15 May
1:00pm - 4:30pm
1 March - 30 September
10:00am - 5:00pm

Admission:
£4.00, children under 16 free

Charities:
Port Logan Hall receives 40%, the net remaining to SG Beneficiaries

WOODFALL GARDENS
Glasserton DG8 8LY
Ross and Liz Muir
E: woodfallgardens@btinternet.com www.woodfall-gardens.co.uk

This lovely three acre 18th century triple walled garden has been thoughtfully restored to provide year round interest. Many mature trees and shrubs including some less common species; herbaceous borders and shrub roses surround the foundations of original greenhouses; grass borders; a parterre; extensive beds of fruit and vegetables; a herb garden; a small woodland walk. This unusual garden is well worth a visit.

Other Details: Teas and home baking on 19 June only.

Directions: Two miles south-west of Whithorn at junction of A746 and A747 (directly behind Glasserton Church).

Disabled Access:
Partial

Opening Times:
Sundays
19 June & 10 July
10:30am - 4:30pm
By arrangement on request

Admission:
£4.00, children free must be accomp. by responsible adult

Charities:
Glasserton Parish Church & Macmillan Cancer Support each receive 20%, the net remaining to SG Beneficiaries

Each visit you make to one of our gardens in 2016 will raise money for our beneficiary charities:

In addition, funds will be distributed to a charity of the owner's choice.
For South West Scotland, these include:

Alzheimer Scotland, Dumfries Branch

Alzheimer's Research

Caerlaverock - Wildfowl and Wetlands Trust

Cloverglen Support Services Ltd

Compassion in World Farming

Corsock and Kirkpatrick Durham Church

Dogs for the Disabled

Dunscore Church

Friends of Kirkcudbright Swimming Pool

Friends of Loch Arthur Community

Glasserton Parish Church

Kirkandrews Church

Kirkmahoe Parish Church

Kirkpatrick Durham Church

Loch Arthur Community (Camphill Trust)

Macmillan Cancer Support

Macmillan Nurses

Marie Curie

Palliative Care Unit, Dumfries Hospital

Peter Pan Moat Brae Trust

Poppy Scotland

Port Logan Hall

RBGE

ROKPA Tibetan Charity

The Crichton Trust

The Jo Walters Trust

The Kirkcudbright Hospital League of Friends

The South of Scotland Wildlife Hospital

SOUTH EAST SCOTLAND

Scotland's Gardens 2016 Guidebook is sponsored by **INVESTEC WEALTH & INVESTMENT**

EDINBURGH & WEST LOTHIAN

Linlithgow

Edinburgh

Dalkeith

MIDLOTHIAN

Haddington

EAST LOTHIAN

Dunbar

Berwick-upon-Tweed

BERWICKSHIRE

Peebles

PEEBLESSHIRE

Galashiels

ETTRICK & LAUDERDALE

Jedburgh

ROXBURGHSHIRE

Hawick

BERWICKSHIRE

Scotland's Gardens 2016 Guidebook is sponsored by **INVESTEC WEALTH & INVESTMENT**

District Organiser

Mrs F Wills	Anton's Hill, Coldstream TD12 4JD
	E: berwickshire@scotlandsgardens.org

Treasurer

Mr F Wills	Anton's Hill, Coldstream TD12 4JD

Gardens open on a specific date

Anton's Hill, Leitholm, Coldstream	Sunday 22 May	2:00pm	- 5:00pm
East Gordon Smiddy, Gordon	Sunday 26 June	11:00am	- 5:00pm
Lennel Bank, Coldstream	Sunday 3 July	10:30am	- 5:00pm
Netherbyres, Eyemouth	Sunday 3 July	2:00pm	- 5:00pm
Anton's Hill, Leitholm, Coldstream	Sunday 10 July	11:00am	- 4:00pm
Kames, Greenlaw	Sunday 17 July	2:00pm	- 5:00pm

Gardens open regularly

Bughtrig, near Leitholm, Coldstream	Daily	11:00am	- 5:00pm

Gardens open by arrangement

Anton's Hill, Leitholm, Coldstream	On request	01890 840203
Lennel Bank, Coldstream	On request	01890 882297
Netherbyres, Eyemouth	1 May - 31 August	01890 750337

Key to symbols

	New in 2016		Homemade teas		Accommodation
	Teas		Dogs on a lead allowed		Plant stall
	Cream teas		Wheelchair access		Scottish Snowdrop Festival

GARDEN LOCATIONS
IN BERWICKSHIRE

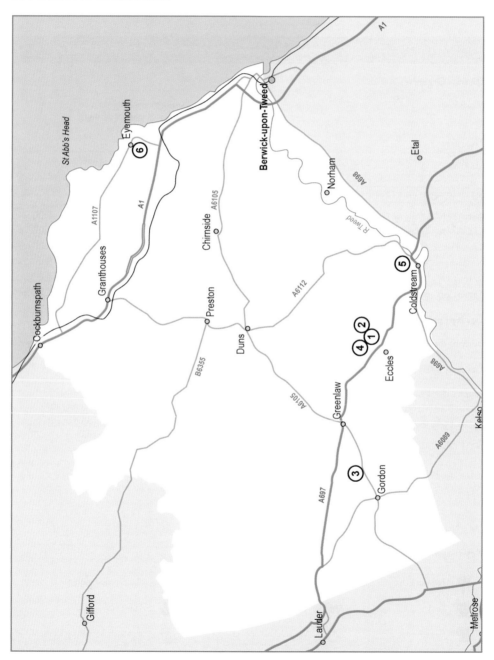

ANTON'S HILL
Leitholm, Coldstream TD12 4JD
Mr and Mrs F Wills T: 01890 840203
E: cillawills@antonshill.co.uk

A well treed mature garden which has been improved and added to since 1999. There are woodland walks and over 20 different varieties of oaks. The garden in spring has azaleas and rhododendrons, primroses and bluebells. There is a stumpery, a well planted pond, shrubberies and herbaceous borders, topiary elephant family of yew, shrub rose walk, leading to an acer glade with martagon lilies. There is a further pond planted with dogwood and gunnera with a hosta island.

Directions: Signposted off B6461, west of Leitholm.

Disabled Access:
Full

Opening Times:
Sunday 22 May
2:00pm - 5:00pm
Sunday 10 July
11:00am - 4:00pm
By arrangement on request

Admission:
£4.00

Charities:
Christ Church, Duns receives 40% (May), Oakfield, Easton Maudit receives 40% (Jul) net remaining to SG Beneficiaries

BUGHTRIG
Near Leitholm, Coldstream TD12 4JP
Mr and Mrs William Ramsay T: 01890 840777
E: ramsay@bughtrig.co.uk

A traditional hedged Scottish family garden with an interesting combination of sculpture, herbaceous plants, shrubs, annuals and fruit. It is surrounded by fine specimen trees which provide remarkable shelter.

Other Details: There will be plants for sale.

Directions: Quarter of a mile east of Leitholm on B6461.

Disabled Access:
Partial

Opening Times:
1 June - 1 September
11:00am - 5:00pm

Admission:
£4.00, children £1.00

Charities:
Donation to SG Beneficiaries

EAST GORDON SMIDDY
Gordon TD3 6JY
Martyn and Judith Welch

A garden newly created from farmland in 2008 with wonderful panoramic views towards the Cheviot Hills. Herbaceous borders, shrubbery, extensive vegetable garden and fruit trees. There is a pond, woodland and wildflower meadow. The whole garden is divided by mature hornbeam hedging, grass pathways and interesting corners to sit and contemplate.

Directions: On A6105 between Gordon and Greenlaw at East Gordon. On top of the hill at the farm entrance.

Disabled Access:
Full

Opening Times:
Sunday 26 June
11:00am - 5:00pm

Admission:
£5.00, children free

Charities:
Sustrans receives 40%, the net remaining to SG Beneficiaries

BERWICKSHIRE

KAMES
Greenlaw TD10 6UL
Mr & Mrs D Jenkinson

An old and well established garden with shrubs and herbaceous plants, with a superb view of the Cheviot Hills. There is a very attractive large landscaped lake, together with further pond, and a new woodland walk.The abandoned walled garden is currently five years into a restoration project and progressing well.

Other Details: Teas by the lake.

Directions: Take the A697 onto B6461 signposted Leitholm to Kames.

Disabled Access:
Full

Opening Times:
Sunday 17 July
2:00pm - 5:00pm

Admission:
£5.00, children free

Charities:
The Daisy Chain Trust receives 40%, the net remaining to SG Beneficiaries

LENNEL BANK
Coldstream TD12 4EX
Mrs Honor Brown T: 01890 882297

Lennel Bank is a terraced garden overlooking the River Tweed, consisting of wide borders packed with shrubs and perennial planting, some unusual. The water garden, built in 2008, is surrounded by a rockery and utilises the slope ending in a pond. There is a small kitchen garden with raised beds in unusual shapes. Different growing conditions throughout the garden from dry, wet, shady and sunny lend themselves to a variety of plants, which hopefully enhance interest in the garden.

Directions: On A6112 Coldstream to Duns road, one mile from Coldstream.

Disabled Access:
None

Opening Times:
Sunday 3 July
10:30am - 5:00pm
By arrangement on request

Admission:
£5.00

Charities:
British Heart Foundation receives 40%, the net remaining to SG Beneficiaries

NETHERBYRES
Eyemouth TD14 5SE
Col S J Furness T: 01890 750337

A unique 18th century elliptical walled garden. Annuals, roses, herbaceous borders, fruit and vegetables in summer.

Other Details: Plant stall on 3 July. Light refreshments.

Directions: Half a mile south of Eyemouth on A1107 to Berwick.

Disabled Access:
Full

Opening Times:
Sunday 3 July
2:00pm - 5:00pm
By arrangement
1 May - 31 August

Admission:
£5.00, concessions £4.00, children free

Charities:
Gunsgreen House Trust receives 40%, the net remaining to SG Beneficiaries

EAST LOTHIAN

Scotland's Gardens 2016 Guidebook is sponsored by **INVESTEC WEALTH & INVESTMENT**

District Organiser

Frank Kirwan

Humbie Dean, Humbie, East Lothian EH36 5PW
E: eastlothian@scotlandsgardens.org

Area Organisers

Bill Alder

Granary House, Kippielaw, Haddington EH41 4PY

Mark Hedderwick

Gifford Bank, Gifford EH41 4JE

Julie Parker

Steading Cottage, Stevenson, Haddington EH41 4PU

Judy Riley

The Old Kitchen, Tyninghame House, Tyninghame
EH42 1XW

June Tainsh

Amisfield Walled Garden, Haddington EH41 3TE

Treasurer

Joan Johnson

The Round House, Woodbush, Dunbar EH42 1HB

Humbie Dean

EAST LOTHIAN

Gardens open on a specific date

Shepherd House, Inveresk, Musselburgh	Saturday 20 February	11:00am	4:00pm
Shepherd House, Inveresk, Musselburgh	Sunday 21 February	11:00am	4:00pm
Winton House, Pencaitland	Sunday 10 April	12:00pm	4:30pm
Shepherd House, Inveresk, Musselburgh	Saturday 7 May	11:00am	4:00pm
Shepherd House, Inveresk, Musselburgh	Sunday 8 May	11:00am	4:00pm
Humbie Dean, Humbie	Thursday 12 May	2:00pm	6:00pm
Tyninghame House and The Walled Garden, Dunbar	Sunday 15 May	1:00pm	5:00pm
Traprain Garden Circle	Wednesday 25 May	11:00am	6:00pm
Humbie Dean, Humbie	Thursday 26 May	2:00pm	6:00pm
Stenton Village, East Lothian	Sunday 5 June	2:00pm	5:30pm
Humbie Dean, Humbie	Thursday 9 June	2:00pm	6:00pm
Dirleton Village, North Berwick	Sat/Sun 11/12 June	2:00pm	6:00pm
Traprain Garden Circle	Wednesday 15 June	11:00am	6:00pm
Inveresk Village, Musselburgh	Sunday 19 June	2:00pm	5:00pm
Humbie Dean, Humbie	Thursday 23 June	2:00pm	6:00pm
Inveresk Lodge Garden, Musselburgh	Thursday 23 June	11:00am	12:00pm
Greywalls, Gullane	Saturday 25 June	2:00pm	5:00pm
Traprain Garden Circle	Wednesday 29 June	11:00am	6:00pm
Tyninghame House and The Walled Garden, Dunbar	Sunday 3 July	1:00pm	5:00pm
Humbie Dean, Humbie	Thursday 7 July	2:00pm	6:00pm
Newhailes , Newhailes Road, Musselburgh	Friday 8 July	2:00pm	3:00pm
Gifford Village and Broadwoodside, Gifford	Sunday 10 July	1:00pm	5:00pm
Athelstaneford Village	Sunday 4 September	2:00pm	6:00pm
Humbie Dean, Humbie	Thursday 7 July	2:00pm	6:00pm

Gardens open regularly

Shepherd House, Inveresk, Musselburgh	9 February - 3 March and 12 April - 14 July Tuesdays and Thursdays	2:00pm	4:00pm

Key to symbols

 New in 2016

 Teas

 Cream teas

 Homemade teas

 Dogs on a lead allowed

 Wheelchair access

 Accommodation

 Plant stall

 Scottish Snowdrop Festival

GARDEN LOCATIONS IN EAST LOTHIAN

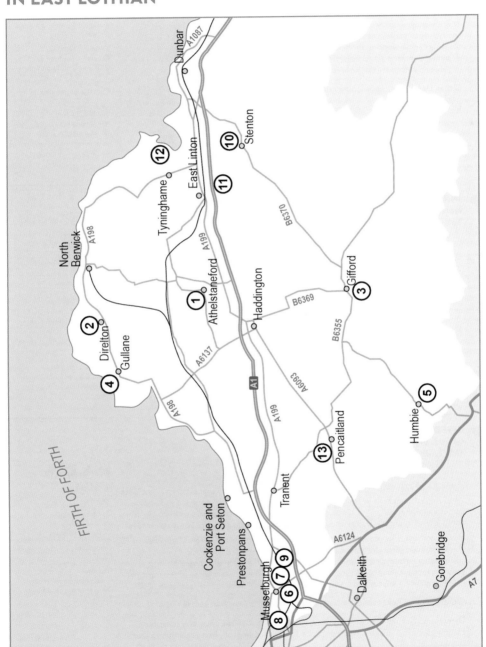

EAST LOTHIAN

ATHELSTANEFORD VILLAGE
EH39 5BE
Gardeners of Athelstaneford

There is huge variety in this village of keen gardeners: the hidden gardens of the Estate cottages reveal rare and unusual plants, vegetable plots, bee friendly plantings and a working model train. A large garden with formal areas has a newly designed contemporary area and orchard opening to the landscape. Explore further in gardens dotted through the small village and just beyond the boundary.

Other Details: Teas available in the village hall.

Directions: The village is on the B1343.

Disabled Access:
Partial

Opening Times:
Sunday 4 September
2:00pm - 6:00pm

Admission:
£5.00, children free

Charities:
The Village Hall, Village School and Village Church receive 40%, the net remaining to SG Beneficiaries

DIRLETON VILLAGE
North Berwick EH39 5EH
The Gardeners of Dirleton and Historic Scotland

Dirleton is a beautiful conservation village with a large green, historic church and castle. Gardens of various sizes and types, including that of Dirleton Castle, are open throughout the village.

Other Details: Parking, tickets and maps are available at the green. Teas will be served in the Church Hall.

Directions: Dirleton Village is two miles west of North Berwick off the A198.

Disabled Access:
Partial

Opening Times:
Saturday 11 June
2:00pm - 6:00pm
Sunday 12 June
2:00pm - 6:00pm

Admission:
£5.00, children free

Charities:
RNLI and Dog Rescue receive 40%, the net remaining to SG Beneficiaries

GIFFORD VILLAGE AND BROADWOODSIDE
Gifford EH41 4QY
The Gardeners of Gifford and Mr & Mrs Robert Dalrymple

Gifford: Laid out in the 18th century, Gifford retains much of its original charm. It includes a beautiful church built in 1708, the Lime Avenue of Yester House and a wide range of gardens all within walking distance of each other. The gardens vary in size and type, from compact and informal, to large and formal with a wide range of plants, shrubs and trees.

Broadwoodside: Planted in and around a farm steading, rescued from dereliction. Two sheltered courtyards are encircled by the old buildings; outside planting extends into surrounding farmland and woods. "This is one of Scotland's finest contemporary private gardens, with excellent structure, imaginative use of objects, and some of the most eye-catching planting in Scotland ... who could ask for more." *Scotland for Gardeners, 2014.*

Other Details: Tickets and garden maps available from the village hall.

Directions: Gifford sits between the A1 and A68 roads about five miles south of Haddington. The village is well signposted from Haddington, Pencaitland and Duns.

Disabled Access:
Partial

Opening Times:
Sunday 10 July
1:00pm - 5:00pm

Admission:
£6.00

Charities:
Local charities will receive 40%, the net remaining to SG Beneficiaries

4 GREYWALLS
Gullane EH31 2EG
Mr and Mrs Giles Weaver
www.greywalls.co.uk

Six acre formal garden, attributed to Gertrude Jekyll, surrounding Greywalls
Hotel, on the edge of Muirfield golf course with stunning views over East Lothian
and the Firth of Forth. One of the highlights of the garden is the walls - straight
walls and curved walls create rooms and vistas; radiating paths link entrances and
exits. Everywhere there are places to sit, in sun and in shade. Featured in the BBC
Beechgrove Garden in September 2015.

Other Details: Lunches and teas will be available in the hotel on the day.

Directions: Signposted on the A198 southeast of Gullane. From Edinburgh take A1
south, then A198 to Gullane last turning on left side. From south take A1 north to
Haddington, Gullane is signposted. Further information is on our website.

Disabled Access:
Partial

Opening Times:
Saturday 25 June
2:00pm - 5:00pm

Admission:
£5.00, accompanied children
free

Charities:
Leuchie House receives
40%, the net remaining to
SG Beneficiaries

5 HUMBIE DEAN
Humbie EH36 5PW
Frank Kirwan T: 07768 996382
E: frank.kirwan@which.net www.humbiedean.com

A two acre ornamental and woodland garden at 600 feet under single-handed
renovation and major extension since 2008. The aim is to provide interest
throughout a long season. A limited palette of plants with hosta, primula,
meconopsis and spring bulbs; herbaceous and shrubaceous planting; bluebell
meadow; mature and recent azalea and rhododendron planting. A short woodland
walk has been created.

Other Details: Access-exit to the woodland walk is via multiple sets of steps.

Directions: Enter Humbie from A68, pass school and village hall on the left then
immediately turn right into the lane. Take second left. Humbie Dean is on left
between two small bridges.

Disabled Access:
None

Opening Times:
Thursdays
12 May, 26 May, 9 June,
23 June, 7 July and 21 July
2:00pm - 6:00pm

Admission:
£5.00

Charities:
Trellis Scotland receives
40%, the net remaining to
SG Beneficiaries

EAST LOTHIAN

6 INVERESK LODGE GARDEN
24 Inveresk Village, Musselburgh EH21 7TE
The National Trust for Scotland T: 0131 653 5599
E: inveresk@nts.org.uk www.nts.org.uk

Tucked away behind stone walls in the charming village of Inveresk, this delightful hillside garden offers an oasis of calm and a year-round feast for the senses. The garden is split into two main areas-sloping lawns and borders at the top of the hill, and the wilder woodland and ponds below, both alive with birdsong and wildlife. You'll also be drawn to the beautiful restored Edwardian conservatory which is home to an aviary. The garden is a true treat for the senses with scented plants and birdsong.

Other Details: Secret Inveresk - learn more about the nature and history of Inveresk with its colourful herbaceous beds, attractive shrubs, old roses and abundant wildlife through a guided walk in this lovely garden.

Directions: OS Ref - NT348716 Road - A6124, south of Musselburgh, six miles east of Edinburgh. Cycle - one mile from NCN 1. Bus - LRT from Edinburgh city centre.

Disabled Access:
Partial

Opening Times:
Thursday 23 June
11:00am - 12:00pm

Admission:
£2.00 for guided walk.
Normal admission applies.

Charities:
Donation to SG Beneficiaries

7 INVERESK VILLAGE
Musselburgh EH21
The Gardeners of Inveresk

A collection of five walled gardens, including Shepherd House, in an historic village. Each has its own individual character displaying a wide variety of interesting and unusual trees, shrubs and plants.

Directions: South side of Musselburgh, Inveresk Village Road - A6124.

Disabled Access:
Partial

Opening Times:
Sunday 19 June
2:00pm - 5:00pm

Admission:
£7.00, children free

Charities:
Horatio's Garden receives
40%, the net remaining to
SG Beneficiaries

© NTS

NEWHAILES

Newhailes Road, Musselburgh EH21 6RY
The National Trust for Scotland T: 0844 493 2125
E: gardens@nts.org.uk www.nts.org.uk

An 18th century designed landscape surrounds the main house and includes a raised walkway, the enchanting and mysterious shell grotto, tea house, a water garden and a number of different walks and paths. In 2015 the Trust embarked upon a major project to restore several areas of the landscape including the Flower Garden, Ha ha and the Walled Kitchen Garden utilizing extensive archive research including the papers of Miss Christian Dalrymple and archaeological excavations.

Other Details: We are undertaking an exciting conservation project to restore the Newhailes historic landscaped garden. Join us as we reveal the history and future of this beautiful garden. Dogs are welcome on leads in the grounds.

Directions: By car Newhailes Road (A6095). Lothian Buses 30, 26 and 44. First Buses 140 and 141. National Cycle Route 1. Newhailes is a 20 minute walk from Newcraighall Station.

Disabled Access:
Partial

Opening Times:
Friday 8 July
2:00pm - 3:00pm
for guided talk.

Admission:
Guided talk £2.00,
non-member parking £2.00
Normal admission applies if
visiting the house.

Charities:
Donation to SG Beneficiaries

SHEPHERD HOUSE

Inveresk, Musselburgh EH21 7TH
Sir Charles and Lady Fraser T: 0131 665 2570
E: annfraser@talktalk.net www.shepherdhousegarden.co.uk

Shepherd House and its one acre garden form a walled triangle in the middle of the 18th century village of Inveresk. The main garden is to the rear of the house where the formality of the front garden is continued with a herb parterre and two symmetrical potagers. A formal rill runs the length of the garden, beneath a series of rose and clematis arches and connects the two ponds. There is a growing collection of specialist snowdrops which are mainly grown in beds and borders some of which will be displayed in our "Snowdrop Theatre". An addition to the garden in 2014 was a Shell House, designed by Lachlan Stewart. The garden has been featured in many magazines and in 2015 appeared on ITV in Alan Titchmarsh's *Britain's Best Back Gardens*. Charles and Ann have also published a book *Shepherd House Garden* which is for sale at Open Days, by application to Shepherd House or the website.

Other Details: Prints and cards by Ann Fraser will be on sale at weekend openings. The garden will also open on Sunday 19 June 2:00pm to 5:00pm as part of the Inveresk Village opening.

Directions: The garden is near Musselburgh. From A1 take A6094 exit signed Wallyford and Dalkeith and follow signs to Inveresk.

Disabled Access:
Partial

Opening Times:
Saturday 20 February
& Sunday 21 February
11:00am - 4:00pm
for the Snowdrop Festival
Saturday 7 May
& Sunday 8 May
11:00am - 4:00pm
for tulips
Tuesdays and Thursdays
9 February - 3 March
& 12 April - 14 July
2:00pm - 4:00pm

Admission:
£5.00, children free

Charities:
Horatio's Garden receives
40%, the net remaining to
SG Beneficiaries

EAST LOTHIAN

 TRAPRAIN GARDEN CIRCLE
EH41
The Gardeners of Traprain

Disabled Access:
Partial

Opening Times:
Wednesdays
25 May, 15 June, 29 June
11:00am - 6:00pm

Admission:
£15.00 for unlimited access
to all three gardens over the
three days.
Or £5.00 per garden for a
single visit.
Tickets available at all open
gardens.

Charities:
Trellis Scotland receives
40%, the net remaining to
SG Beneficiaries

1. Garvald Grange Haddington EH41 4LL (Caroline Straker)
The owners have transformed this garden over the last 24 years from a bare
landscape into a haven for wildlife. Beehives feature in the orchard and vegetables,
shrubs, roses and herbaceous plants grow in the small walled garden beside the
house, under a huge walnut tree. There are two ponds with a resident population of
mallard and several new woods plus mature oak coppice and other hardwoods.

Directions: On the B6370 heading east, take the turn immediately after the
turning signposted for Garvald Village.

2. Granary House Kippielaw EH41 4PY (Bill and Margaret Alder)
A small but well stocked cottage style garden just to the north of Traprain Law.
Planted by Margaret Alder who trained at the Waterperry Horticultural College
and worked at the Oxford Botanical Gardens, the garden has many unusual plants
and shrubs. A small walled area leads through to a lawn, borders and a pond. There
are extensive views westward to the Pentlands and beyond and northwards to Fife.

Directions: From A199 passing East Linton follow the signs to Whittingehame and
turn right at Traprain Farm down a small lane for ½ mile.

3. Stevenson Steading Walled Garden Haddington EH41 4PU (Mr & Mrs N Parker)
A two acre walled garden, early summer herbaceous borders; espaliered roses and
climbers; over sixty different hostas; woodland walk along the Tyne.

Directions: Stevenson Steading Walled Garden - Two miles east of Haddington on
the road to Hailes Castle.

 STENTON VILLAGE
East Lothian EH42 1TE
The Gardeners of Stenton Village

Disabled Access:
Partial

Opening Times:
Sunday 5 June
2:00pm - 5:30pm

Admission:
£5.00, children free

Charities:
Leuchie House receives
40%, the net remaining to
SG Beneficiaries

Stenton (Stane Toon) with its ancient cottages of purple hued sandstone and
pantiled roofs has been awarded *outstanding conservation* status.

There is a thriving Horticultural Society and the gardens, large and small, are of
extraordinary variety and interest.
Stenton is also renowned for its generous teas on Open Days.

Directions: Follow signs from A199/A1.

12 TYNINGHAME HOUSE AND THE WALLED GARDEN
Dunbar EH42 1XW
Tyninghame Gardens Ltd and Mrs C.Gwyn

Splendid 17th century pink sandstone Scottish baronial house, remodelled in 1829 by William Burn, rises out of a sea of plants. The gardens include herbaceous border, formal rose garden, Lady Haddington's Secret Garden with old fashioned roses and an extensive wilderness spring garden with magnificent rhododendrons, azaleas, flowering trees and bulbs. Grounds also include a one mile beech avenue to the sea. The formal walled garden combines the lawn, sculpture and yew hedges, an apple walk, extensive herbaceous planting including roses and peonies with an informal arboretum. The Romanesque ruin of St Baldred's Church commands views across the Tyne Estuary and Lammermuir Hills. Tyninghame has been awarded 'Outstanding' for every category in the Inventory of Gardens and Designed Landscapes of Scotland.

Other Details: Champion Trees: Two British and seven Scottish.

Directions: Gates on A198 at Tyninghame Village.

Disabled Access:
Full

Opening Times:
Sunday 15 May
1:00pm - 5:00pm
Sunday 3 July
1:00pm - 5:00pm

Admission:
£5.00, children free

Charities:
The Lynton Centre (East Linton) receives 40% (May), MND Scotland receives 40% (July), the net remaining to SG Beneficiaries

13 WINTON HOUSE
Pencaitland EH34 5AT
Sir Francis Ogilvy Winton Trust T: 01875 340222
www.wintonhouse.co.uk

The gardens continue to develop and improve. In addition to the natural areas around Sir David's Loch and the Dell, extensive mixed borders are taking shape for the terraces and walled garden. In spring a glorious covering of daffodils makes way for cherry and apple blossoms. Enjoy an informative tour of this historic house and walk off delicious lunches and home baking around the estate.

Directions: Entrance off B6355 Tranent/Pencaitland Road.

Disabled Access:
Full

Opening Times:
Sunday 10 April
12:00pm - 4:30pm

Admission:
£4.00
Guided House Tours
£5.00/£3.00, children under 10 free

Charities:
Marie Curie receives 40%, the net remaining to SG Beneficiaries

© Tony Marsh

EDINBURGH & WEST LOTHIAN

Scotland's Gardens 2016 Guidebook is sponsored by **INVESTEC WEALTH & INVESTMENT**

District Organiser

Victoria Reid Thomas	Riccarton Mains Farmhouse, Currie EH14 4AR E: edinburgh@scotlandsgardens.org

Area Organisers

Nicky Lowe	2/17 Powderhall Rigg, Edinburgh EH7 4GA
Caroline Pearson	42 Pentland Avenue, Edinburgh EH13 0HY

Treasurer

Michael Pearson	42 Pentland Avenue, Edinburgh EH13 0HY

Gardens open on a specific date

101 Greenbank Crescent, Edinburgh	Sunday 1 May	2:00pm - 5:00pm
Moray Place and Bank Gardens, Edinburgh	Sunday 1 May	2:00pm - 5:00pm
Roscullen, 1 Bonaly Road, Edinburgh	Sunday 8 May	2:00pm - 5:00pm
Redcroft, 23 Murrayfield Road, Edinburgh	Saturday 14 May	2:00pm - 5:00pm
Brighton Gardens, Portobello, Edinburgh	Sunday 15 May	2:00pm - 5:00pm
Redcroft, 23 Murrayfield Road, Edinburgh	Sunday 15 May	2:00pm - 5:00pm
Roscullen, 1 Bonaly Road, Edinburgh	Sunday 15 May	2:00pm - 5:00pm
Dr Neil's Garden, Duddingston Village	Saturday 21 May	2:00pm - 5:00pm
Dr Neil's Garden, Duddingston Village	Sunday 22 May	2:00pm - 5:00pm
Dean Gardens, Edinburgh	Sunday 5 June	2:00pm - 5:00pm
The Glasshouses at the Royal Botanic Garden Edinburgh	Sunday 12 June	10:00am - 5:00pm
Malleny Garden, Balerno	Tuesday 28 June	10:00am - 11:00am
Balerno Lodge, 36 Johnsburn Road, Balerno	Saturday 9 July	2:00pm - 5:00pm
Rivaldsgreen House, 48 Friars Brae, Linlithgow	Saturday 23 July	12:00pm - 5:00pm
Craigentinny and Telferton Allotments, Edinburgh	Sunday 7 August	2:00pm - 5:00pm
45 Northfield Crescent, Longridge, Bathgate	Saturday 13 August	2:00pm - 5:00pm
45 Northfield Crescent, Longridge, Bathgate	Sunday 14 August	2:00pm - 5:00pm
Hunter's Tryst, 95 Oxgangs Road, Edinburgh	Sunday 14 August	2:00pm - 5:00pm
Redhall Walled Garden, 97 Lanark Road, Edinburgh	Friday 26 August	2:00pm - 5:00pm

EDINBURGH & WEST LOTHIAN

Gardens open regularly

Newliston, Kirkliston	1 May - 4 June except Mondays and Tuesdays	2:00pm - 6:00pm
Redhall Walled Garden, 97 Lanark Road, Edinburgh	Monday to Friday	9:00am - 3:30pm
The Glasshouses at the Royal Botanic Garden Edinburgh	March - September	10:00am - 5:00pm
	February & October	10:00am - 4:00pm
	Nov, Dec & Jan	10:00am - 3:00pm
	Closed 25 Dec & 1 Jan	

Gardens open by arrangement

61 Fountainhall Road, Edinburgh	1 April - 30 October	0131 667 6146
Hunter's Tryst, 95 Oxgangs Road, Edinburgh	On request	0131 477 2919
Laverockdale House, 66 Dreghorn Loan, Edinburgh	1 August - 31 August	0131 441 7936
Redcroft, 23 Murrayfield Road, Edinburgh	23 September - 14 October	0131 337 1747

Three photos of Fountainhall Road © Andrea Jones

Key to symbols

  New in 2016

 Homemade teas

Accommodation

Teas

 Dogs on a lead allowed

Plant stall

Cream teas

Wheelchair access

 Scottish Snowdrop Festival

GARDEN LOCATIONS IN
EDINBURGH & WEST LOTHIAN

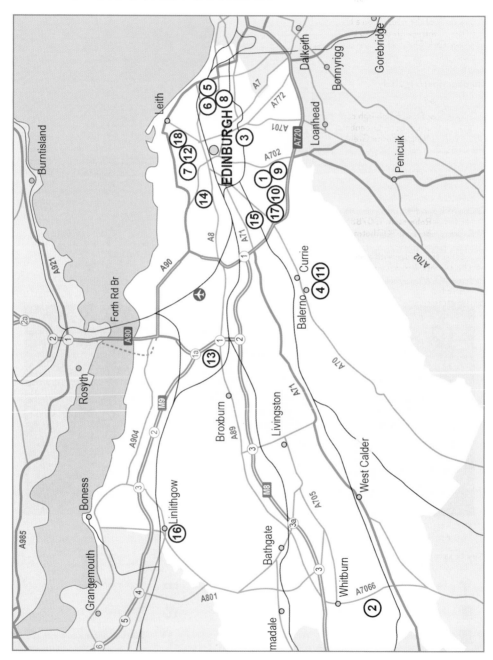

1 101 GREENBANK CRESCENT

Edinburgh EH10 5TA
Mr and Mrs Jerry and Christine Gregson T: 0131 447 6492
E: jerry_gregson@yahoo.co.uk

The front of the house is on a busy town bus route, but the back of the house is in the country, with views to the Pentland Hills and over the adjoining Braidburn Valley Park. The garden shows what can be done on a steeply sloped site: paths and steps join a variety of distinct areas and terraces, each with a different character. The aim is to have colour, contrast and interest all year round.

Other Details: This is a child friendly garden. There will be live music (weather permitting).

Directions: From Edinburgh centre, take A702 through Morningside. Continue on and then turn right on Greenbank Crescent at Greenbank Church. On the 5 and 16 bus routes: stop opposite Greenbank Row.

Disabled Access:
None

Opening Times:
Sunday 1 May
2:00pm - 5:00pm

Admission:
£4.00

Charities:
St Columba's Hospice receives 40%, the net remaining to SG Beneficiaries

2 45 NORTHFIELD CRESCENT

Longridge, Bathgate EH47 8AL
Mr Jamie Robertson T: 07885 701642
E: jamierobertson04@hotmail.co.uk

A delightful garden with a wide variety of shrubs, herbaceous, bedding and dozens of dahlia plants. Large pond with a small waterfall and a colourful decked area with an attractive selection of bedding plants. There is a vegetable patch with raised bed. A twelve foot by eight foot feature greenhouse showing award winning pot plants. The garden is the current holder of the Oatridge College award and has won several gold medals. The owner has won the *West Lothian Gardener of the Year* prize four times and is chairman of the Livingston and District Horticultural Society.

Directions: From A71- turn right after Breith at traffic lights, go about a mile and turn right into the Crescent.
From Whitburn - take A706 Longridge Road to Longridge and last left into the Crescent.

Disabled Access:
Partial

Opening Times:
Saturday 13 August
2:00pm - 5:00pm
Sunday 14 August
2:00pm - 5:00pm

Admission:
£3.00

Charities:
World Cancer Research receives 40%, the net remaining to SG Beneficiaries

3 61 FOUNTAINHALL ROAD

Edinburgh EH9 2LH
Mrs Annemarie Hammond T: 0131 667 6146
E: froglady@blueyonder.co.uk www.froglady.pwp.blueyonder.co.uk

Large walled town garden in which trees and shrubs form an architectural backdrop to a wide variety of flowering plants. The growing collection of hellebores and trilliums and a large variety of late blooming flowers provide interest from early March to late October. In addition, there are now several alpine beds which include a large collection of Sempervivums. Three ponds, with and without fish, have attracted a lively population of frogs.

Directions: See Contact Details on website.

Disabled Access:
Full

Opening Times:
By arrangement
1 April - 30 October

Admission:
£4.00

Charities:
Froglife receives 40%, the net remaining to SG Beneficiaries

BALERNO LODGE
36 Johnsburn Road, Balerno EH14 7DX
Gilly Corstorphine

Balerno Lodge is a two acre mature garden consisting of rhododendrons, azaleas, shrubbery and a small pretty stream leading into a pond. Within the walled garden there is a large central herbaceous border and a newly created insect friendly bed.

Other Details: Plant stall run by Macplants Nursery.

Directions: A70 to Balerno, leave school on the left, over a small roundabout up Johnsburn Road and it is the second opening on the right.
Bus 44A.

Disabled Access:
Full

Opening Times:
Saturday 9 July
2:00pm - 5:00pm

Admission:
£4.00

Charities:
Canine Partners receives 40%, the net remaining to SG Beneficiaries

---

BRIGHTON GARDENS
14 East Brighton Crescent, Portobello, Edinburgh EH15 1LR
The Gardeners of Brighton

Brighton Place and East and West Brighton Crescent belong to a unified Georgian development around two parks. Five gardens will be open, ranging from small to over half an acre and from formal to intimate, all with interesting planting. In spring, magnolias, rhododendrons and bulbs are prominent.

Other Details: Tickets and a summary map to all gardens will be available from 14 East Brighton Crescent, at the corner of Brighton Place and Brighton Crescent. Teas are available from the many nearby cafes on Portobello High Street and the Promenade, a list and map will be provided.

Directions: Buses 21, 42 and 49 to Brighton Place, and 15, 26, 40 and 45 to Portobello High Street. Brighton Place intersects Portobello High Street just east of the bus stops.

Disabled Access:
Partial

Opening Times:
Sunday 15 May
2:00pm - 5:00pm

Admission:
£5.00 for entrance to all five gardens

Charities:
All proceeds to SG Beneficiaries

CRAIGENTINNY AND TELFERTON ALLOTMENTS
Telferton Road, off Portobello Road, Edinburgh EH7 6XG
The Gardeners of Craigentinny and Telferton
craigentinnytelferton.btck.co.uk

Established in 1923, this independent allotment site is a tranquil and charming space. Hidden away in a built up area, the local community benefit from growing their own vegetables and fruit. Come and enjoy tea, home baking and chat with our friendly plot holders.

Other Details: Various workshops will be organised for the day.

Directions: Park on Telferton Road. Lothian Regional Transport buses 15, 26, 45.

Disabled Access:
Partial

Opening Times:
Sunday 7 August
2:00pm - 5:00pm

Admission:
£3.00, children free

Charities:
The Craigentinny Telferton Allotments receives 40%, the net remaining to SG Beneficiaries

DEAN GARDENS
Edinburgh EH4 1QE
Dean Gardens Management Committee
www.deangardens.org

Nine acres of semi-woodland garden with spring bulbs on the steep banks of the Water of Leith in central Edinburgh. Founded in the 1860s by local residents, the Dean Gardens contains part of the great structure of the Dean Bridge, a Thomas Telford masterpiece of 1835. Lawns, paths, trees, and shrubs with lovely views to the weir in the Dean Village and to the St Bernard's Well. There is also a children's play area.

Other Details: There will also be live music.

Directions: Entrance at Ann Street or Eton Terrace.

Disabled Access:
Partial

Opening Times:
Sunday 5 June
2:00pm - 5:00pm

Admission:
£3.00, children free

Charities:
All proceeds to
SG Beneficiaries

DR NEIL'S GARDEN
Duddingston Village EH15 3PX
Dr Neil's Garden Trust
E: info@drneilsgarden.co.uk   www.drneilsgarden.co.uk

Wonderful secluded, landscaped garden on the lower slopes of Arthur's Seat including conifers, heathers, alpines, physic garden, herbaceous borders and ponds. Thompson's Tower with the Museum of Curling and beautiful views across Duddingston Loch.

Directions: Kirk car park on Duddingston Road West and then follow signposts through the Manse Garden.

Disabled Access:
Partial

Opening Times:
Saturday 21 May
2:00pm - 5:00pm
Sunday 22 May
2:00pm - 5:00pm

Admission:
£3.00

Charities:
Dr Neil's Garden Trust
receives 40%, the net
remaining to SG Beneficiaries

HUNTER'S TRYST
95 Oxgangs Road, Edinburgh EH10 7BA
Jean Knox T: 0131 477 2919
E: jean.knox@blueyonder.co.uk

Well stocked, mature, medium-sized town garden comprising herbaceous/shrub beds, lawn, vegetables and fruit, water feature, seating areas and trees. This is a garden that has been transformed from a wilderness thirty years ago and continues to evolve. This hidden treasure of a garden was featured on *The Beechgrove Garden* in June 2015.

Directions: From Fairmilehead crossroads head down Oxgangs Road to Hunter's Tryst roundabout, last house on the left. Take buses 4, 5, 18 or 27. The bus stop is at Hunter's Tryst and the garden is opposite.

Disabled Access:
None

Opening Times:
Sunday 14 August
2:00pm - 5:00pm
By arrangement on request

Admission:
£4.00

Charities:
Lothian Cat Rescue receives
40%, the net remaining to
SG Beneficiaries

EDINBURGH & WEST LOTHIAN

LAVEROCKDALE HOUSE
66 Dreghorn Loan, Edinburgh EH13 0DB
Susan Plag T: 01314417936
E: laverockdalegarden@gmail.com www.laverockdalehouse.com

The garden at the Sir Robert Lorimer designed Laverockdale House sits on the boundary between city and countryside with the Pentland Hills as a backdrop. From the terrace the view of the garden is very special as the sweeping lawn leads to the spectacular pond and waterfalls fed from the Bonaly Burn. The garden features large areas of planting with herbaceous perennials, shrubs, annuals, a raised vegetable garden and mixed mature woodland.

Other Details: Homemade teas available on request.

Directions: Top of Dreghorn Loan, carry on straight ahead up lane.

Disabled Access:
Partial

Opening Times:
By arrangement 1 - 31 August for groups

Admission:
£4.00

Charities:
Scottish Love in Action (SLA) receives 40%, the net remaining to SG Beneficiaries

MALLENY GARDEN
Balerno EH14 7AF
National Trust for Scotland T: 0131 653 5599
E: rnaismith@nts.org.uk www.nts.org.uk

This hidden treasure is a walled garden surrounded by woodland, found just outside Balerno, a suburb of Edinburgh. The garden is a haven for plant lovers thanks to its large variety of colourful and fragrant flowers, plants and trees. Beside the garden there is also an unoccupied doocot with an unusual saddle-backed roof and a fountain. The grounds are separated from Balerno by a stream, further enhancing the feel of seclusion, privacy and peacefulness.

Other Details: National Plant Collection®: 19th Century Shrub Roses. Malleny in Bloom-a rare opportunity to savour the scents of Malleny with a morning stroll through this beautiful garden at the peak of the rose display and learn more about the walled garden and surrounding woodlands.

Directions: In Balerno off A70 Lanark Road. Buses LRT 44 and First 44.

Disabled Access:
Partial

Opening Times:
Tuesday 28 June
10:00am - 11:00am

Admission:
£2.00 for guided walk
Normal admission applies

Charities:
Donation to SG Beneficiaries

MORAY PLACE AND BANK GARDENS
Edinburgh EH3 6BX
The Residents of Moray Place and Bank Gardens

Moray Place: Private garden of 3½ acres in Georgian New Town. Shrubs, trees and beds offering atmosphere of tranquillity in the city centre.

Bank Gardens: Nearly six acres of secluded wild gardens with lawns, trees and shrubs with banks of bulbs down to the Water of Leith. Stunning vistas across Firth of Forth.

Other Details: Disabled access Moray Place only.

Directions:
Moray Place - enter by north gate in Moray Place.
Bank Gardens - enter by the gate at top of Doune Terrace.

Disabled Access:
Partial

Opening Times:
Sunday 1 May
2:00pm - 5:00pm

Admission:
£4.00

Charities:
The Euan Macdonald Centre for Motor Neurone Disease Research receives 40%, the net remaining to SG Beneficiaries

NEWLISTON
Kirkliston EH29 9EB
Mr and Mrs R C Maclachlan T: 0131 333 3231
E: mac@newliston.fsnet.co.uk

Eighteenth century designed landscape with good rhododendrons and azaleas. The house, designed by Robert Adam, is also open.

Directions: Nine miles west of Edinburgh city centre, four miles south of the Forth Road Bridge, off the B800 between Newbridge and Kirkliston.

Disabled Access:
Partial

Opening Times:
1 May - 4 June
2:00pm - 6:00pm except
Mondays and Tuesdays

Admission:
£4.00

Charities:
Children's Hospice
Association receives 40%,
the net remaining to
SG Beneficiaries

REDCROFT
23 Murrayfield Road, Edinburgh EH12 6EP
James and Anna Buxton T: 0131 337 1747
E: annabuxtonb@aol.com

A walled garden surrounding an Arts and Crafts villa which provides an unexpected haven off a busy road. Planted and maintained with shape and texture in mind. In early May there should be a fine display of flowering shrubs including rhododendrons, tulips and other bulbs. In the autumn the herbaceous border has a renewed flourish and there should be autumn crocuses, nerines, dahlias and usually plentiful apples.

Other Details: Our chosen charity is Horatio's Garden which is located at the Spinal Injuries Unit at the Southern General Hospital in Glasgow.

Directions: Murrayfield Road runs north from Corstorphine Road to Ravelston Dykes. There is easy parking available which is free. Buses 26, 31 and 38; get off at Murrayfield Stadium.

Disabled Access:
Full

Opening Times:
Saturday 14 May
2:00pm - 5:00pm
Sunday 15 May
2:00pm - 5:00pm
By arrangement
23 September - 14 October

Admission:
£4.00

Charities:
Horatio's Garden receives
40%, the net remaining to
SG Beneficiaries

REDHALL WALLED GARDEN
97 Lanark Road, Edinburgh EH14 2LZ
Scottish Association for Mental Health T: 0131 443 0946
E: redhall@samhservices.org.uk

Redhall Walled Garden, part of SAMH, provides a unique setting for a remarkable mental health service. It is a working garden, with a rich history and in a beautiful location. Georgian Palladium Summerhouse with Terrace Garden, formal Herb Garden, Roundhouse, Bee and Butterfly Garden, Bog Garden, pond and wildlife area. There are also fruits, vegetables, herbaceous, shrubs and lovely walks.

Directions: There is disabled parking available at the garden, for other cars parking is on the main street. On the LRT 44 bus route.

Disabled Access:
Full

Opening Times:
Friday 26 August
2:00pm - 5:00pm
Weekdays 9:00am - 3:30pm

Admission:
£4.00, concessions £2.50,
children free

Charities:
Redhall Walled Garden
SAMH receives 40%, the net
remaining to SG Beneficiaries

RIVALDSGREEN HOUSE
48 Friars Brae, Linlithgow. EH49 6BG
Dr Ian Wallace T: 01506845700
E: Ianwjw1940@gmail.com

Mature two acre garden with lovely mixed herbaceous, rose and tree planting.

Other Details: Teas will be available priced £2.50.

Directions: For final directions if necessary call the number listed above. There is car parking available.

Disabled Access:
Partial

Opening Times:
Saturday 23 July
12:00pm - 5:00pm

Admission:
£4.00

Charities:
St Peter's Episcopal Church, Linlithgow receives 20%, the Order of St John receives 20%, the net remaining to SG Beneficiaries

---

ROSCULLEN
1 Bonaly Road, Edinburgh EH13 0EA
Mrs Anne Duncan T: 0131 441 2905

Fabulous spring garden with numerous varieties of tulips. There are also beautiful rhododendrons and azaleas.

Other Details: Plant stall run by Kevock Gardens

Directions: From city take the left fork at the traffic lights at the top of Colinton village. Bonaly Road is the third road along on the left. Parking is best on Grant Avenue. On the LRT 10 bus route.

Disabled Access:
Partial

Opening Times:
Sunday 8 May
2:00pm - 5:00pm
Sunday 15 May
2:00pm - 5:00pm

Admission:
£4.00

Charities:
Brooke Hospital for Animals and Friends of The Royal Botanic Garden Edinburgh each receive 20%, the net remaining to SG Beneficiaries

---

THE GLASSHOUSES AT THE ROYAL BOTANIC GARDEN EDINBURGH
20A Inverleith Row, Edinburgh EH3 5LR
Royal Botanic Garden Edinburgh T: 0131 248 2909
www.rbge.org.uk

The Glasshouses with 10 climatic zones are a delight all year. The Orchids and Cycads House brings together primitive cycads which dominated the land flora some 65 million years ago, and a diverse range of orchids, the most sophisticated plants in the world. In summer, giant water lilies, Victoria amazonica, are the star attraction in the Tropical Aquatic House. Plants with vibrant flowers and fascinating foliage thrive in the Rainforest Riches House and the complex ecosystems of life in the world's deserts are explored in the Arid Lands House. Collections of gingers (Zingiberaceae) and vireya rhododendrons and a case housing carnivorous plants are among other attractions.

Other Details: Closes 30 mins after last admission.

Directions: Located off the A902, one mile north of city centre. Entrances at Inverleith Row and Arboretum Place. Lothian Buses 8, 23 and 27 stop close to the East Gate entrance on Inverleith Row. The Majestic Tour Bus stops at Arboretum Place.

Disabled Access:
Full

Opening Times:
Sunday 12 June 10am - 5pm
Opens 10am daily (except 25 Dec/1 Jan) Glasshouse closes Mar - Sept 5pm, Feb & Oct 4pm, Nov - Jan 3pm

Admission:
£5.50, conc. £4.50, u16 free (incls donation to Garden, for prices without donation check rbge.org.uk).

Charities:
Donation to SG Beneficiaries

ETTRICK & LAUDERDALE

Scotland's Gardens 2016 Guidebook is sponsored by **INVESTEC WEALTH & INVESTMENT**

Area Organisers

Mrs M Kostoris	Wester Housebyres, Melrose TD6 9BW
Mrs P Litherland	Laidlawstiel House, Clovenfords, Galashiels TD1 1TJ
Mrs D Warre	Peace Cottage, Synton Parkhead, Ashkirk TD7 4PB
	E: ettrick@scotlandsgardens.org

Treasurer

Mrs D Muir	Torquhan House, Stow TD1 2RX

Gardens open on a specific date

The Yair, Galashiels	Sunday 5 June	2:00pm	-	6:00pm
Laidlawstiel House, Clovenfords, Galashiels	Sunday 12 June	2:00pm	-	5:00pm
Harmony Garden with Priorwood Garden, Melrose	Saturday 30 July	10:00am	-	5:00pm

Priorwood Garden

Key to symbols

	New in 2016		Homemade teas		Accommodation
	Teas		Dogs on a lead allowed		Plant stall
	Cream teas		Wheelchair access		Scottish Snowdrop Festival

GARDEN LOCATIONS IN ETTRICK & LAUDERDALE

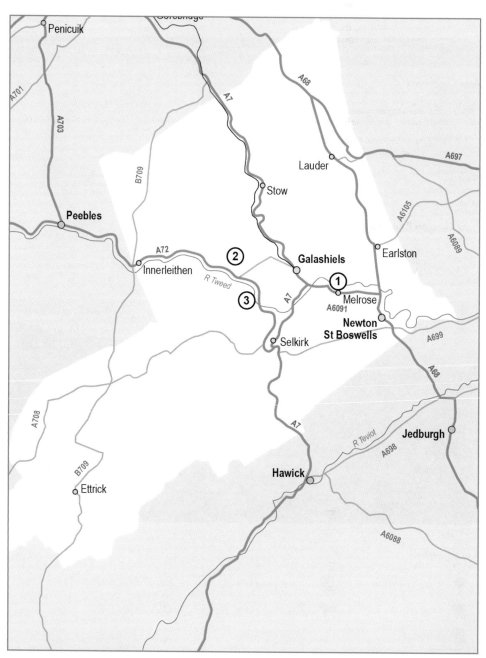

HARMONY GARDEN WITH PRIORWOOD GARDEN
St Mary's Road, Melrose TD6 9LJ
The National Trust for Scotland T: 01896 822493
E: sdunnet@nts.org.uk www.nts.org.uk

Harmony Garden: Wander through this tranquil garden, wonderful herbaceous borders, lawns, fruit and vegetable plots, and enjoy fine views of the Abbey and Eildon Hills.

Priorwood Garden: Overlooked by the Abbey ruins, this unique garden produces plants for a superb variety of dried flower arrangements made and sold here. The orchard also contains many historic apple varieties. Come along for a tour of Priorwood Garden with our knowledgeable staff to learn about the wide variety of dried flowers grown including annuals, herbs and perennials. See the unique flower drying room and discover the traditional skills of this colourful and aromatic ancient art.

Other Details: Seasonal fruits and vegetable sales on trolley at the entrance of Harmony. Plant stall and dried flowers arrangements are available at Priorwood.

Directions: Off A6091, in Melrose, opp. Abbey. First Bus from Edinburgh & Peebles.

Disabled Access:
Full

Opening Times:
Saturday 30 July
10:00am - 5:00pm

Admission:
Normal Trust admission applies.

Charities:
Donation to SG Beneficiaries

LAIDLAWSTIEL HOUSE
Clovenfords, Galashiels TD1 1TJ
Mr and Mrs P Litherland

Walled garden containing herbaceous border, fruit, and vegetables in raised beds. There are also colourful rhododendrons and azaleas as well as splendid views down to the River Tweed.

Directions: A72 between Clovenfords and Walkerburn, turn up the hill signposted for Thornielee. The house is on the right at the top of the hill.

Disabled Access:
None

Opening Times:
Sunday 12 June
2:00pm - 5:00pm

Admission:
£4.00, children free

Charities:
CLIC Sargent receives 40%, the net remaining to SG Beneficiaries

THE YAIR
Galashiels TD1 3PW
Mr and Mrs W Thyne
E: didi@theyair.co.uk

Attractive mixed borders round classical house, herbaceous, shrubs and specimen trees. Enjoy walking along the River Tweed, through the glen and up to see the old semi-tended walled garden.

Other Details: There will be a cake stall as well as a plant stall.

Directions: On A707 between Caddonfoot and Selkirk. Turn in at Yair Bridge, at traffic lights.

Disabled Access:
Partial

Opening Times:
Sunday 5 June
2:00pm - 6:00pm

Admission:
£5.00, children under 16 free

Charities:
Caddonfoot Parish Church Appeal receives 40%, the net remaining to SG Beneficiaries

MIDLOTHIAN

Scotland's Gardens 2016 Guidebook is sponsored by INVESTEC WEALTH & INVESTMENT

District Organiser

Mrs Sarah Barron DL	Laureldene, Kevock Road, Lasswade EH18 1HT E: midlothian@scotlandsgardens.org

Area Organisers

Mrs Margaret Drummond	Pomathorn House, Penicuik EH26 8PJ
Mrs Kathleen Hill	Law House, 27 Biggar Road, Silverburn EH26 9LJ
Mrs Eilidh Liddle	21 Craigiebield Crescent, Penicuik EH26 9EQ

Treasurer

Mrs Margaret Drummond	Pomathorn House, Penicuik EH26 8PJ

Gardens open on a specific date

Kevock Garden and Greenfield Lodge, Lasswade	Sunday 10 April	12:00pm	- 5:00pm
Huntly Cottage, Moorfoot, by Temple	Saturday 7 May	1:00pm	- 5:00pm
Newhall, Carlops	Wednesday 22 June	2:00pm	- 4:30pm
Newhall, Carlops	Wednesday 29 June	2:00pm	- 4:30pm
Newhall, Carlops	Wednesday 6 July	2:00pm	- 4:30pm
1 Standpretty, Fuschiebridge, by Gorebridge	Sunday 10 July	2:00pm	- 5:00pm
Newhall, Carlops	Wednesday 13 July	2:00pm	- 4:30pm
Eskbank Gardens, 23 Lasswade Road, Eskbank	Sunday 17 July	1:00pm	- 5:00pm
Newhall, Carlops	Wednesday 20 July	2:00pm	- 4:30pm
Newhall, Carlops	Wednesday 27 July	2:00pm	- 4:30pm
Silverburn Village, near Penicuik	Sunday 7 August	12:30pm	- 5:00pm
Harvieston Walled Garden, Gorebridge	Sunday 14 August	2:00pm	- 5:00pm
Huntly Cottage, Moorfoot, by Temple	Saturday 3 September	1:00pm	- 5:00pm

Key to symbols

	New in 2016		Homemade teas		Accommodation
	Teas		Dogs on a lead allowed		Plant stall
	Cream teas		Wheelchair access		Scottish Snowdrop Festival

GARDEN LOCATIONS IN MIDLOTHIAN

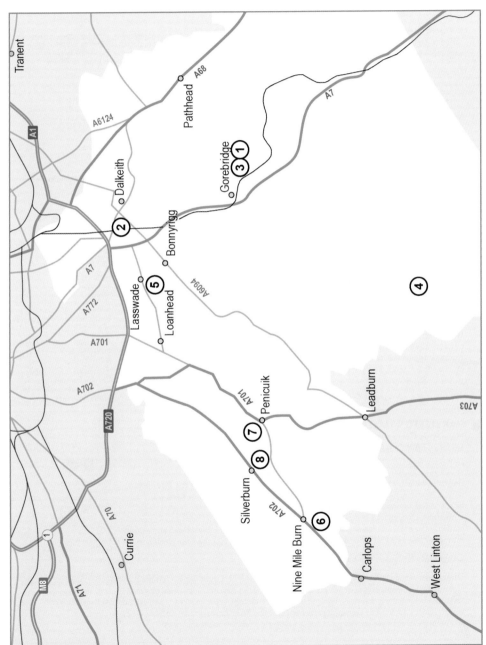

1 STANDPRETTY

Fuschiebridge, by Gorebridge EH23 4QG
Mrs K Adam
E: susan.adam@akadamia.co.uk

A small tranquil cottage garden, set on high ground above Gorebridge, overlooking the Gore Glen and Pentland Hills. There are informal borders and island beds with a range of shrubs, herbaceous and woodland plants. Small raised beds form a colourful vegetable garden, along with herbs and hens. Lovely local walks.

Directions: From A7 take the turning signposted Fushiebridge and Catcune (½ mile beyond the B6372 Temple/Gorebridge crossroads). Drive up the hill, around the hairpin bend, over a stone railway bridge and Standpretty is the second house on the left with an ivy leaf gate. Parking will be stewarded and available on the main road beyond the house.

Disabled Access:
None

Opening Times:
Sunday 10 July
2:00pm - 5:00pm

Admission:
£4.00, children free

Charities:
Pancreatic Cancer receives 40%, the net remaining to SG Beneficiaries

ESKBANK GARDENS

23 Lasswade Road, Eskbank EH22 3EE
The Gardeners of Eskbank

Eskbank lies on the south-western edge of the historic town of Dalkeith. An interesting variety of small and medium-sized modern suburban gardens will be open, which have a broad range of planting styles and design. The gardens are located primarily in Wishart Place, Lasswade Road and Eskfield Grove.

Other Details: Entry at 23 Lasswade Road where a map will be provided, there will also be a plant stall and second-hand gardening books will be on sale.

Directions: Gardens are all located on and in the streets close to the A768, Eskbank to Lasswade and Loanhead Road. From Edinburgh take the A772 and B6392 to Eskbank Toll or A7 from other directions. New Borders Railway line from Edinburgh or Tweedbank stops at Eskbank Station a few minutes' walk from all gardens. Lothian Buses 3, 39, 40, 49 to Eskbank Toll.

Disabled Access:
Partial

Opening Times:
Sunday 17 July
1:00pm - 5:00pm

Admission:
£5.00, accompanied children free

Charities:
Alzheimer Scotland (Mid & East Lothian Services) receives 20%, Glencorse Church, Penicuik receives 20%, the net remaining to SG Beneficiaries

HARVIESTON WALLED GARDEN

Harvieston Cottage, Gorebridge, Midlothian EH23 4QA
Lorna and Bill Crook

Beautiful walled garden, dating from the early 19th century and part of the Harvieston Estate. It has been carefully redesigned over 20 years by the current owners, who have created a wonderful contemporary garden, full of interesting and unusual trees and shrubs. Divided into several spaces with informal borders, island beds and a prairie garden with perennial planting and unusual grasses. A large vegetable garden and a pond with water lilies, iris and other damp loving plants. Lots to interest the keen gardener.

Other Details: Teas in the garden and a good plant stall.

Directions: A7 south from Edinburgh - junction with B6372, Gorebridge - Temple crossroads. Just beyond crossroads on left side of A7 is the new entrance drive to Walled Garden. Parking along driveway. Limited parking at front entrance, reserved for disabled visitors. Buses 33 & 29 to Gorebridge terminus, at the B6372 crossroads, X95 bus stops just before Gorebridge/Temple junction. ¼ mile walk from the bus stop.

Disabled Access:
Partial

Opening Times:
Sunday 14 August
2:00pm - 5:00pm

Admission:
£4.00, accompanied children free

Charities:
Pancreatic Cancer receives 40%, the net remaining to SG Beneficiaries

HUNTLY COT
Moorfoot, by Temple, Midlothian EH23 4TF
Peter de Vink

A unique garden, set in one of Midlothian's most beautiful and tranquil locations, nestling below the Moorfoots and Huntly Cot Hills. At a height of over 850 feet, there are spectacular views, across Gladhouse Reservoir to the Pentland Hills. At its centre is a beautiful heart-shaped heather garden, with a natural spring burn, perfectly complementing the garden's moorland setting. Cloud-pruned shrubs and trees create structure in the garden and the herbaceous borders surrounding the house, provide tastefully planted colour combinations throughout the year. Daffodils and rhododendrons in spring and the heathers come to life in autumn. Whatever time of year you visit, a warm welcome is assured in this charming hillside garden.

Directions: A7 south to Gorebridge/Temple crossroads. Turn onto B6372 go past Temple and on, past Rosebery Reservoir, at sharp right-hand bend in road (B6372 Penicuik), continue straight on signposted Moorfoot 1½ miles. Turn into Moorfoot Farm and continue on road. Follow yellow signs.

Disabled Access:
Partial

Opening Times:
Saturdays
7 May and 3 September
1:00pm - 5:00pm

Admission:
£5.00, accompanied children under 16 free

Charities:
Marie Curie Cancer Care receives 40% (May), the net remaining to SG Beneficiaries and all proceeds to SG Beneficiaries (September)

KEVOCK GARDEN AND GREENFIELD LODGE
Lasswade EH18 1HT
Prof and Mrs.David Rankin and Dr and Mrs David Farqharson

Two beautiful and contrasting gardens in the Kevock Conservation Area of Lasswade.

Kevock Garden EH18 1HT
A wonderful, compact hillside garden created on the south facing slopes of the North Esk Valley. A plantsman's garden, it is designed as a series of terraces, with azaleas and unusual shrubs, many of Sino-Himalayan origin, infilled with a range of rare woodland plants and bulbs. There is a pond and bog garden with primula, iris and other damp loving plants.

Greenfield Lodge EH8 1HE
A charming, two acre, woodland garden with mature specimen trees, rhododendrons, magnolias, and other interesting shrubs. In the spring the garden is full of hellebores and bulbs. There is a large productive vegetable garden and pond.

Other Details: Soup and rolls available at lunch, teas in the afternoon. Interesting plant stall with a range of unusual plants at Kevock Garden.

Directions: Kevock Road lies off the A768, Loanhead/Lasswade Road. Five minutes from the Edinburgh City Bypass, Lasswade Junction and also on the 31 Lothian Bus route to Polton/Bonnyrigg. Follow sign post to Edinburgh and Lasswade Riding Centre and yellow signs. Access to Greenfield Lodge is via a local footpath from Kevock Road.

Disabled Access:
Partial

Opening Times:
Sunday 10 April
12:00pm - 5:00pm

Admission:
£5.00, accompanied children under 16 free

Charities:
Wellbeing of Women receives 40%, the net remaining to SG Beneficiaries

6 NEWHALL
Carlops EH26 9LY
John and Tricia Kennedy T: 01968 660206
E: tricia.kennedy@newhalls.co.uk

Traditional 18th century walled garden with huge herbaceous border, shrubberies, fruit and vegetables. Stunning glen running along the North Esk river in the process of restoration (stout shoes recommended). Large pond with evolving planting. Young arboretum and collection of Rosa pimpinellifolia. In *Good Gardens Guide* 2010, *Scottish Field*, *Gardens Monthly*, *Scotland on Sunday*.

Other Details: Do it yourself teas and coffees will be available.

Directions: On A702 Edinburgh/Biggar, ¼ mile after Ninemileburn and a mile before Carlops. Follow signs.

Disabled Access:
Partial

Opening Times:
Wednesdays
22 and 29 June
6, 13, 20 and 27 July
2:00pm - 4:30pm

Admission:
£4.00

Charities:
Stable Life receives 40%, the net remaining to SG Beneficiaries

7 SILVERBURN VILLAGE
Near Penicuik EH26 9LJ
The Gardeners of Silverburn

Nestling in the foothills of the Pentlands, Silverburn has a selection of village gardens of varying size and planting styles, all growing at 800 feet. There are wonderful views of the Pentlands and surrounding areas and many ideas for growing plants in exposed locations. Come and have tea in Silverburn Village Hall with its Beechgrove Community Garden. There are lovely local walks across the Pentland Hills and good quality plants for sale.

Other Details: Soup and rolls and homemade teas in Village Hall. Dogs welcome on lead please.

Directions: A702, Edinburgh/Biggar Road, thirteen miles south of Edinburgh and one mile before Ninemileburn.

Disabled Access:
Partial

Opening Times:
Sunday 7 August
12:30pm - 5:00pm

Admission:
£4.00

Charities:
Silverburn Community receives 40%, the net remaining to SG Beneficiaries

1 Standpretty

PEEBLESSHIRE

Scotland's Gardens 2016 Guidebook is sponsored by **INVESTEC WEALTH & INVESTMENT**

District Organiser

Mrs R Parrott	An Sparr, Medwyn Road, West Linton EH46 7HA
	E: peeblesshire@scotlandsgardens.org

Area Organisers

Mr J Bracken	Gowan Lea, Croft Road, West Linton EH46 7DZ
Mr Graham Buchanan-Dunlop	The Potting Shed, Broughton Pl, Broughton ML12 6HJ
Ms R Hume	Llolans, Broughton ML12 6HJ
Lesley McDavid	Braedon, Medwyn Road, West Linton EH46 7HA

Treasurer

Mr J Bracken	Gowan Lea, Croft Road, West Linton EH46 7DZ

Gardens open on a specific date

Kailzie Gardens, Peebles	Sunday 7 February	Dawn	-	Dusk
The Peeblesshire Garden Trio - Haystoun	Saturday 28 May	1:30pm	-	5:00pm
8 Halmyre Mains, West Linton	Sunday 29 May	10:00am	-	12:00pm
The Peeblesshire Garden Trio - Haystoun & Glen House	Sunday 29 May	1:30pm	-	5:00pm
Stobo Japanese Water Garden, Home Farm, Stobo	Wednesday 8 June	2:00pm	-	7:30pm
Stobo Japanese Water Garden, Home Farm, Stobo	Thursday 9 June	2:00pm	-	7:30pm
The Potting Shed, Broughton Place, Broughton	Wednesday 15 June	11:00am	-	5:00pm
West Linton Village Gardens, West Linton	Sunday 19 June	2:00pm	-	5:00pm
The Peeblesshire Garden Trio - The Cottage	Wednesday 22 June	1:30pm	-	5:00pm
The Potting Shed, Broughton Place, Broughton	Wednesday 22 June	11:00am	-	5:00pm
The Peeblesshire Garden Trio - Glen House	Thursday 23 June	1:30pm	-	5:00pm
The Peeblesshire Garden Trio - Haystoun	Wednesday 29 June	1:30pm	-	5:00pm
The Potting Shed, Broughton Place, Broughton	Wednesday 29 June	11:00am	-	5:00pm
The Potting Shed, Broughton Place, Broughton	Wednesday 6 July	11:00am	-	5:00pm
Portmore, Eddleston	Wednesday 13 July	1:00pm	-	5:00pm
The Potting Shed, Broughton Place, Broughton	Wednesday 13 July	11:00am	-	5:00pm
8 Halmyre Mains, West Linton	Sunday 17 July	2:00pm	-	5:00pm
Drumelzier Old Manse, Drumelzier, near Broughton	Sunday 17 July	2:00pm	-	5:00pm
Portmore, Eddleston	Wednesday 20 July	1:00pm	-	5:00pm
The Potting Shed, Broughton Place, Broughton	Wednesday 20 July	11:00am	-	5:00pm
The Peeblesshire Garden Trio - The Cottage	Thursday 21 July	1:30pm	-	5:00pm
Portmore, Eddleston	Wednesday 27 July	1:00pm	-	5:00pm

PEEBLESSHIRE

Portmore, Eddleston	Wednesday 3 August	1:00pm	- 5:00pm
Portmore, Eddleston	Wednesday 10 August	1:00pm	- 5:00pm
Portmore, Eddleston	Wednesday 17 August	1:00pm	- 5:00pm
Portmore, Eddleston	Wednesday 24 August	1:00pm	- 5:00pm
The Peeblesshire Garden Trio - The Cottage & Glen House	Thursday 25 August	1:30pm	- 5:00pm
Portmore, Eddleston	Wednesday 31 August	1:00pm	- 5:00pm
Portmore, Eddleston	Wednesday 7 September	1:00pm	- 5:00pm
Dawyck Botanic Garden, Stobo	Sunday 9 October	10:00am	- 5:00pm

Gardens open regularly

Dawyck Botanic Garden, Stobo	Daily from 1 Feb - 30 Nov		
	April - September	10:00am	- 6:00pm
	March and October	10:00am	- 5:00pm
	February and November	10:00am	- 4:00pm
Kailzie Gardens, Peebles	1 January - 5 March	Dawn	- Dusk
	6 March - 30 October	10:00am	- 5:00pm
	31 October - 31 December	Dawn	- Dusk

Gardens open by arrangement

Portmore, Eddleston	1 June - 7 September	07825 294388

Plant sales

8 Halmyre Mains, West Linton	Sunday 29 May	10:00am	- 12:00pm

Key to symbols

	New in 2016		Homemade teas		Accommodation
	Teas		Dogs on a lead allowed		Plant stall
	Cream teas		Wheelchair access		Scottish Snowdrop Festival

GARDEN LOCATIONS
IN PEEBLESSHIRE

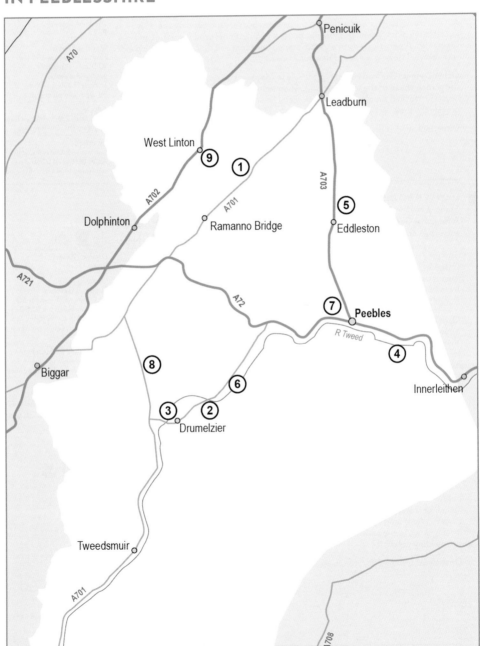

8 HALMYRE MAINS
West Linton EH46 7BX
Joyce Andrews and Mike Madden T: 07774 609 547
E: agentromanno@gmail.com

A half-acre organic garden with deep herbaceous borders surrounding the main lawn. Raised plots, greenhouse, keder house and polytunnel producing fruit and vegetables. A pergola leads to a sizable composting area and then down to the pond with restyled viewing areas and new sun house.

Other Details: Our early season plant sale in May gives an opportunity to preview the garden ahead of the main opening, when there will be a further sale. There will be a well-stocked supply of plants with many having grown in the garden. Teas will be provided in the nearby Lamancha Hub on the 17 July only.

Directions: Five miles South of Leadburn Junction on the A701 (Moffat).

Disabled Access:
Full

Opening Times:
Plant sale Sunday 29 May
10:00am - 12:00pm
garden also open.
Sunday 17 July 2:00pm -
5:00pm also plant stall

Admission:
Plant sale £2.00, children free
July - £4.00, children free

Charities:
Lamancha & District Comm
Assoc receives 40%, the net
remaining to SG Beneficiaries

DAWYCK BOTANIC GARDEN
Stobo EH45 9JU
A Regional Garden of the Royal Botanic Garden Edinburgh T: 01721 760 254
www.rbge.org.uk/dawyck

Stunning collection of rare trees and shrubs. With over 300 years of tree planting, Dawyck is a world-famous arboretum with mature specimens of Chinese conifers, Japanese maples, Brewer's spruce, the unique Dawyck beech and Sequoiadendrons from North America which are over 45 metres tall. Bold herbaceous plantings run along the burn. Range of trails and walks. Fabulous autumn colours.

Other Details: National Plant Collection®: Larix and Tsuga. Open for the Snowdrop Festival 30 January - 13 March. A range of trails and walks are on offer. Visit the new hydro-electric scheme at the Scrape Burn. Lunches and teas using local produce are available in the cafe overlooking scenic woodland. Last entry one hour before garden closes.

Directions: Eight miles southwest of Peebles on B712.

Disabled Access:
Partial

Opening Times:
Sunday 9 October
10:00am - 5:00pm for SG
Daily 1 Feb-30Nov 10:00am
Closes: Apr to Sep 6pm, Mar
& Oct 5pm, Feb & Nov 4pm.

Admission:
£6.50, conc £5.50, u16 free
(incls donation to garden, for
prices without donation check
rbge.org.uk).

Charities:
Donation to SG Beneficiaries

DRUMELZIER OLD MANSE
Drumelzier, Near Broughton, ML12 6JD
Mr and Mrs Julian Birchall

A traditional Manse garden in attractive Upper Tweed Valley. Colourful herbaceous border within walled garden. Unusual selection of plants throughout the garden including rare Meconopsis "Hensol Violet". There is a rock border and kitchen garden. Wide variety of shrubs planted in the last 15 years in the lower garden leading down to the path along burn with primulas and hostas. Beautiful setting and surrounding walks.

Directions: On the B712, ten miles west of Peebles. Broughton two miles.

Disabled Access:
Partial

Opening Times:
Sunday 17 July
2:00pm - 5:00pm

Admission:
£4.00, children free

Charities:
John Buchan Museum,
Peebles receives 20%, Stobo
and Drumelzier Church
receives 20%, the net
remaining to SG Beneficiaries

KAILZIE GARDENS
Peebles EH45 9HT
Lady Buchan-Hepburn T: 01721 720007
E: angela.buchanhepburn@btinternet.com www.kailziegardens.com

Semi-formal walled garden with shrubs and herbaceous borders, rose garden and excellent display of plants in large Victorian greenhouses. Woodland and burnside walks among spring bulbs, snowdrops, bluebells, rhododendrons and azaleas. The garden is set among fine old trees including a larch planted in 1725. Osprey watch with live CCTV recordings of Ospreys nesting in the recently extended nature centre. Kailzie has been featured on *Landward* and *The Beechgrove Garden*.

Other Details:
Champion Trees: Larch planted 1725

Wild garden and woodland walks open throughout the year, including for the Snowdrop Festival 30 January - 13 March.

Walled garden open 6 March - 30 October.

Children's play area. Restaurant and tearoom open daily during the summer months. See website for spring and winter restaurant hours. For groups and concessions please call 01721 720007.

Directions: Two and a half miles east of Peebles on B7062.

Disabled Access:
Partial

Opening Times:
Sun 7 Feb Dawn - Dusk
for the Snowdrop Festival
1 January - 5 March
Dawn - Dusk
6 March - 30 October
10:00am - 5:00pm
31 October - 31 December
Dawn - Dusk

Admission:
1 January - 5 March £3.50
6 March - 1 May £4.50,
concessions £3.50.
2 May - 31 October £5:00
concessions £4.50, under
fives free.

Charities:
Erskine Hospital receives
40%, the net remaining to
SG Beneficiaries

PORTMORE
Eddleston EH45 8QU
Mr and Mrs David Reid T: 07825 294388
www.portmoregardens.co.uk

Lovingly created by current owners over the past 20 years the gardens surrounding the David Bryce mansion house contain mature trees and offer fine views of the surrounding countryside. Large walled garden with box-edged herbaceous borders planted in stunning colour harmonies, potager, rose garden, pleached lime walk and ornamental fruit cages. The Victorian glasshouses contain fruit trees, roses, geraniums, pelargoniums and a wide variety of tender plants. There is an Italianate grotto, water garden with shrubs and meconopsis and woodland walks lined with rhododendrons, azaleas and shrub roses. Starred in *Good Gardens Guide* and featured in Kenneth Cox's book *Scotland for Gardeners*.

Other Details: Self service refreshments on Wednesday openings. Homemade cream teas for groups over 15 people by prior arrangement.

Directions: Off A703 one mile north of Eddleston. Bus 62.

Disabled Access:
Partial

Opening Times:
Wednesdays 13, 20 27 Jul,
3, 10, 17, 24, 31 Aug & 7 Sept
1:00pm - 5:00pm
By arrangement 1 June - 7 Sept
Except between 1 - 13 July

Admission:
£6.00

Charities:
Firrholm Day Unit (Dementia
Specialist Resource Centre)
Peebles receives 40%, the net
remaining to SG Beneficiaries

STOBO JAPANESE WATER GARDEN
Home Farm, Stobo EH45 8NX
Hugh and Georgina Seymour T: 01721 760245
E: hugh.seymour@btinternet.com

June and October are the prime months to visit this secluded woodland garden.
While water is probably the main feature of the garden now, the layout echoes
facets of a more conventional Japanese garden - stepping stones, humpback
bridges, the 40 feet waterfall, azaleas and rhododendrons, acers and other specialist
trees and shrubs, many of far eastern origins. Several Japanese lanterns and a tea
house still remain from when the garden was created in the early years of the last
century.

Other Details: Self service tea/coffee available. Guided tours available for groups of
12 or more - also lunches/teas/coffee. B&B at Home Farm House.
Some areas may be slippery or rough under foot so please wear appropriate
footwear (and use alternative paths) There is ongoing work on trees and shrubs.

Directions: Off B712. Follow signs for Stobo Castle then yellow signs on the drive.

Disabled Access:
Partial

Opening Times:
Wednesday 8 June
2:00pm - 7:30pm
Thursday 9 June
2:00pm - 7:30pm

Admission:
£5.00, children free

Charities:
Stobo & Drumelzier Kirk
receives 40%, the net
remaining to SG Beneficiaries

THE PEEBLESSHIRE GARDEN TRIO
EH45
The Tennant Family, Mrs David Coltman and Mr John Irvine

1. Glen House Glen Estate, Innerleithen EH44 6PX
Surrounding the outstanding Scots baronial mansion designed by David Bryce
in the mid-19th century, Glen House gardens are laid out on a series of shallow
terraces overhanging the glen itself, which offers one of the loveliest 'designed
landscapes' in the Borders. The garden expands from the formal courtyard through
a yew colonnade, and contains a fine range of trees, long herbaceous border and
pool garden with pergola, all arranged within the curve of slopes sheltering the
house. The gardens range over a series of terraces and therefore give very limited
access to wheelchair users.
Directions: Follow B709 out of Innerleithen for approximately 2½ miles. Right turn
at signpost for Glen Estate.

2. Haystoun Peebles EH45 9JG
A 16th century house (not open) which has a charming walled garden with an
ancient yew tree, herbaceous beds and vegetable garden. There is a wonderful
burnside walk, created since 1980, with azaleas, rhododendrons and primulas leading
to a small ornamental loch (cleared in 1990), with stunning views up Glensax valley.
Directions: Cross River Tweed in Peebles to south bank and follow garden open sign
for approximately 1 mile.

3. The Cottage 36 Main Street, Station Road West Linton EH46 7BT
The garden (which is devoted to flowers and flowering shrubs) is designed to be as
secluded as possible having mature Scots pines at one end and hedges of various
types dividing it into a number of areas with different layouts. There is a cottage
garden with annuals, perennials and flowering shrubs and a small enclosed garden
with access through arches, designed as a peaceful place to sit in. The main garden,
which includes a lily pond, provides colour from late spring to late autumn when
viewed from the house. There are three borders containing perennials and a
flowering shrub border.
Directions: From the A702 head through the village past the church on your right,
this is now Station Road and The Cottage will be on your right.

Other Details: For further information or to book your ticket, email Rose Parrott
at parrott@btinternet.com. Teas will be served at local tea rooms, details of these
will be given with your ticket.

Disabled Access:
Partial

Opening Times:
Haystoun
Saturday 28 May
1:30pm - 5:00pm

Haystoun & Glen House
Sunday 29 May
1:30pm - 5:00pm

The Cottage
Wednesday 22 June
1:30pm - 5:00pm

Glen House
Thursday 23 June
1:30pm - 5:00pm

Haystoun
Wednesday 29 June
1:30pm - 5:00pm

The Cottage
Thursday 21 July
1:30pm - 5:00pm

The Cottage & Glen House
Thursday 25 August
1:30pm - 5:00pm

Admission:
Open ticket covering all three
gardens and all seven dates
£13.00.
Single entry to either Glen
House or Haystoun £5.00
and to The Cottage £3.00.

Charities:
The Conservation
Foundation, Ben Walton Tust
and St Columba's Hospice
receives 40%, the net
remaining to SG Beneficiaries

THE POTTING SHED
Broughton Place, Broughton, Biggar ML12 6HJ
Jane and Graham Buchanan-Dunlop T: 01899 830574
E: buchanandunlop@btinternet.com

A one acre garden, begun from scratch in 2008, on an exposed hillside at 900 feet. It contains herbaceous plants, climbers, shrubs and trees, all selected for wind resistance and ability to cope with the poor, stony soil. There are (usually) fine views to the Southern Uplands.

Other Details: Lunch and tea available at Laurel Bank in Broughton Village. T: 01899 830462.

Directions: Signposted from the main A701 Edinburgh - Moffat Road, immediately north of Broughton Village.

Disabled Access:
Partial

Opening Times:
Wednesdays
15, 22, 29 June and
6, 13, 20 July
11:00am - 5:00pm

Admission:
£4.00, children free

Charities:
Borders Forest Trust receives 40%, the net remaining to SG Beneficiaries

WEST LINTON VILLAGE GARDENS
West Linton EH46 7EL
West Linton Village Gardeners T: 01968 660328
E: parrott@btinternet.com

Several gardens will be opening this year some situated near the golf course and others in the heart of the village. There is a pleasant tree lined walk up to the golf course albeit a little steep. The gardens all vary in size, content, style and interest including features such as stone and wood carvings, a rust shed with sedum roof and insect hotel, large herbaceous borders, specimen trees and shrubs. As well as gardeners that love to chat about their gardens come rain or shine.

Directions: A701 or A702 and follow signs.

Disabled Access:
Partial

Opening Times:
Sunday 19 June
2:00pm - 5:00pm

Admission:
£4.00

Charities:
The Ben Walton Trust receives 40%, the net remaining to SG Beneficiaries

ROXBURGHSHIRE

Scotland's Gardens 2016 Guidebook is sponsored by **INVESTEC WEALTH & INVESTMENT**

District Organiser

Mrs Sally Yonge	Newtonlees House, Kelso TD5 7SZ E: roxburghshire@scotlandsgardens.org

Area Organiser

Mrs Marion Livingston	Bewlie House, Lilliesleaf, Melrose TD6 9ER

Treasurer

Mr Peter Jeary	Kalemouth House, Eckford, Kelso TD5 8LE

Gardens open on a specific date

West Leas, Bonchester Bridge	Sunday 5 June	2:00pm - 6:00pm
Easter Weens, Bonchester Bridge, Hawick	Sunday 3 July	2:00pm - 5:30pm
Corbet Tower, Morebattle, near Kelso	Saturday 9 July	2:00pm - 5:00pm
Yetholm Village Gardens, Town Yetholm	Sunday 10 July	1:00pm - 5:30pm
West Leas, Bonchester Bridge	Sunday 31 July	2:00pm - 6:00pm

Gardens open regularly

Floors Castle, Kelso	25 March - 30 April	10:30am - 4:00pm
	1 May - 30 September	10:30am - 5:00pm
	1 October - 30 October	11:00am - 4:00pm
Monteviot, Jedburgh	1 April - 31 October Closed 27 - 28 May	12:00pm - 5:00pm

Gardens open by arrangement

West Leas, Bonchester Bridge	On request	01450 860711

Key to symbols

	New in 2016		Homemade teas		Accommodation
	Teas		Dogs on a lead allowed		Plant stall
	Cream teas		Wheelchair access		Scottish Snowdrop Festival

GARDEN LOCATIONS
IN ROXBURGHSHIRE

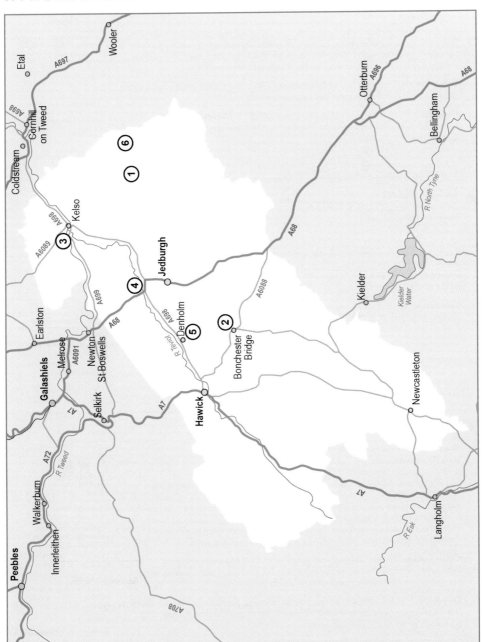

ROXBURGHSHIRE

1 CORBET TOWER
Morebattle, Near Kelso TD5 8AQ
Simon and Bridget Fraser

Charming Scottish Victorian garden set in parklands in the foothills of the Cheviots. The established garden includes a formal box parterred rose garden with old fashioned roses, a well stocked, traditional, walled vegetable and cutting garden, terraced lawns around the Victorian house and medieval peel tower. The gardens are approached via an attractive woodland walk with lime avenue.

Other Details: Delicious homemade teas and refreshments, cake and produce stall, plant stall and Ann Fraser greetings cards and prints.

Directions: From A68 north of Jedburgh take A698 for Kelso. At Kalemouth (Teviot Smokery) follow B6401 to Morebattle, then road marked Hownam to Corbet Tower.

Disabled Access:
Partial

Opening Times:
Saturday 9 July
2:00pm - 5:00pm

Admission:
£5.00

Charities:
The Children's Society receives 40%, the net remaining to SG Beneficiaries

2 EASTER WEENS
Bonchester Bridge, Hawick TD9 8JQ
Roger and Alison Curtis

Formal garden set within former stable courtyard and informal grounds surrounding, designed by Percy Cane in 1958. Terraced rhododendron bank, vegetable gardens and woodland walks. Pear-shaped walled garden approx ½ mile to the south, accessed through grazed parkland.

Directions: The property is on the B6357 on the Jedburgh side of Bonchester Bridge, just north of Bonchester Care Home. Parking is available in the farm yard.

Disabled Access:
Partial

Opening Times:
Sunday 3 July
2:00pm - 5:30pm

Admission:
£5.00, children £1.00

Charities:
Lavender Touch receives 20%, Hobkirk Church receives 20%, the net remaining to SG Beneficiaries

3 FLOORS CASTLE
Kelso TD5 7SF
The Duke of Roxburghe T: 01573 223333
www.floorscastle.com

The Walled and Millennium Gardens are situated within the grounds of Floors Castle. Meander through the formal Millennium Parterre and soak up the spectacular visions of colour, texture and the most delicious scents around the four herbaceous borders in one of the finest Victorian kitchen gardens in Scotland. Enjoy the adventure playground, Terrace Cafe and Castle Kitchen deli shop. Explore the wider Estate which offers woodland and riverside walks.

Other Details: Terrace Cafe open all year round. Last admission one hour before closing time. Please check our website for possible closures and details of concessionary admission prices and family tickets.

Directions: Floors Castle can be reached by following the A6089 from Edinburgh; the B6397 from Earlston or the A698 from Coldstream. Go through Kelso, up Roxburgh Street to the Golden Gates.

Disabled Access:
Partial

Opening Times:
25 March - 30 April
10:30am - 4:00pm
1 May - 30 September
10:30am - 5:00pm
1 October - 30 October
11:00am - 4:00pm

Admission:
Castle, Gardens & Grounds:
£12.50
Gardens & Grounds: £6.50

Charities:
Donation to SG Beneficiaries

MONTEVIOT

Jedburgh TD8 6UQ
Marquis & Marchioness of Lothian T: 01835 830380
www.monteviot.com

A series of differing gardens including a herb garden, rose garden, water garden linked by bridges, and river garden with herbaceous shrub borders of foliage plants.

New in 2015 - The Garden of Persistent Imagination - planted with rose and clematis avenues leading to a Moonstone Gate.

Directions: Turn off A68, three miles north of Jedburgh on to B6400.

Disabled Access:
Partial

Opening Times:
1 April - 31 October
12:00pm - 5:00pm
Closed 27 - 28 May

Admission:
£5.00, children under 16 free. RHS members free with membership card

Charities:
Donation to SG Beneficiaries

WEST LEAS

Bonchester Bridge TD9 8TD
Mr and Mrs Robert Laidlaw T: 01450 860711
E: ann.laidlaw@btconnect.com

The visitor to West Leas can share in the exciting and dramatic project on a grand scale still in the making. At its core is a passion for plants allied to a love and understanding of the land in which they are set. Collections of perennials and shrubs, many in temporary holding quarters, lighten up the landscape to magical effect. New dams and water features and woodland planting ongoing for 2016.

Other Details: Opening on 5 June for early summer colour and 31 July for high summer colour.

Directions: Signposted off the Jedburgh/Bonchester Bridge Road.

Disabled Access:
Partial

Opening Times:
Sunday 5 June
2:00pm - 6:00pm
Sunday 31 July
2:00pm - 6:00pm
By arrangement on request

Admission:
£4.00

Charities:
Macmillan Cancer Support, Borders Appeal receives 40%, the net remaining to SG Beneficiaries

West Leas © Bernie Gajos

YETHOLM VILLAGE GARDENS
Town Yetholm TD5 8RL
The Gardeners of Yetholm Village

The village of Town Yetholm is situated at the north end of the Pennine Way and lies close to the Bowmont Water in the dramatic setting of the foothills of the Cheviots. A variety of gardens with their own unique features have joined the Yetholm Village Gardens Open Day this year. In addition The Yew Tree Allotments running along the High Street will open again providing an ever popular feature. The day offers visitors the chance to walk through several delightful gardens planted in a variety of styles and reflecting many distinctive horticultural interests. From newly established, developing and secret gardens, to old and established gardens there is something here to interest everyone. The short walking distance between the majority of the gardens provides the added advantage of being able to enjoy the magnificence of the surrounding landscape to include Staerough and The Curr which straddle both the Bowmont and Halterburn Valleys where evidence of ancient settlements remains.

Other Details: Champion Trees: The Old Yew Tree in Yew Tree Lane. Attractions include the ever popular music, local woodturning products at Almond Cottage, a bric-a-brac stall, home baking and produce stall plus an excellent plant stall supported by Woodside Plant Centre is planned for the afternoon. Tickets are available in the local village hall. Dogs on leads allowed. Cream teas £2.00.

Directions: Equidistant between Edinburgh and Newcastle. South of Kelso in the Scottish Borders take the B6352 to Yetholm Village. Ample parking available along the High Street.

Disabled Access:
Partial

Opening Times:
Sunday 10 July
1:00pm - 5:30pm

Admission:
£4.00, children under 10 free

Charities:
Riding for the Disabled Association - Borders Group receives 40%, the net remaining to SG Beneficiaries

Each visit you make to one of our gardens in 2016 will raise money for our beneficiary charities:

In addition, funds will be distributed to a charity of the owner's choice. For South East Scotland, these include:

Alzheimer Scotland

Borders Forest Trust

British Heart Foundation

Brooke Hospital for Animals

Caddonfoot Parish Church Appeal

Canine Partners

Children's Hospice Association

Christ Church, Duns

CLIC Sargent

Dog Rescue

Dr Neil's Garden Trust

Erskine Hospital

Firrholm Day Unit (Dementia)

Friends of The Royal Botanic Garden Edinburgh

Froglife

Glencorse Church, Penicuik

Gunsgreen House Trust

Hobkirk Church

Horatio's Garden

Lamancha & District Community Association

Lavender Touch

Leuchie House

Lothian Cat Rescue

Macmillan Cancer Support

Marie Curie

MND Scotland

Oakfield, Easton Maudit

Pancreatic Cancer

Penicuik Development Trust

Redhall Walled Garden SAMH

Riding for the Disabled Association

RNLI

Scottish Love in Action

Silverburn Community Ltd

St Columba's Hospice

St Peter's Episcopal Church, Linlithgow

Stable Life

Stobo and Drumelzier Church

Sustrans

The Ben Walton Trust

The Children's Society

The Conservation Foundation

The Craigentinny Telferton Allotments

The Daisy Chain Trust

The Euan Macdonald Centre for Motor Neurone Disease

The Lynton Centre

The Order of St John

Trellis Scotland

Wellbeing of Women

World Cancer Research

GET INVOLVED WITH SCOTLAND'S GARDENS

OPEN YOUR GARDEN

Opening your garden is a fun and rewarding experience, as one of our openers put it, "Well worth all the hard work for such a fantastic day." Many gardens open year after year; some for more than 80 years! Try it - you might just get hooked too.

BUY OUR GUIDEBOOK

This lists all the garden openings, trails and events for the year.

HELP WITH THE OPEN DAYS

- Welcome visitors at the gate
- Bake some delicious homebaking to sell
- Serve the teas and sell plants
- Find out how people heard about us
- Grow plants to sell on the day
- Take photos

HELP TO PROMOTE SCOTLAND'S GARDENS

- Would you write an article for a newspaper?
- Could you help by tweeting?
- Are you a dedicated Facebook follower?
- Would you like to write a blog for us?

VISIT A GARDEN

A lovely way to see other people's gardens; get design ideas, enjoy the home baking, discover new ways to deal with slimey slugs and also raise money for charity.

COME TO AN EVENT

Take part in one of our workshops, enjoy the Snowdrop Festival, come to a plant sale, or explore a garden trail.

Or, just let all your friends and family know about Scotland's Gardens and encourage them to visit us at **WWW.SCOTLANDSGARDENS.ORG**

WOULD YOU LIKE TO OPEN YOUR GARDEN FOR CHARITY?

If you would like information on how to open your garden for charity please write at the address below, call 01 22 37 or email …@scotlandsgar…

We welcome gardens large and small and also groups of gardens.

To: Scotland's Gardens, 23 Castle Street, Edinburgh EH2 3DN

Please send me more information about opening my garden for charity.

Name _____

Address _____

_____

Postcode _____ Tel _____

Email _____

VISIT OUR
WEBSITE
for last minute offers

the National Trust
for Scotland
a place for everyone

SCOTTISH BREAKS

Enjoy a relaxing break surrounded by breathtaking Scottish scenery in our extensive range of self-catering accommodation

Find out more and book online at **www.nts.org.uk**
or call **0131 458 0305** to request a brochure

The National Trust for Scotland for Places of Historic Interest or Natural Beauty is a charity registered in Scotland, Charity Number SC 007410

INDEX OF GARDENS

G

H

I

K

OUR GUIDEBOOK FOR 2017

ORDER NOW
and your copy will be posted to you on publication.

Send order to:

Scotland's Gardens, 23 Castle Street, Edinburgh EH2 3DN

Please send me ____ copy / copies of our **Guidebook for 2017**,
price £5.00 with FREE UK p&p, as soon as it is available.

I enclose a cheque / postal order made payable to Scotland's Gardens.

Name _____

Address _____

_____

Postcode _____

Copies of our Guidebook for 2017 may also be purchased on our website:
www.scotlandsgardens.org

Experts in country living
for over 150 years.

Jamie Macnab
Savills Edinburgh
0131 247 3711
jmacnab@savills.com

Andrew Perratt
Savills Glasgow
0141 222 5875
aperratt@savills.com

Ruaraidh Ogilvie
Savills Tayside
01356 628628
rogilvie@savills.com

Fiona Gormley
Savills Aberdeen
01224 971122
fgormley@savills.com

savills

savills.co.uk

FINNEY'S
HOME & LEISURE

Manufacturers of the finest
quality solid teak furniture

FREE DELIVERY

◇ **CHAIRS**
◇ **BENCHES**
◇ **TABLES**
◇ **LOUNGERS**

LUXURIOUS OUTDOOR LIVING

Unit1, 403-405 Edgeware Road, London NW2 6LN
Mobile: 07588 774494
Email: marshallfinney@hotmail.co.uk

www.finneysleisure.com